Discover
Yorkshire's Wildlife

Your guide to Yorkshire Wildlife Trust's nature reserves

Peacock

Discover Yorkshire's Wildlife

Designed by Sally Henderson at Yorkshire Wildlife Trust.

This revised second edition printed 2017.
First paperback edition printed 2012 in the United Kingdom.
A catalogue record for this book is available from the British Library.

ISBN 978-0-9509460-4-7

Published by Yorkshire Wildlife Trust.

For more copies of this book, please email info@ywt.org.uk
or call 01904 659570.

The production of this book has been generously supported by the
players of the People's Postcode Lottery and the following companies:

Contents

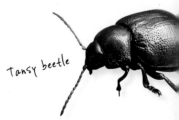

Tansy beetle

Introduction

Whatever the season, Yorkshire is a fantastic place to discover wildlife. Whether you are a seasoned naturalist or a beginner taking your first steps into the wonderful world of wildlife, the county has plenty to offer. What makes Yorkshire so special is the incredibly varied landscape and climate, with a corresponding range of habitats and wildlife.

Red kite

Yorkshire Wildlife Trust is the largest charity dedicated solely to nature conservation in the county. Over several decades and with the support of local people and funding bodies, the Trust has safeguarded an impressive number of wildlife havens, which represent many of the habitats and wildlife characteristic of the county. The majority of these safeguarded habitats, conserved as nature reserves, can be found within the pages of this book. Many of the sites are owned by the Trust, but some are managed in partnership with various landowners. A small number of fragile or tiny sites have been added as footnotes to entries for nearby nature reserves. Finally, there are also a few Trust nature reserves which have not made it into this book as they have been deemed to be hazardous to visitors or access restrictions are in place.

Sheffield and Rotherham Wildlife Trust manage a range of sites and have worked in partnership with Yorkshire Wildlife Trust in the production of this book in order to provide readers with a comprehensive picture of the Wildlife Trust nature reserves in the county. These sites are included with the South Yorkshire nature reserves, but bear the Sheffield and Rotherham Wildlife Trust logo.

Sadly, Yorkshire's wildlife has continued to decline and the Trusts continue to work hard to reverse this trend. Without the valiant efforts of both charities over the last several decades, Yorkshire's wildlife would have undoubtedly fared even worse and many of the special places highlighted in this book would have been lost.

Both Yorkshire Wildlife Trust and Sheffield and Rotherham Wildlife Trust are actively implementing the Wildlife Trusts' vision for Living Landscapes and Living Seas. Nature reserves and other protected areas are key parts of this vision, but for wildlife to have a more secure future conservation must work at a landscape scale. For more information about this vision, please visit **www.ywt.org.uk** or **www.wildsheffield.com**.

Discover Yorkshire's Wildlife will hopefully inspire you to don your walking boots, grab your hand lens or binoculars and get out into Yorkshire's countryside. For those less mobile, or who visit the county only occasionally, the book may help you reminisce about Yorkshire's fabulous wildlife.

Love Yorkshire, Love Wildlife

Give **Yorkshire's wildlife** a brighter future!

Yorkshire's wildlife is declining and with your help we will stop it.

Yorkshire Wildlife Trust has worked for over 70 years to defend our wildlife and to look after the precious havens you will find within the pages of this book. Your support will help us continue this essential work. We need your voice to strengthen ours, to make decision makers take notice and to give Yorkshire's wildlife a brighter future.

JOIN TODAY

Visit www.ywt.org.uk/membership

Call 01904 659570

Pop into one of our centres

Living Seas Centre at Flamborough, Potteric Carr, Spurn, Stirley Community Farm at Huddersfield, or our York office.

Common seal

Foreword by John Lawton

Yorkshire has been described as "God's own county". Well, it is. Not only is Yorkshire the largest county in England, it hosts two National Parks (the North York Moors and the Yorkshire Dales), with a third (the Peak District) creeping across the south-west county boundary.

The geology of Yorkshire literally underpins the county's wonderful wildlife, with rocks from every geological period spanning the Ordovician to the Cretaceous. Rifle Butts Quarry reveals a major unconformity between the Lower Jurassic and the Upper Cretaceous near Market Weighton. The North Sea coast is spectacular (and among the most rapidly eroding in the UK), the relentless erosion providing the material for Spurn Point. The last great run of the English chalk thrusts out into the sea at Flamborough Head, with its spectacular seabird cliffs.

The Yorkshire Naturalists Trust (as it was originally known) was founded in 1946 – the second Naturalists Trust in the UK after Norfolk. In 1944, two blocks of relict fen-woodland at Askham Bog (just outside York) became available for sale, and were bought by the 'chocolate barons' Sir Francis Terry and Arnold Rowntree; Yorkshire Wildlife Trust was founded with the primary objective of receiving these two parts of Askham Bog as a gift, which it duly did in 1946. The Trust did not complete its ownership of Askham (a nice touch) until its Golden Jubilee in 1996.

From this small beginning (a single nature reserve, and eleven 'subscribers' plus Terry as President and Rowntree as Vice-President) the Trust has grown steadily so that today we have just over 100 nature reserves, and over 41,000 members (the second largest in the country). On the way we became Yorkshire Wildlife Trust in 1983. The Trust's first public appeal for money was in 1955, to raise £500 to purchase Moorlands (a woodland) near York as our second nature reserve. The Trust acquired Spurn Point from the War Office in 1959 thanks to unstinting efforts of Dr Edward Wilfred Taylor, the then (honorary) President. The Trust's first paid Executive Officer (Lt. Col. John Newman) was not appointed until 1968. Now we have over 100 staff and about 500 regular volunteers.

The remarkable and exciting growth of the Trust reflects the huge interest that exists in the UK in natural history and the environment. It is also necessary, because threats to wildlife and wild places continue unabated. Yorkshire Wildlife Trust's precious nature reserves are a fundamental (but by no means the only) part of our efforts to protect the county's natural heritage. And what superb nature reserves we have. All the sites are important, and you will find them described in this book. But some are more notable than others, and are of national and international significance. They include Spurn, Fen Bog (an upland valley mire), Strensall Common (heathland on the Vale of York), Potteric Carr (a fantastic wetland complex near Doncaster), Wheldrake Ings (ancient lowland hay-meadows in the Lower Derwent Valley), Southerscales (limestone pavements on Ingleborough), and Flamborough Cliffs. No other county in England can boast such a rich variety of nationally important sites. But many smaller, less well-known nature reserves are gems in their own right, and all are worth a visit.

Enjoy them, and love Yorkshire and her wonderful wildlife.

Sir John Lawton, President

Banded demoiselle

Foreword by Rob Stoneman

Yorkshire: England's largest and most magnificent county. This is a county defined by its incredible wildlife and celebrated landscape, which Yorkshire Wildlife Trust and all its supporters are devoted to maintaining and enriching.

Yorkshire. The very word captures the magic of the place – the Yorkshire coast, the Yorkshire Dales, the Yorkshire Wolds, the great Yorkshire cities. A county rich in diversity, of the people who live here, of its landscape and of its wildlife. From the seabird cliffs of Flamborough to the shimmering muds of the Humber; from the fast-tumbling streams arising on lonely moors to those same rivers gracing the riverside parks of Sheffield or Leeds. This is a truly grand and magnificent county.

Yet, there is no room for complacency. The stark truth is that Yorkshire's amazing wildlife is much diminished. Its essential biodiversity remains (just) but its bio-abundance has rapidly declined. Clouds of butterflies replaced by just a few; murmurations of starling now a rare sight; water voles clinging on; our meadow flora restricted to just 2% of its pre-WWII range. It could have been worse if it were not for the unstinting efforts of the two Wildlife Trusts in Yorkshire – Sheffield and Rotherham Wildlife Trust and the older Yorkshire Wildlife Trust.

With the decline of wildlife continuing especially in the arable lowlands of Yorkshire, both Trusts have adopted a radical mission of 'Living Landscapes and Seas' that are so rich in wildlife they can cope with the massive change that is sweeping upon us in the shape of climate change. At the heart of this mission remains our nature reserves and protected area network – Marine Protected Areas (MPAs) at sea; Local Wildlife Sites (LWS), Sites of Special Scientific Interest (SSSI) and nature reserves on land. This network becomes ever more important.

First, our nature reserves provide places where we can show how land can be managed in a way that sustains lots of wildlife – both its diversity and abundance. A great place to see a bittern or a murmuration of starlings is Potteric Carr, near Doncaster. Potteric Carr, though, is much more than just a nature reserve – it stores water in times of flood and its reedbeds take carbon from the atmosphere and lay it down as fen peat. As a stress-busting escape from the daily bustle of South Yorkshire urban life, there can be no better medicine than a walk round this nature reserve.

Second, our nature reserves are the cathedrals of nature conservation, where we inspire, educate and involve people in nature conservation. If we want to ensure Yorkshire remains a truly grand county, we must restore its wildlife heritage. And, as hard as the Wildlife Trusts and others might try, that involves all of Society – farmers, planners, politicians and everyday folk who make millions of daily decisions that could impact on that wildlife.

And third, and most excitingly of all, our nature reserves are the place to start the restoration of our wildlife from. They are the gene pool: the places where the diversity of wildlife still remains; the places from which we can restore Yorkshire's bio-abundance and create landscapes that are rich in wildlife and sustains the grandness of this incredible county of ours.

Across Yorkshire, the Trusts manage over 100 of these magical places: for the common and the rare; out of the way and smack in the middle of the city; and always for the many rather than the privileged few. Enjoy these gems, dream of an even grander and more magnificent future for Yorkshire and stay involved.

Rob Stoneman, Chief Executive

Puffins

Winter

In the depths of winter, those brave enough to venture outside can enjoy some wonderful wildlife experiences. With a bit of planning and warm clothes, some special winter visitors and spectacular flocks may be seen.

With short days and long cold nights, many birds and mammals are very active during the day and can therefore be more visible. Snow cover betrays the presence of unseen mammals by the tracks they leave. Shortly after dawn and just before dusk is usually best for seeing wildlife, when sites are mostly undisturbed. An early morning walk at many of the Trust's nature reserves can yield sightings of foxes, roe deer or even a fishing otter for the lucky few.

Spectacular flocks of wintering wildfowl are a feature of the Trust's wetlands at this time of year. Tens of thousands of wigeon, teal, pintail, mallard and shoveler bring welcome colour to a rather monochrome landscape. Bolton-on-Swale Lake, Denaby Ings, North Cave Wetlands and Wheldrake Ings are great places to enjoy this spectacle. Look out for hunting peregrines and merlins too, which also seek out these flocks. Potteric Carr offers great views of wildfowl and can be combined

Starlings

with an hour or two watching for bitterns. Whilst these reedbed specialists have bred here in recent years, numbers in the winter are swelled with the arrival of migrants from the continent and with short days there is a good chance of seeing one on the nature reserve. Look out for them stalking slowly along the water's edge, or flying low over the reedbeds at dusk, looking surprisingly owl-like, despite being in the heron family. Don't forget to look up too, as Potteric Carr hosts a spectacular roost of starlings at this time of year, and their swirling aerobatics known as a murmuration is a spectacular sight.

Bittern

DEC	JAN	FEB
Hunting peregrines at Wheldrake Ings	Wintering bitterns and wildfowl at Potteric Carr	Sunbathing adders at Allerthorpe Common

Potteric Carr

Spring

The faded hues of winter give way to a riot of colour as wildflowers spring up in our woodlands and the air begins to fill with bird song and the hum of bees. With summer migrant birds arriving daily, this really is an exciting time!

As spring approaches, our flocks of wintering birds start to slip away north and east. Large herds of Iceland-bound whooper swans often pause for a rest at Yorkshire's wetlands, sometimes in large numbers. By early March the first hardy wheatears and sand martins will be arriving back in the county and later in the month chiffchaffs will be heard singing in the woodlands. With trees yet to leaf, it is the time woodland flowers come into their own, with January's snowdrops rapidly being replaced by wood anemones, dog violets and early purple orchids. At Allerthorpe Common, Fen Bog and Greno Woods look for adders basking in sheltered spots on sunny days from February onwards, whilst the first brimstone butterflies should be on the wing. By late April and May, some of our woodlands, including Grass Wood, and North Cliffe Wood are carpeted with a lilac haze of bluebells, spangled by white wood anemones and greater stitchwort.

Now is a brilliant time to get up and out early in order to hear the dawn chorus of birds as the summer migrants add their voices to those of our resident songsters. Along the River Ouse in York search for emerald-green tansy beetles along the riverbanks, one of Yorkshire's rarest and most lovely insects. If you miss them now, try again from mid-July when the second brood will emerge.

Out on the coast, seabirds will be thronging the cliffs at Flamborough Head, with thousands of puffins, guillemots, razorbills and kittiwakes battering the senses with sights, sounds and smells throughout the spring. Try Flamborough Cliffs for some of the best views of puffins on the UK mainland, but do so before the middle of July to avoid disappointment.

Guillemots

MAR	APR	MAY
Returning avocets and little ringed plovers at North Cave Wetlands	A carpet of woodland flowers at Hetchell Wood	Seabirds and migrant birds at Flamborough Cliffs

Wood anemones

Summer

The long, lazy days of summer provide opportunities to explore orchid-filled meadows, watch dragonflies battle over our wetlands and thrill over the sights, sounds and smells of our seabird colonies.

June is arguably one of the best months for the wildlife enthusiast and the month to get involved with the Wildlife Trusts' 30 Days Wild challenge, which encourages everyone to do something 'wild' every day of June.

In summer, the chalk grassland nature reserves of Kiplingcotes, Ledston Luck Sprotbrough Flash and Wharram Quarry look stunning with a host of orchids and other flowering plants in bloom. Thistle broomrape will be flowering at Wharram Quarry and at Ripon Loop: look carefully for the flower spikes emerging from the base of thistles. In the Dales, the meadows will be looking spectacular, with many rare species present to excite the visitor. With warming temperatures, insects become abundant. Among the most noticeable are butterflies. Marbled whites are a favourite and can be found on sites on the Yorkshire Wolds and also at sites along the magnesian limestone ridge that runs down the centre of Yorkshire. Brockadale and Ledsham Bank are great places to look for them, with dark green fritillaries joining them later in the summer. On the North York Moors, small pearl-bordered fritillaries can be found at Fen Bog often feeding on nectar from the heather near the car park. On the bog itself, large heath butterflies can be found. Look out for bog bush-crickets here too, along with spectacular golden-ringed dragonflies and

Keeled skimmer

keeled skimmers. Many of the Trust's sites are great for the dragonfly enthusiast, with Filey Dams, Staveley Nature Reserve, Saltmarshe Delph and Thorpe Marsh all well worth a look.

As the sun sets in the sky, don't be tempted to head home as many of our wetlands are great for bats. Those with pale bellies that are skimming low over the water like hovercrafts are likely to be Daubenton's bats, whilst large bats hunting high overhead may well be noctules.

30 DAYS WILD

To find out more, visit
www.mywildlife.org.uk/30dayswild

JUN	JUL	AUG
Thistle broomrape at Wharram Quarry	Golden-ringed dragonflies and keeled skimmers at Fen Bog	Clustered bellflowers at Brockadale

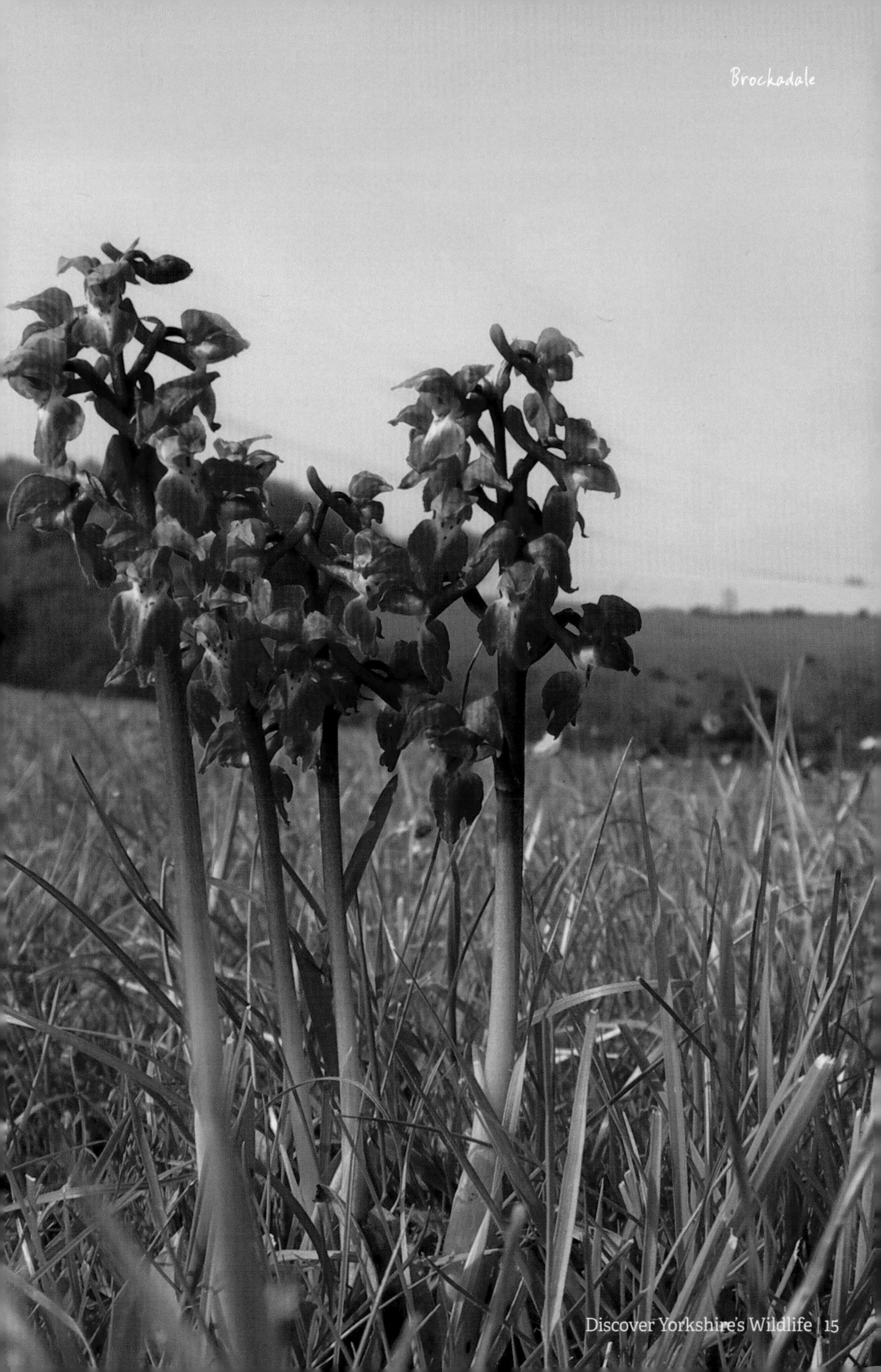

Brockadale

Autumn

The fresh green of summer is replaced by yellow, orange and red as leaves begin to fall. Deer bellow on frosty mornings, winter migrant birds begin to return and our wildlife starts to prepare for the winter.

For many birds, autumn migration starts early, with green sandpipers and spotted redshanks heading south from late June. Numbers build during the late summer and into autumn, providing a spectacular sight at Trust nature reserves on the Humber estuary: Kilnsea Wetlands, Paull Holme Strays, Spurn and Welwick Saltmarsh.

This is a great time to explore Yorkshire's seashore, particularly along the North Yorkshire coast, where low tide reveals wildlife-rich rockpools. Look out to sea as early autumn is ideal for seeing harbour porpoises, particularly from Flamborough Cliffs and Spurn. The chances of seeing a minke whale or something even rarer from the Yorkshire coast seems to be increasing. As the autumn harvest of bright orange sea buckthorn berries at Spurn ripens, along with the deep red hawthorn berries in the hedgerows, large numbers of migrant birds arrive in Yorkshire. With poor weather and an onshore wind vast flocks of redwings, fieldfares and blackbirds can be seen along the coast, arriving from the North Sea, as well as woodcocks, goldcrests and the occasional long-eared owl.

Things are relatively quiet in the woods, but it is the best time to seek out fungi as in the damp, cool conditions, the fruiting bodies of many species are on show: try Low Wood, where there are at least 36 species. As autumn progresses large numbers of wildfowl and wading birds arrive to spend the winter in our county and the last of the summer visitors depart. Our resident wildlife make their final preparations for winter and the naturalist can reminisce about the wonderful moments shared with Yorkshire's wildlife during the year.

Sea buckthorn

Blackbird

SEPT
Rockpooling at South Landing, Flamborough

OCT
Autumn bird migration at Spurn

NOV
Fungi at Low Wood

Fly agaric

Enjoy your visit!

The nature reserves in this book provide excellent opportunities for you to experience some of Yorkshire's best wildlife and landscapes, and to learn more about our natural heritage. It is worth remembering that nature reserves are wild places and conditions can be hazardous at times. Also, visiting a nature reserve can be frustrating if you visit at a time of day when wildlife is less active or in a season when the specialities are not present. These pages will give you some information and tips about visiting the Trust's sites safely and responsibly, and how to get the most from your visit.

Access

Yorkshire Wildlife Trust is keen for people to visit its nature reserves and tries hard to make them accessible by creating paths, installing boardwalks, viewing hides, car parking, kissing gates, interpretation and signage. However, some sites by their very nature can be challenging to access, due to their isolated location, the difficult terrain such as wet ground, steep slopes or dense vegetation or the fragility of their habitats. Some remote sites may have little more than a welcome sign and an entrance gate. We work with disability groups to provide access for less mobile people where practical and when funding allows. For information about the accessibility of a particular site please call **01904 659570**.

Planning your visit

To ensure a safe and enjoyable visit please go properly equipped with good walking shoes or wellies and sensible clothing for the weather conditions, plus sun screen and insect repellent if appropriate. Binoculars, a notebook, camera, field guides and other equipment may enhance your visit. You can visit the Trust's shop at Potteric Carr or the online shop **www.ywt.org. uk/shop** to purchase some of these items.

Before you visit make sure you are familiar with the access information for the nature reserve you intend to visit, whether dogs are permitted (check before you leave home!), where you can park or what public transport is available. The fact file, postcode, grid references and maps in this guide should help. If visiting an isolated site on your own, make sure you tell somebody where you are going and when you will be back. Please make sure that you do not leave valuables on display in your car. Also, make sure you are aware of the facilities available on or close to the site.

Rockpooling

The vast majority of Yorkshire Wildlife Trust nature reserves do not have toilets, refreshments or shelter, so please make allowances for this.

When should you visit?

Visiting a nature reserve hoping to see a particular plant or animal can often lead to disappointment and even when species such as otters are present you have to be very lucky to see one. Timing your visit to when few other visitors are present such as dawn and dusk, during the week, or even when the weather is not so good, could mean that there may have been less disturbance which could lead to that once in a lifetime sighting. Even more importantly, check whether the wildlife you hope to see is present at the time of year you plan to visit. Many insects, birds and plants are seasonal and may only be found for a short period of time and visiting outside of their season will mean you won't find them. Weather conditions can also play a role. For example, sites such as Spurn and Flamborough Cliffs can be exceptional for watching migrating birds, but this spectacle is much influenced by the weather and season.

Help Yorkshire Wildlife Trust keep its nature reserves havens for wildlife and people, by following this code:

■ Dogs, even if well behaved, disturb wildlife by their mere presence. Please check that dogs are permitted to visit and if so please keep your dog under control and on a short lead at all times, taking particular care during spring and summer, and when grazing animals or ground-nesting birds are present.

■ Please clean up after your dog and take this and any litter away with you.

■ Sheep, ponies and cattle are often used to graze our nature reserves. Please avoid disturbing these animals and take great care when in the vicinity of grazing animals if you have a dog with you. Cows with calves can be aggressive towards dogs, so if you are approached under these circumstances, it is advisable to let go of your dog until the danger has passed.

■ If you wish to report an incident or injured grazing animal please call **01302 570077**.

■ Please do not remove any plants or animals from nature reserves.

■ Please keep to the paths wherever possible. Close all gates and avoid trespass or disturbance to adjacent property.

■ Please be considerate to other visitors to the site. This is particularly important in viewing hides – respect the quiet! If a hide is busy, don't be a 'hide-hog', give others a chance to sit down if you have been there a while.

■ Take care to avoid disturbing birds or other animals especially during the spring and early summer when they are breeding.

■ Some sites are subject to flooding following heavy rainfall or snowmelt, so please take special care at these times.

ADEL DAM

NEAREST POSTCODE
LS16 8AG

NEAREST TOWN
Leeds

GRID REFERENCE
SE 272 414

PUBLIC TRANSPORT
Take the bus from Leeds or Otley and alight at Golden Acre Park or the Mercure Parkway Hotel.

DIRECTIONS
Park in the Golden Acre car park (off A660). Take the underpass and follow the path to the right of the lake. Past the lake, join a bridle path below Golden Acre Dam and carry on to the nature reserve entrance. There are wheelchair-friendly paths from the car park to the nature reserve and to Marsh Hide (a RADAR key is required for wheelchair users at the site entrance).

OTHER INFORMATION
Size: 8 ha

A café and toilets are available in the adjacent Golden Acre Park.

TOP TIP Spring flowers put on a wonderful show, while kingfishers might be chanced upon at any time.

Emerged from a centuries-old working dam and the surrounding land, this tranquil nature reserve is a rare combination of wet and dry woodland, which surrounds a lake and pond frequently visited by kingfishers – the number one attraction. The masses of bluebells and fungi in season are also exceptional.

This woodland nature reserve straddles Adel Beck which runs through a shallow valley with the former dam central to the site. Mature native and exotic trees can be found in the mixed woodland, with more than 36 species in total. Alder and willow dominate the wet woodland, with sphagnum moss on the ground. Beech, oak, holly, rowan, yew and ash are found in the dry woodland alongside introduced species like Corsican pine and Norway maple, which are indicative of its past.

Broad buckler ferns and brambles cover the floor, with fine showings of bluebells and marsh marigolds in the spring and foxgloves in the summer. Fungi flourishes amongst the standing and lying dead trees.

Stop at Marsh Hide to look over the pond and feeding station for sightings of tits, chaffinch, nuthatch and great spotted woodpecker. Moorhen, coot, mandarin and tufted ducks can be seen bringing up their families in summer from the newly replaced Lake Hide. Kingfishers breed at Adel Dam: if you are patient and lucky you will catch a flash of their bright blue. Birds of prey also frequent the site, with resident sparrowhawks and visits from red kites and buzzards. The more elusive species to look for include water rail and lesser spotted woodpeckers. Other visitors include badgers and roe deer, plus a family of foxes.

Noted for its special ecology since 1830, the site has been a nature reserve since 1968. Once an operational dam, it fell into disuse with the gradual demise of the water power industry. It then became a central feature of a Victorian garden, around which many exotic trees were planted. The dam was later breached in the 1930s, allowing water to escape to form the current shallow lake.

A loyal supporters' group work here, carrying out general maintenance and welcoming visitors. Management plans are in place to increase diversity in the dry woodland by reducing sycamores and replanting with low-to-mid canopy shrubs and trees, as well as developing more reedbed along the lakeshore.

Kingfisher

Location

Golden Acre Park

Arthington Road

A660

Bridlepath

Adel Beck

Marsh Hide

Lake Hide

N

0   100m

Bakery Café & Toilets

Otley

Golden Acre Park

A660

Leeds

Hotel

Arthington Road

Adel Dam

N

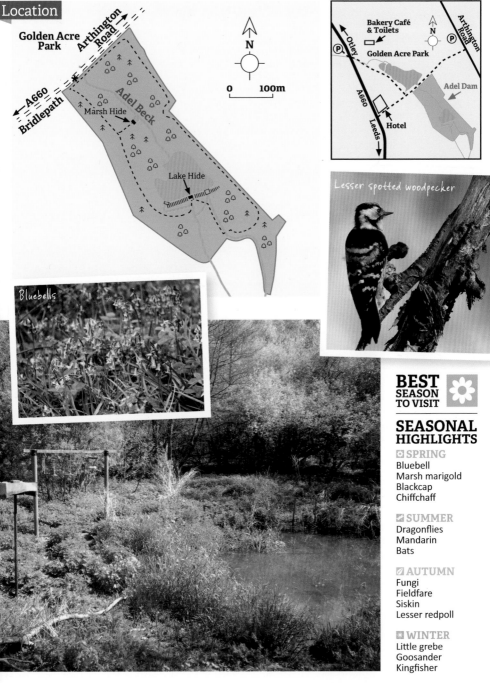

Lesser spotted woodpecker

Bluebells

BEST SEASON TO VISIT

SEASONAL HIGHLIGHTS

✣ SPRING
Bluebell
Marsh marigold
Blackcap
Chiffchaff

☑ SUMMER
Dragonflies
Mandarin
Bats

☑ AUTUMN
Fungi
Fieldfare
Siskin
Lesser redpoll

✣ WINTER
Little grebe
Goosander
Kingfisher

AGDEN BOG

Sheffield & Rotherham

Situated in the beautiful Bradfield Dale, on the northwest corner of Agden Resevoir, Agden Bog Nature Reserve is a classic example of a peat bog mostly disappeared from our landscape. Rich in plant life, purple moor-grass and heath spotted orchids provide a touch of colour.

NEAREST POSTCODE
S6 6LJ

NEAREST TOWN
Sheffield

GRID REFERENCE
SK 252 930

PUBLIC TRANSPORT
A bus runs from Hillsborough to Bradfield, just over half a mile away.

DIRECTIONS
Access from the A6102, taking the High Bradfield road at Oughtibridge. From High Bradfield turn right, halfway down the hill to Low Bradfield. Drive round Agden Resevoir and park off-road on the left, just before the bend and opposite the houses.

OTHER INFORMATION
Size: 2 ha

TOP TIP Pick up a magnifying glass or hand lens for a visit here to help appreciate the finer beauty of the sphagnum mosses and sundews.

A gden Bog is most notable for its plants and flowers, although birds, mammals and amphibians all thrive here. Plant life varies from moist sphagnum moss beds, which hold copious amounts of water, to purple moor-grass fields, with extensive bracken beds and birch woodland breaking it up.

Round-leaved sundew and cranberry are common amongst the moss, whilst in early summer hundreds of flowering heads poke through as heath spotted orchids start to bloom. These flowers are followed by the golden spikes of bog asphodel and later in season by the lilac globes of devil's-bit scabious, popular with many pollinating insects. The aptly named adder's-tongue fern may also be found.

Mammals are a common sight here, with brown hare and roe deer regularly spotted. Birds including nightjar, spotted flycatcher, siskin, lesser redpoll and common sandpiper have all been recorded nesting nearby, whilst black grouse also use the site. Common toads, common frogs and common lizards are all plentiful, whereas golden-ringed dragonflies are more exceptional, yet breed here and can sometimes be seen hawking over the site or sunning on a clump of grasses. The remnants of the peat bog here are today unusual in the landscape, although once they would have been common. Draining of the soils for agriculture in the surrounding area dried out the sphagnum moss and crops were put in their place. Over the past few years Yorkshire Wildlife Trust has tried to preserve the special habitat that remains.

Whilst currently managed by Yorkshire Wildlife Trust, this site is in the process of being transferred to Sheffield and Rotherham Wildlife Trust due to its closer proximity to them.

Devil's-bit scabious

Location

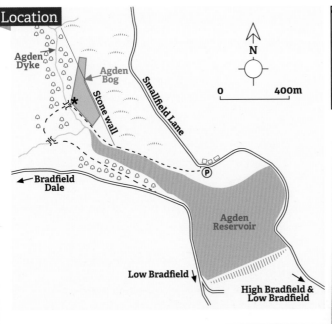

Agden Dyke
Agden Bog
Smallfield Lane
Stone wall
N
0   400m
Bradfield Dale
P
Agden Reservoir
Low Bradfield
High Bradfield & Low Bradfield

Huddersfield
A616
Stocksbridge
A6102
A629
A61
35A
35
Agden Bog
High Bradfield
Low Bradfield
Oughtibridge
B6087
A61
Sheffield

Adder's-tongue fern

BEST SEASON TO VISIT

SEASONAL HIGHLIGHTS

✹ SPRING
Cuckoo
Swallow
Sedge warbler
Reed warbler

✹ SUMMER
Heath spotted orchid
Marsh orchid
Devil's-bit scabious
Golden-ringed dragonfly
Nightjar

✹ AUTUMN
Black grouse
Starling

✹ WINTER
Peregrine
Merlin

ALLERTHORPE COMMON

NEAREST POSTCODE
YO42 4RU

NEAREST TOWN
Pocklington

GRID REFERENCE
SE 761 475

PUBLIC TRANSPORT
Buses between York and Hull stop at Barmby Moor village, which is just over two miles away.

DIRECTIONS
Turn south off the A1079 near the petrol station at Barmby Moor, signed Sutton. Turn left to Thornton and park in the car park about half a mile on the right. Cross the road and follow the main track until you reach a line of pylons. Turn right and the nature reserve is a short distance along on the right.

OTHER INFORMATION
Size: 6 ha

TOP TIP Visit early on a sunny morning between February and April, for close-up views of basking adders. Do not get too close as they have a venomous bite if threatened.

Bees buzzing around sweet-smelling purple spikes of heather, a green woodpecker 'yaffling' from the woodland edge, an adder shyly slithering into the undergrowth below prickly coconut-scented gorse bushes make up just some of the sights, sounds and smells of Allerthorpe Common.

Allerthorpe Common is alive with wildlife throughout the year and supports a surprising range of habitats for such a small pocket of lowland heath – wet heath, dry heath, acid grassland, woodland, scrub and open water are all waiting to be discovered.

The lowland heath habitat found here once stretched right across the Vale of York, but now only remains in isolated fragments. This habitat and the wildlife it supports is now rare across the UK. Much of the flat, fertile land it is found on has been used by humans over time for agriculture and development, meaning nationally we have lost over 80% of the habitat since 1800. As a result the areas we have left are even more important for wildlife.

Ling heather, tormentil, sheep's fescue and wavy hair-grass grow on the drier areas of the site. Whereas in the damper areas cross-leaved heath, purple moor grass and the locally rare St John's wort grow, as well as nationally rare May lily. Patches of gorse scrub provide shelter for birds and their network of roots support a healthy population of adders. Come spring listen out for the song of woodlark. Areas of mature birch and willow woodland add yet another dimension to the site: great spotted woodpecker may sometimes be seen here. One large pool and several smaller ponds support numerous damselfly and dragonfly species including black darter and blue-tailed damselfly.

Sitting within Forestry Commission woodland, the site has historically been an oasis for wildlife typical of lowland heaths. It was designated as a SSSI in 1965, being one of the best areas of the Common, and has been managed by Yorkshire Wildlife Trust since 1966. More recently, the Forestry Commission has felled large tracts of coniferous forest and the land is now returning to lowland heath allowing species from the nature reserve to colonise.

On-site grazing using rare breed longhorn cattle helps keep tree saplings and some of the coarse competitive grasses that can take over the heath in check. On top of this volunteers work regularly to control bramble and bracken that can become a problem and remove any birch saplings that the cattle have missed.

Adder

Location

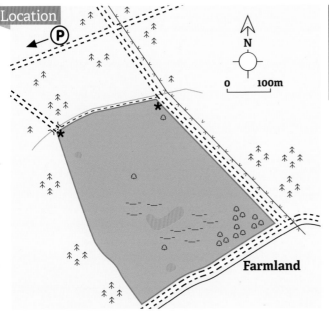

N

0   100m

Farmland

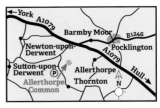

Tormentil and cross-leaved heath

BEST SEASON TO VISIT

SEASONAL HIGHLIGHTS

▣ SPRING
May lily
Adder
Green woodpecker
Woodlark
Willow warbler

▨ SUMMER
Tormentil
Ling heather
Marsh cinquefoil
Broad-bodied chaser

▨ AUTUMN
Woodcock
Siskin
Lesser redpoll

▣ WINTER
Jay
Coal tit
Treecreeper

ASHBERRY

NEAREST POSTCODE
YO62 5LE

NEAREST TOWN
Helmsley

GRID REFERENCE
SE 568 845

PUBLIC TRANSPORT
A bus service runs to nearby Helmsley from Scarborough, Malton and York. In the summer months Moorsbus run a service between Helmsley and Rievaulx.

DIRECTIONS
½ miles west of Rievaulx and about 3 miles north-west of Helmsley. If approaching from Helmsley, take the B1257 Stokesley road for approximately 1½ miles and take a left hand turning onto Scawton road. Descend through the woods, turn left across the River Rye and turn right towards Old Byland after a further ¼ mile.

OTHER INFORMATION
Site designation: SSSI
Size: 52 ha

Dogs are allowed on the public right of way. Very limited roadside parking, access to the nature reserve is via a small gate. The site can be very wet in places, even during the summer, so wellies are advised.

TOP TIP Look for globeflowers in June: the best spot is just past the wooden gate.

One of the finest ancient woodlands in Yorkshire, Ashberry Nature Reserve is bordered by flower-rich limestone grassland on the valley sides and a marshy valley bottom through which a crystal clear stream flows.

Glacial melt water carved out the steep valley sides of Ashberry Nature Reserve, cutting through different rock layers and exposing geology that has heavily influenced the habitats that have established here.

The very thin soils on the upper slopes of the valley support areas of unimproved limestone grassland and woodland with a very high diversity of specialised plant species. The middle and lower slopes of the valley are also wooded, and contain a range of bird species including nuthatch, treecreeper and sometimes wood warbler.

Along the valley bottom runs tributaries of the River Rye. Here there are areas of neutral grassland, mire and carr woodland. Where the calcium-rich springs that flow through the nature reserve reach the valley bottom extensive areas of calcareous marsh exist, with many rare plant and insect species associated. These include marsh helleborine, bird's-eye primrose, globeflower, marsh hawk's-beard and grass-of-Parnassus. Black bog-rush occurs in two of the larger areas of springs and common butterwort and marsh lousewort are widespread. Red, fallow and roe deer are present in the area and can be seen early in the morning or at dusk. The sooty-black chimney sweeper is a day-flying moth that can be seen in the grasslands. Freshwater shrimps and white-clawed crayfish can be found in the stream that flows through the site.

Marsh helleborine

Bird's-eye primrose

Location

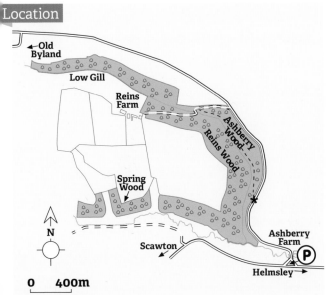

Chimney sweeper moth

BEST SEASON TO VISIT

SEASONAL HIGHLIGHTS

⊞ SPRING
Wood anemone
Orange-tip
Blackcap
Chiffchaff

☑ SUMMER
Globeflower
Marsh helleborine
Bird's-eye primrose
Chimney sweeper
White-clawed crayfish

☑ AUTUMN
Fallow deer
Red deer

⊞ WINTER
Great spotted woodpecker
Marsh tit
Nuthatch

ASHES PASTURE

NEAREST POSTCODE
LA6 3JF

NEAREST TOWN
Hawes

GRID REFERENCE
SD 776 784

PUBLIC TRANSPORT
Nearest train station is Ribblehead, from where it is a 1½ mile walk along the road to the nature reserve.

DIRECTIONS
Off the B6479 1 mile south of the B6255 junction (Ribblehead).

OTHER INFORMATION
Site designation: SSSI, SAC
Size: 6 ha

TOP TIP Make a day of it and tour around the habitats of Ingleborough visiting the nearby nature reserves at Salt Lake Quarry, Brae Pasture and South House Pavement. If this leaves you peckish don't forget the pub at Ribblehead or tea rooms in Horton-in-Ribblesdale.

An idyllic location in Ribblesdale adds to the charm of this diverse grassland nature reserve. In spring and summer the grassland is dotted with orchids and other flowering plants and buzzing with bumblebees.

Positioned near the head of Ribblesdale this nature reserve enjoys fabulous views of the surrounding dale and meadows. Ashes Pasture consists of a mosaic of grassland types including acid pasture, fen meadow and calcareous flushes along with a small wooded gully on the eastern boundary. In spring and summer it is at its most colourful with a good show of orchids including common and heath spotted, early purple, fragrant, frog and northern marsh. A profusion of other flowering plants such as devil's-bit scabious, great burnet, saw-wort, betony, lousewort and ragged robin add to the colour along with globeflower, wood cranesbill and marsh marigold on the lower slopes.

The area is great for breeding birds and in spring you may be rewarded with views of the 'bubbling' display of curlews and the parachute display of meadow pipits. Black grouse are occasionally reported nearby and management of the nature reserve includes boosting potential black grouse habitat by creating a mosaic of tall and short vegetation and providing a range of food sources from shoots and buds to invertebrates to feed chicks.

The area of gully woodland on the eastern boundary follows a stream and adds further diversity. Plants found here include bluebells in spring followed by angelica, meadowsweet and giant bellflower.

Ashes Pasture is grazed by cattle and sheep in autumn and winter, following the traditional grazing regime of the area, which helps to maintain its diverse flora. The nature reserve and the surrounding land is designated as a SSSI and there is a great view of the traditionally managed hay meadows and field barns typical of the Yorkshire Dales.

There aren't any paths around this nature reserve currently and we ask visitors to be aware of the fragile nature of the flowering plants.

Greater butterfly orchid

Common carder bee

Location

Common spotted orchid

BEST SEASON TO VISIT

SEASONAL HIGHLIGHTS

SPRING
Curlew
Common spotted orchid
Fragrant orchid
Wood cranesbill

SUMMER
Skylark
Greater butterfly orchid
Devil's-bit scabious

AUTUMN
Painted lady
Common carder bee

WINTER
Meadow pipit

ASKHAM BOG

NEAREST POSTCODE
YO23 2UB

NEAREST TOWN
York

GRID REFERENCE
SE 575 481

PUBLIC TRANSPORT
Buses stop adjacent to Askham Bog on the A64 and in the nearby village of Copmanthorpe. A cycle track links up to both York and Tadcaster.

DIRECTIONS
Take the A1036 turn off on the A64 on the approach to York and then turn a sharp left into the car park (marked by a large Yorkshire Wildlife Trust sign) after the first set of traffic lights. From the car park follow the path into the nature reserve. If coming from York, take Tadcaster Road south. At the traffic lights for the Askham Bar Park & Ride continue straight on rather than turning right, cross a railway bridge and the car park is on your right.

OTHER INFORMATION
Site designation: SSSI
Size: 44 ha

The boardwalk is a short loop which can be accessed at all times. Wellies are required for the rest of the site which is boggy with deep pools and ditches. Dogs on leads are permitted on the boardwalk only.

TOP TIP Look around the edges of the car park for bee orchids which flower in June.

Magnificent royal ferns, rare gingerbread sedge and spectacular displays of water violets are to be found in this mosaic of fen, woodland and meadow.

Askham Bog is a remarkable survivor of the ancient fenlands of Yorkshire. It occupies the site of an ancient lake, left behind by a retreating glacier 15,000 years ago. The low hill to the south of the nature reserve, along which the A64 runs is the terminal moraine from that glacier. Since Roman times the site has been used by local communities as a source of peat for fuel, resulting in a mosaic of habitats and a legacy of ditches, probably originally used for peat extraction.

The edges of the Bog are kept alkaline by water draining from the moraine and harbour the greatest diversity of plants and insects, including marsh orchids, marsh violet and meadow thistle. The colony of gingerbread sedge in Far Wood is the largest in England and some of the royal ferns are huge and probably very old.

The site was once renowned for water beetles and though some rare species still occur many were lost when the adjacent Challoner's Whin was used as a municipal dump in the late 20th Century. There is still an exceptional number of moths with rare species such as fen square-spot recorded here. Breeding birds are abundant, including common buzzard, willow and marsh tits, grasshopper, sedge and reed warblers. In winter woodcock are sometimes flushed from the undergrowth and large twittering flocks of goldfinches, siskins and lesser redpolls can be heard and seen feeding on birch and alder seeds. Roe deer and foxes are seen regularly, and the pond is a great spot to watch newts, while overhead many dragonflies including migrant and southern hawkers can be seen on warm summer days.

The very beginnings of Yorkshire Wildlife Trust, Askham Bog was purchased in 1946 by sweet manufacturers Francis Terry and Arnold Rowntree, and the Trust set up to care for it. Since then the site has been carefully managed to restore it to the haven for wildlife it once was. Grazing by Trust cattle, traditional hay cuts in the meadows and the hardwork of an active volunteer group has happily seen much of the wildlife return.

Royal fern

Location

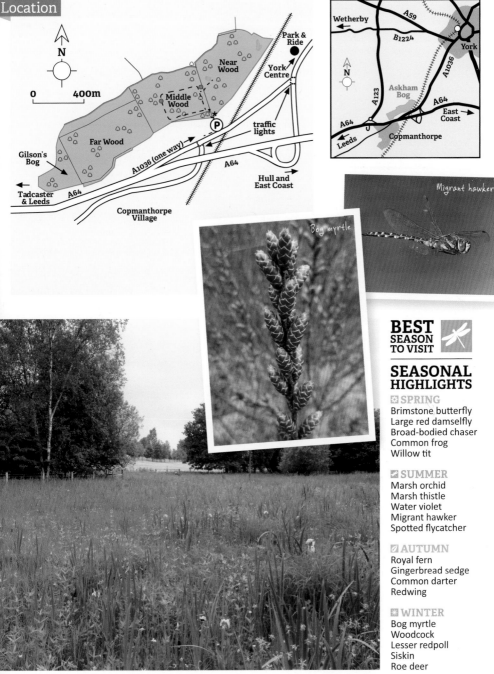

N

0 — 400m

Near Wood

Middle Wood

Far Wood

Gilson's Bog

Tadcaster & Leeds

A64

A1036 (one way)

Copmanthorpe Village

Park & Ride

York Centre

traffic lights

A64

P

Hull and East Coast

Wetherby

A59

B1224

York

A1036

N

Askham Bog

A123

A64

A64

Leeds

Copmanthorpe

East Coast

Migrant hawker

Bog myrtle

BEST SEASON TO VISIT

SEASONAL HIGHLIGHTS

✿ SPRING
Brimstone butterfly
Large red damselfly
Broad-bodied chaser
Common frog
Willow tit

☀ SUMMER
Marsh orchid
Marsh thistle
Water violet
Migrant hawker
Spotted flycatcher

🍂 AUTUMN
Royal fern
Gingerbread sedge
Common darter
Redwing

❄ WINTER
Bog myrtle
Woodcock
Lesser redpoll
Siskin
Roe deer

BARLOW COMMON

NEAREST POSTCODE
YO8 8EZ

NEAREST TOWN
Selby

GRID REFERENCE
SE 633 285

PUBLIC TRANSPORT
Bus services are available from Selby, which pass near the entrance to the nature reserve.

DIRECTIONS
Approach Barlow Common from the A1041 Selby to Snaith road. On reaching the brown nature reserve sign turn onto Barlow Road and travel for approximately ½ mile. The nature reserve is over the bridge on the left, where there is also a car park.

OTHER INFORMATION
Site designation: Local Nature Reserve (LNR)
Size: 37 ha

TOP TIP Visit in early summer to experience the rich carpet of wildflowers on the common, including bee, pyramidal and common spotted orchids.

Painted lady

With a mosaic of habitats to explore on this former brownfield site, Barlow Common is well worth a look. Tranquil lakes host grey herons and kingfishers year round, whilst early summer brings the meadow areas alive with common spotted orchids and viper's bugloss.

Barlow Common, a recent addition to Yorkshire Wildlife Trust's portfolio, is perfect for a family day out. With habitats spanning from wetland areas and wildflower meadows to mature woodland, this delightful nature reserve is home to a diverse range of wildlife.

Visitors are encouraged to listen out for the loud, laughing call of a green woodpecker and to keep watch for grass snakes basking in the sun.

In summer, butterflies including peacock, red admiral and painted lady feast on flowering teasels, whilst dramatically-marked cinnabar moth caterpillars are visible on ragwort – striped yellow and black as a vivid warning to would-be predators.

Flowers including evening primrose, lady's bedstraw, wild basil and common centaury provide a stunning display, whilst ox-eye daisies and orchids also draw visitors in.

On the far ponds ducks, geese and swans raise young in the spring; whilst under the water dragonfly larvae and newts are waiting to be discovered during pond dipping events hosted by the Trust.

Come winter the teasels, flowering now ended for the year, provide seeds for incoming flocks of finches. Sharp-eyed visitors may also glimpse a timid roe deer or fox wandering the site.

Up until the early 1900s local people grazed cattle, pigs and sheep, after which the site was purchased by a local rail company and used it as a ballast tip. Later, in 1983, British Rail reclaimed the land and capped the tip using local soils. Selby District Council then acquired the site in 1986 and managed it until March 2013, when the Trust took over its care.

Today, Trust staff and volunteers undertake a number of conservation tasks onsite, including control of invasive species such as Himalayan balsam, grass cutting and woodland management. The team also maintains the pathways and removes trees posing a danger making this a pleasant and safe site to visit.

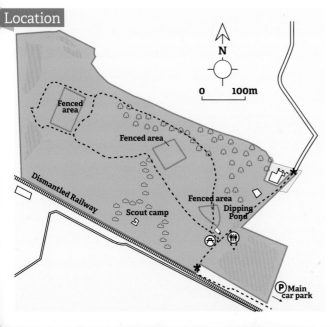

N

0   100m

Fenced area

Fenced area

Fenced area

Dismantled Railway

Scout camp

Dipping Pond

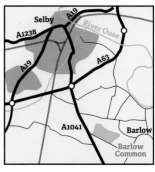

Selby
A19
A1238
River Ouse
A19
A63
A1041
Barlow
Barlow Common

Long-tailed tit

P Main car park

BEST SEASON TO VISIT

SEASONAL HIGHLIGHTS

✿ SPRING
Grey heron
Kingfisher
Reed bunting

✿ SUMMER
Common spotted orchid
Red admiral
Grass snake
Cuckoo

✿ AUTUMN
Fox
Great spotted woodpecker

✿ WINTER
Roe deer
Long-tailed tit
Siskin
Swan

BARNSLEY CANAL – WILTHORPE

NEAREST POSTCODE
S71 1RD

NEAREST TOWN
Barnsley

GRID REFERENCE
SE 346 078

PUBLIC TRANSPORT
Buses from Barnsley
Interchange to Honeywell
– Athersley South stop
near the site.

DIRECTIONS
From M1 take A628 to
Barnsley Centre. Take A61
north to Smithies, take
Smithies Lane on left at
traffic lights. Pass fishing
pond on right, after 200m
park in small car park on
right opposite Barnsley
College Smithies annex.

**OTHER
INFORMATION**
Site designation:
Local Wildlife Site
Size: 17.3 ha

TOP TIP Follow the
footpath from the car park until
you get the stunning views
over the Dearne reedbeds on
your right.

Barnsley canal at Willthorpe is the gateway into the
Upper Dearne Valley. Industrial history and wildlife
coexist in this extensive wetland habitat

A sinuous site comprising the course of the now-defunct
Barnsley Canal gives great views over the wild, Upper
Dearne Valley, its cut-off meanders and sprawling
reedbeds, a mile from Barnsley town centre.

Barnsley Canal finally succumbed to mining subsidence and was
closed in 1953. It now comprises of some stretches of open water
with silted swamp areas and reedbeds.

To the south of the site, accessed via Smithies Lane from the
car park, is an open semi-improved grassland where exquisite
bee orchids can be found in summer. The hedge to the north of
the canal is the longest stretch of continuous hedge in Barnsley. It
provides foraging for flocks of tits including willow tits, thrushes and
bullfinches. From the car park walking west, the canal bed is at first
dry, with crack willow growing in the bed. This soon gives way to a
wetter marsh before opening up into open water. Continuing down
the footpath, past the old footbridge across the canal on the left,
the open water provides ideal habitat for amphibians including great
crested newts. The water plants are interesting and include the only
population of frogbit in the Barnsley area.

Many footpaths can be found in this area. There is a continuous
footpath to follow from Barnsley Canal to the east across Smithies
Lane, through the area known as "the Fleets" into the western end
of Dearne Valley Country Park where you are reacquainted with
another stretch of the Barnsley Canal which still
contains water.

Self-set trees along the banks shade out
the open water and plant communities of the
canal and pose a threat to the integrity of the
canal walls. We are sensitively removing these
saplings and creating a better open canopy in
this pioneer woodland for willow tits
to colonise.

Yorkshire wildlife Trust manage the park
in partnership with Barnsley Council for the
benefit of local people and wildlife.

Frogbit

Location

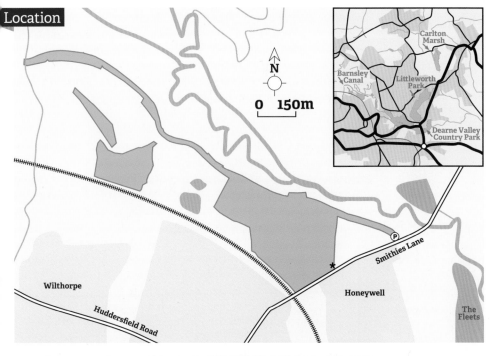

Carlton Marsh

Barnsley Canal

Littleworth Park

Dearne Valley Country Park

N

0   150m

Wilthorpe

Smithies Lane

Honeywell

Huddersfield Road

The Fleets

 BEST SEASON TO VISIT

SEASONAL HIGHLIGHTS

✦ SPRING
Willow tit
Grasshopper warbler
Great crested newt

☀ SUMMER
Reed bunting
Frogbit
Field scabious
Yellow flag iris

🍂 AUTUMN
Mallard
Teal
Gadwall
Green woodpecker

❄ WINTER
Water rail
Bullfinch
Kingfisher
Great spotted woodpecker

BIRCH WOOD

NEAREST POSTCODE
YO62 5NA

NEAREST TOWN
Helmsley

GRID REFERENCE
SE 569 919

PUBLIC TRANSPORT
None available

DIRECTIONS
Birch Wood is located just over 7 miles north of Helmsley on the B1257, immediately adjacent to the road. Parking is available in a large lay-by just past the nature reserve entrance (if heading north, it is on the right of the road). Care should be taken when walking from the lay-by to the nature reserve as there is no footpath.

OTHER INFORMATION
Size: 16 ha

TOP TIP
Visit in late May and early June to see the bluebells in flower.

Birch Wood is a stunning piece of ancient woodland barely touched by the hand of man for decades. Lying within the boundary of the North York Moors National Park, the nature reserve faces across the picturesque valley towards the roots of the Hambleton Hills and boasts some of the most spectacular views in the area.

Birch Wood is primarily a mix of oak, birch and sycamore, with a healthy understorey of rowan, hazel, hawthorn, elder, ferns and more. There is also a reasonable amount of holly, which the Trust manages by reducing periodically to avoid it taking over the woodland. Because of the high deer population in the area, very few new trees other than the holly ever manage to establish due to grazing damage, so a handful of small glades have been planted with young oaks and protected from browsing. This ensures a diversity of different-aged trees within the wood, and therefore the continuation of its existence.

Traditionally, Birch Wood would have had several different 'industrial' uses throughout its life. The woodland itself would have provided basic firewood, but also more specialist material such as hazel coppice for hurdle and wattle making, and evidence of this is still apparent in some of the mature coppice stools that can be seen around the woodland. Farmers would also have pollarded trees in the woodland centuries ago to use the young branches and leaves as winter fodder for cattle and sheep in the days before mineral supplements were available, and this can still be seen in the gnarled shape of the few surviving veteran oaks. The site has also been quarried for the sandstone bedrock and there are several excavated grottos in the high parts of the wood.

Wildlife is in absolute abundance here as it is so relatively undisturbed. Great spotted woodpeckers and redstarts can be found within the wood, plus a wide range of other small birds. As well as the deer, there is clear evidence of foxes, badgers, hedgehogs and grey squirrels throughout the wood, and there is also a healthy variety of small mammals. All these larger species thrive on a diverse insect population.

Great spotted woodpecker

Location

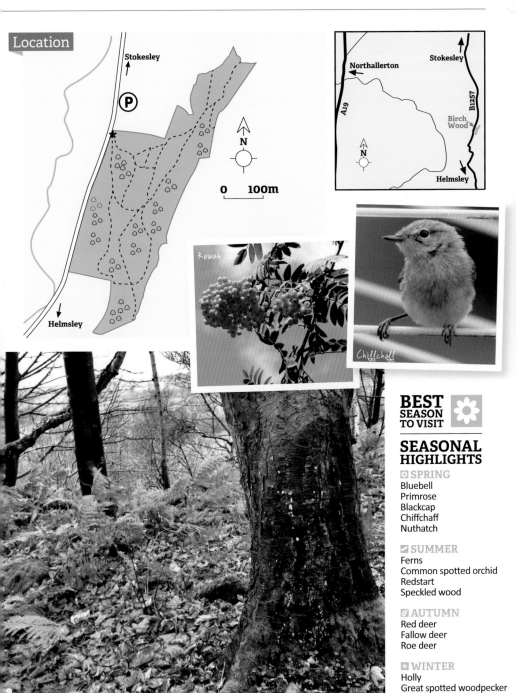

Stokesley

P

Helmsley

N

0 100m

Northallerton

Stokesley

A19

B1257

Birch Wood

Helmsley

N

Rowan

Chiffchaff

BEST SEASON TO VISIT

SEASONAL HIGHLIGHTS

SPRING
Bluebell
Primrose
Blackcap
Chiffchaff
Nuthatch

SUMMER
Ferns
Common spotted orchid
Redstart
Speckled wood

AUTUMN
Red deer
Fallow deer
Roe deer

WINTER
Holly
Great spotted woodpecker
Stoat

BISHOP MONKTON (RAILWAY CUTTING)

Cut into the magnesian limestone belt, this stretch of the now disused railway provides ideal conditions for lime-loving species, creating a small haven for wildlife tucked away in an intensively agricultural landscape. The rich abundance of flowers and sheltered nature of the site provides sun traps for basking insects, and in particular a number of butterflies.

NEAREST POSTCODE
HG3 3QD
....
NEAREST TOWN
Ripon
....
GRID REFERENCE
SE 312 660
....
PUBLIC TRANSPORT
A bus route passes through the village of Burton Leonard a few miles to the south.
....
Directions
The nature reserve lies west of Bishop Monkton. From Harrogate take the Bishop Monkton turning off the A61 Ripon road. Please park in the large layby before crossing Monkton Moor bridge in the direction of the village. The entrance to the site is through a gate close to the bridge on the south side of the road.
....
OTHER INFORMATION
Site designation: SSSI
Size: 2 ha

TOP TIP With over 70 species of moths recorded, try visiting in the evening to find some of them yourself.

P art of the Harrogate to Ripon line of the London and North Eastern Railway, this section became disused in 1967. Once the railway went out of use, nature began to take over, with flourishing wildflowers and the gradual establishment of trees and bushes around the boundaries of the site. The site now comprises an area of rare, unimproved neutral and calcareous grassland, which supports a good range of plants including cowslip, wild marjoram, ox-eye daisy, bird's-foot trefoil, lady's mantle, salad burnet and St John's-wort, creating an attractive swathe of summer colour.

Whilst the line was active, a railway workers' hut with a garden was located by the side of the track and a number of garden plants have survived and are still in evidence there today. Although non-native, these plants provide additional sources of nectar for insects and provide a glimpse into the industrial history of the nature reserve.

The perimeter is bounded by a dense belt of bushes, providing an important habitat for birds, mammals and insects. This scrub is particularly significant in the local area, as the nature reserve is surrounded by arable farmland that provides few such habitats.

In managing this nature reserve, Yorkshire Wildlife Trust aims to maintain the quality and extent of grassland, along with its margin of scrub.

Bird's-foot trefoil

Bullfinch

←A61 (P) Monkton Moor Bridge

Bishop Monkton →

N

0   100m

Ripon
Bishop Monkton
Wormald Green
Bishop Monkton Railway Cutting
A61
Burton Leonard
Harrogate
N

Kestrel

Salad burnet

BEST SEASON TO VISIT

SEASONAL HIGHLIGHTS

SPRING
Cowslip
Bird's-foot trefoil
Hawthorn blossom

SUMMER
Common spotted orchid
Ringlet
Gatekeeper
Salad burnet

AUTUMN
Redwing
Fieldfare
Bullfinch
Roe deer

WINTER
Kestrel
Barn owl
Stoat

BLACKA MOOR

NEAREST POSTCODE
S17 3AH

NEAREST TOWN
Sheffield

GRID REFERENCE
SK 277 806

PUBLIC TRANSPORT
Buses stop between
Sheffield City Centre and
Fox House pub. Alight on
Hathersage Road (A625).

DIRECTIONS
From Sheffield take the
A625 towards Frogatt. The
nature reserve is at Fox
House, before you reach
Frogatt. Car parking is
available on Hathersage
Road, just before the
Stony Ridge Road junction.

**OTHER
INFORMATION**
Contact information:
0114 263 4335
Site designation: LNR, SSSI
Size: 180 ha

TOP TIP **Visit early in
the morning or in the evening
for the best chance of seeing
red deer.**

**Sheffield &
Rotherham**

This magnificent moorland of 180 ha
provides breathtaking scenery and forms
part of a much larger internationally
important wild
landscape.

Stonechat

Blacka Moor provides
spectacular views from
the moorland overlooking
the City of Sheffield below. This
large nature reserve contains a
range of upland species and is
a great place to watch red deer
rutting in the autumn, when the
bellows of impressive stags can
be heard across the landscape.

Unique features on Blacka Moor include the varied heather, the
gradual transition from woodland to open moor and its population of
bilberry bumblebees, *Bombus monticola*. This small upland species
is declining and can be seen mainly in the summer months, though
queens emerge as early as April. The bumblebees have a short tongue
and feed on the nectar of bilberry and heather flowers.

Blacka Moor's diverse migrant bird population includes willow
warbler, blackcap, cuckoo, wheatear, stonechat and whinchat. But, the
ease and regularity of seeing red deer on site – the UK's largest land
mammal – is one of the site's prime attractions.

The nature reserve is full of archaeological features, especially in
the woodlands, which illustrate its past. Charcoal platforms, white coal
kilns, spoil tips, banks and hollow ways are all evidence of the ways

Red deer

in which the woods were used as an integral part
of the local economy. This has led to Sheffield and
Rotherham Wildlife Trust rejuvenating parts of
the woods by restarting some of these woodland
activities. A programme has been put together for
felling small groups of trees, thinning through part
of the woodland, coppicing, controlling non-native
rhododendrons and installing nest boxes. This
work will improve the wood for birds, insects and
woodland plants. The Trust has also reintroduced
cattle grazing on site to help the development of
this rare heathland habitat.

Location

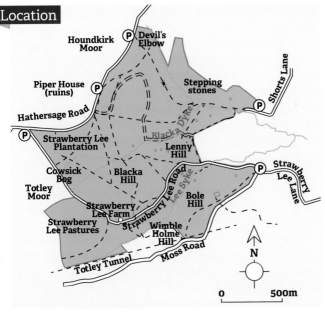

Bell heather

BEST SEASON TO VISIT

SEASONAL HIGHLIGHTS

⊞ SPRING
Willow warbler
Wheatear
Cuckoo
Green hairstreak
Orange underwing

◩ SUMMER
Curlew
Stonechat
Heather
Bilberry bumblebee

◪ AUTUMN
Red deer

⊞ WINTER
Meadow pipit

BOLTON-ON-SWALE LAKE

TOP TIP Check out
the winter gull roost which
sometimes attracts a rarity,
such as a glaucous or Iceland
gull, particularly in late winter.

Created as a result of sand and gravel quarrying, this is one of the few large areas of open water in this part of North Yorkshire and attracts a wide range of breeding and wintering wildfowl.

Once a working sand and gravel quarry, Bolton-on-Swale Lake has been landscaped and allowed to flood to provide suitable habitat for a wide range of wetland bird species. Whilst additional planting of trees and bushes at the lake edge has provided further habitat. The grass is grazed short by sheep belonging to a local farmer, and assisted by a large mixed flock of greylag and Canada geese. The large islands in the lake have mostly been overtaken by bushes and trees, although the Trust plans to clear these to provide nesting opportunities for wading birds such as oystercatcher, which already breed here, and to encourage other species. Great crested grebes, coots and moorhens all breed around the lake.

During the winter months numbers of ducks and wading birds increase and nationally important numbers of wigeon use the site. Smaller numbers of diving ducks, including goldeneye, pochard and tufted duck join the throngs of dabbling ducks which include teal and shoveler. Overwintering wading birds such as lapwing, golden plover and curlew feed on the permanent grasslands surrounding the lake.

The wetlands sometimes attract more unusual visitors: passage migrant species regularly include common sandpipers, arctic and black terns in the spring, and green sandpipers, greenshank and ruff during the late summer and early autumn. The nature reserve is managed by a farming tenant and as such there is limited access around the site, something the Trust is looking to improve in future years. Two hides provide views over the main lake, accessed by a path from the car park.

Shoveler

Oystercatcher

Location

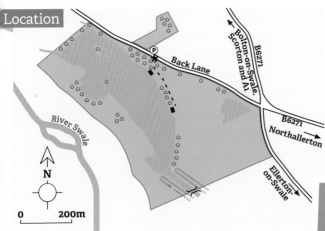

Yellow wagtail

BEST SEASON TO VISIT

SEASONAL HIGHLIGHTS

✷ SPRING
Oystercatcher
Common sandpiper
Sand martin
Yellow wagtail
Sedge warbler

☀ SUMMER
Common darter
Lapwing
Green sandpiper
Greenshank
Ruff

☀ AUTUMN
Great crested grebe

❄ WINTER
Wigeon
Shoveler
Pochard
Tufted duck
Curlew

BOLTON PERCY STATION

NEAREST POSTCODE
YO23 7AW

NEAREST TOWN
Tadcaster

GRID REFERENCE
SE 527 416

PUBLIC TRANSPORT
A bus runs from York to Bolton. Alight opposite Cuckoo Hill Farm, a 15 minute walk from the site.

DIRECTIONS
Just northwest of Bolton Percy village by the railway bridge. From the village head for the bridge then turn right down the track, where the road bends sharply to the left. Parking is by the gate that marks the site entrance.

OTHER INFORMATION
Size: 2 ha

TOP TIP Enjoy a warm June day by combining a visit here with nearby Sherburn Willows and Ledsham Bank.

Nature has taken hold of this old station yard, as bramble scrambles over the old platform and wildflowers grow where rail tracks once ran.

Once a railway goods platform and still lying next to the Leeds-York railway line, this nature reserve covers the old platform and bridge embankments. Areas of the ground are cindery, while in other places you can see the remains of dumped rail-track ballast.

Peacock

In spring, primroses line the railway banks, which suggest limestone was used in their construction. Wildflowers in the grassland includes bird's-foot trefoil, dove's-foot cranesbill and self-heal. Hawthorn lines the boundaries, providing sheltered areas enjoyed by butterflies and moths alike. Common blue butterflies, burnet moths and latticed heath moths can all be found here.

Come summer, garlic mustard and red campion bloom along the hedgerow and attract gatekeeper, wall and small heath butterflies, who also like to take respite in the long tussocky grass. On warm sunny days look out for peacock and red admiral butterflies basking on the old platform. The pond here provides a refuge for great crested newts. Management on site includes bramble control and creating glades perfect for butterflies.

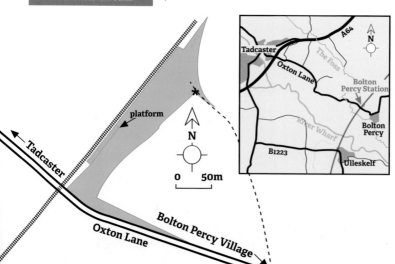

BEST SEASON TO VISIT

SEASONAL HIGHLIGHTS

SPRING
Primrose

SUMMER
Red campion
Peacock
Lesser whitethroat

AUTUMN
Red admiral
Linnet

WINTER
Bullfinch

BRAE PASTURE

Take in the breathtaking views across the Ribble Valley and experience the multitude of plants and flowers in summer.

Whilst only spanning two fields, this nature reserve has an impressive variety of habitats including limestone pavement, acid grassland and a wooded cliff gill. Home to over 150 plant species, several notable ones grow here including the uncommon Oeder's apple moss (so-called because its capsules look like miniature apples) and the rare Alpine bistort found here in one of its most southerly location.

Early purple orchid, violet, primrose and yellow rock-rose all provide colour throughout spring and summer. Butterflies like the small skipper and common blue are attracted in by the rock-rose. Looking out to the surrounding fields, curlew and snipe may also be seen.

NEAREST POSTCODE
BD24 0HU

NEAREST TOWN
Settle

GRID REFERENCE
SD 790 741

PUBLIC TRANSPORT
Nearest train station is in Horton-in-Ribblesdale.

DIRECTIONS
Head north from Horton-in-Ribblesdale village on the B6479. Pass under a railway bridge and travel on for ¾ mile. Pull in on your left past the footpath sign. Access is via a stone stile along the public footpath.

OTHER INFORMATION
Site designation: SSSI
Size: 9 ha

TOP TIP Enjoy the flowers dotted around the meadow and around the limestone pavement in the summer. June is the best time to see them.

Cuckooflower

Rock-rose

BEST SEASON TO VISIT

SEASONAL HIGHLIGHTS

SPRING
Cuckooflower
Barren strawberry

SUMMER
Rock-rose
Alpine bistort
Common blue

AUTUMN
Harebell

WINTER
Stonechat

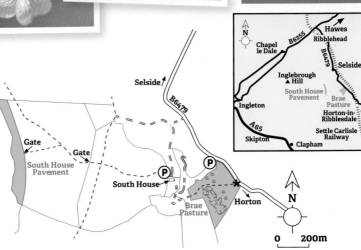

BROADHEAD CLOUGH

NEAREST POSTCODE
HX7 5FB

NEAREST TOWN
Mytholmroyd

GRID REFERENCE
SE 001 250

PUBLIC TRANSPORT
The nearest train station is at Mytholmroyd. Regular buses run from Halifax and Burnley. National Cycle Route 66 crosses the B6138 for cyclists who like a challenge: this is the longest continuous climb in England.

DIRECTIONS
Take the B6138, signposted Littleborough, until ½ mile from Mytholmroyd. Here the houses on the right give way to the fields. Visitors' should park on the road here, vehicles are not permitted on the track. If travelling from Mytholmroyd, Frost Hole public footpath (which is unmarked) will be on your right, before the bridge on Cragg Vale Road. The entrance to the footpath is currently marked with an information board, with the nature reserve marked on it.

OTHER INFORMATION
Site designation: SSSI
Size: 23ha

Some steep climbs and steps; paths can be slippery. To arrange refreshments and education facilities at the Coiners' Barn visit www.bellhousecoiners.com.

TOP TIP Visit at dawn in mid-May to enjoy a beautiful dawn chorus as the woodland wakes up.

Broadhead Clough offers a spectacular Pennine landscape with a dramatic past. This deep valley lies in the bottom of Bell Hole and was better known in the nineteenth century for the notorious Cragg Vale Coiners than its wildlife. From here experience the open, windswept moors and explore the boggy mires of the valley bottom.

The most important habitat of this diverse nature reserve is the rare wet woodland bog areas. A number of small streams flow through the site and spread out to form these boggy areas known as mires. Here tree roots are undermined, causing them to crack or for the trees to fall prematurely, creating the special habitat.

Fallen wood combines with the underlying peat soils, leaves and sphagnum mosses, and rots away to form more peat. This provides the ideal conditions for a remarkable 65 species of moss and liverwort, which include sphagnums and star mosses. Other wetland plants such as rushes and fungi also thrive. Larvae of many invertebrates prosper in this environment, providing food for charismatic birds including curlew, cuckoo, woodpeckers and finches, which rely on the nature reserve for food and shelter.

Managing this site is a delicate operation. Too many trees can lead to the drying out of wetter areas and can shade out sunlight from reaching plants below; too few trees results in dead and rotting wood being removed from the food chain. Trust staff and volunteers work hard to selectively allow light to reach the woodland floor, whilst maintaining moist conditions. The path network and drains are kept clear to ensure visitors can enjoy the site's beauty without impacting on the fragile mire system. Bracken is also kept at bay so that is doesn't outcompete other more delicate plant species.

New visitors to the area should follow the main footpath to the moorland commons above, which allow spectacular views of the surrounding valley. The area's history is also fascinating, home to the notorious Cragg Vale Coiners who produced fake gold coins in the late eighteenth century. Find out more about them at the nearby Coiners' Barn.

Curlew

Location

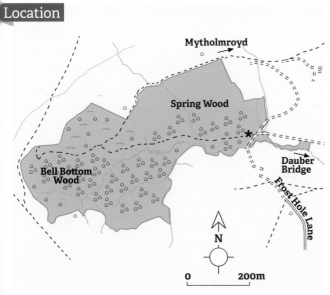

Mytholmroyd

Spring Wood

Bell Bottom Wood

Dauber Bridge

Frost Hole Lane

N

0   200m

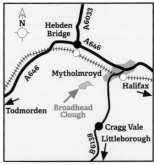

N

Hebden Bridge

A6033

A646

Mytholmroyd

Halifax

Todmorden

A646

Broadhead Clough

Cragg Vale

Littleborough

B6138

Cotton grass

BEST SEASON TO VISIT

SEASONAL HIGHLIGHTS

✚ SPRING
Wood sorrel
Marsh violet
Curlew
Cuckoo
Blackcap

☀ SUMMER
Marsh orchid
Cotton grass
Heather
Harebell
Bird's-foot trefoil

🍂 AUTUMN
Fungi
Jay
Redwing
Fieldfare

❄ WINTER
Woodcock
Red grouse
Tawny owl
Long-tailed tit
Brown hare

BROCKADALE

A visit to Brockadale Nature Reserve is a joy year round, although for the best experience visit in spring when the woodland floor is carpeted in wood anemones, bluebells, primroses, violets and early purple orchids or in summer, when the grassland slopes are alive with butterflies.

NEAREST POSTCODE
WF8 3LJ

NEAREST TOWN
Pontefract

GRID REFERENCE
SE 513 173

PUBLIC TRANSPORT
There is an infrequent bus service from Pontefract to Doncaster which stops at either Wentbridge, Kirk Smeaton or Little Smeaton.

DIRECTIONS
From the A1 in either direction, take the Wentbridge and Kirk Smeaton turn. Drive east along Wentedge Road to Kirk Smeaton and go left through the village to Little Smeaton. Turn left onto Main Street, bear round to the right and then turn left when you meet New Road. Leaving the village, head northwest 0.2 miles up New Road, then turn left down the unmarked Ley's Lane. The car park lies on the left towards the bottom of this lane.

OTHER INFORMATION
Site designation: SSSI
Size: 59 ha

TOP TIP Walk along the south-facing slopes in July to enjoy the wildflowers at their best, with a great chance of both marbled white and dark green fritillary butterflies.

Brockadale is in the valley of the River Went as it flows through a craggy, steep-sided gorge formed after the last ice age when glacial melt-water burst through the magnesian limestone rock. These steep slopes, which have never been ploughed, are now particularly important for their rare grassland habitat. On a bedrock of magnesian limestone, which only exists in a narrow band between Nottingham and Durham, its soil produces excellent farmland, so the flowery slopes only survive as the valley sides are too steep to cultivate.

Around 350 species of plants grow here, some of which are scarce. Early flowers such as cowslip, common dog-violet and spring cinquefoil, well suited to the limestone soil, can be seen in spring. Native plants such as rock-rose follow, as well as orchids, salad burnet, yellow-wort, betony and field scabious. The profusion of large, purple clustered bellflowers is one of the most impressive in the UK and is worth the trip alone. Butterflies abound in the meadows, with the spectacular marbled white and dark green fritillary common in July. Day-flying moths like six-spot burnet and chimney sweepers are common, with close to 300 species of moths having been identified onsite.

Mixed woodland covers the valley floor and dry limestone hill, home to woodland butterflies like speckled wood and white-letter hairstreak, and around 40 species of breeding birds. Great spotted and green woodpeckers, nuthatch and long-tailed tit are resident, whilst warblers such as chiffchaff, willow warbler, blackcap and whitethroat are summer visitors. Yellowhammer and bullfinch are frequently seen and buzzard, kestrel and even the occasional raven may pass overhead.

Where the paths come close to the River Went, look out for dragonflies and damselflies such as the exquisite banded demoiselle and impressive emperor dragonfly. Kingfishers are present year-round but are more often heard than seen as they dart along the river.

The nature reserve was initially purchased by Yorkshire Wildlife Trust in 1966 but has since increased in size following the purchases of additional land, most recently in 2014. The Trust manages the grassland by grazing traditional rare breed cattle and sheep in the autumn and winter, and has support from an active volunteer group, which runs work parties and activities throughout the year.

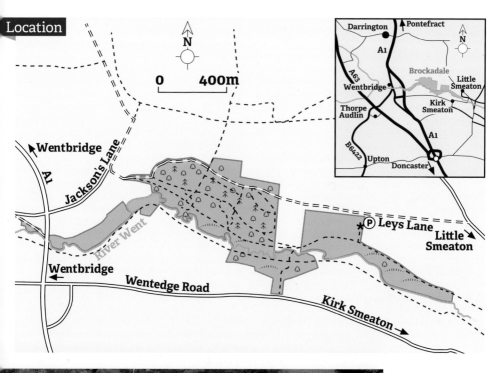

Location

N

0   400m

Darrington   Pontefract

A1

Brockadale

A63   Little Smeaton
Wentbridge

Kirk Smeaton

Thorpe Audlin

A1

B6422   Upton
Doncaster

Wentbridge

Jackson's Lane

A1

River Went

Wentbridge

Wentedge Road

P Leys Lane
Little Smeaton

Kirk Smeaton →

BEST SEASON TO VISIT

SEASONAL HIGHLIGHTS

◆ SPRING
Wood anemone
Spring cinquefoil
Cowslip
Orange-tip
Brimstone

◆ SUMMER
Clustered bellflower
Rock-rose
Field scabious
Dark green fritillary
Marbled white

◆ AUTUMN
Woodland fungi
Redwing
Fieldfare

◆ WINTER
Stinking hellebore
Nuthatch

BURTON LEONARD LIME QUARRIES

NEAREST POSTCODE
HG3 3TE

NEAREST TOWN
Harrogate

GRID REFERENCE
SE 323 629

PUBLIC TRANSPORT
The Ripon-Knaresborough-Harrogate bus passes though Burton Leonard village a short walk away.

DIRECTIONS
No parking exists at the nature reserve which lies along the very narrow Limekiln Lane. Park considerately in Burton Leonard village, which is off the A61, and walk south down the lane. From the junction of Scarah Lane and Limekiln Lane it is ¼ of a mile until the nature reserve entrance on the left of the road.

OTHER INFORMATION
Site designation: SSSI
Size: 3ha

TOP TIP Visit in June to see the orchids at their best and for a good chance of seeing white-letter hairstreaks.

Once a limestone quarry, this nature reserve is now a plant oasis. Butterflies bask in the sun and other insects may be found seeking shelter in this quiet spot. The site's industrial past is still evident, with lime kilns found throughout the nature reserve.

Burton Leonard Lime Quarries comprises a mixture of broadleaved woodland, scrub and magnesian limestone grassland.

This special mix of habitats encourages a rich combination of plant species, some of which are locally rare including squinancywort and autumn gentian. Two small populations of the nationally scarce spring sedge are also present in the grassland areas.

The shallow lime-rich soils are nutrient-poor and support highly botanically diverse magnesian limestone grassland with species including wild thyme, salad burnet, small scabious, fairy flax, bird's-foot trefoil, eyebright, betony, wild basil, harebell, greater knapweed, cowslip and carline thistle. Ash woodland has developed in the northern quarry and calcareous scrub of hawthorn, elder and hazel has grown around the grassland and exposed cliff face of the southern quarry and banks.

Sheltered grassy areas and scrub provide ideal habitats for many butterflies, including dingy skipper, brimstone, green-veined white, meadow brown, ringlet and speckled wood. White-letter hairstreaks are also seen around the elm trees; they are on the wing on warm sunny days between the end of May and the beginning of July.

The site was an active limestone quarry from the 19th Century through to 1941, with the worked stone being burnt in the lime kilns on the site to produce quick lime. This material had a wide variety of uses from construction to agriculture. The remains of four lime kilns can still be seen on site as evidence of the nature reserve's industrial past.

Yorkshire Wildlife Trust leases the nature reserve from Mountgarrett Estates and works to prevent encroachment of trees and shrubs onto the limestone grassland banks by a combination of cutting and grazing. Around the grassland areas, scrub is coppiced on a 20-year rotation, ensuring a wide age range from open areas with flourishing ground flora, to dense thickets rich in berries for birds. The woodland in the northern part of the site is left without intervention.

Meadow brown

Location

Lime Kiln Lane

Burton Leonard

Former refuse tip

Quarry 1

Brier Hill

Quarry 2

Mickle Hill

N

0   100m

River Ure

Ripon

Bishop Monkton

Wormald Green

Burton Leonard

Burton Leonard Lime Quarries

Copgrove

Harrogate

Knaresborough

A61

N

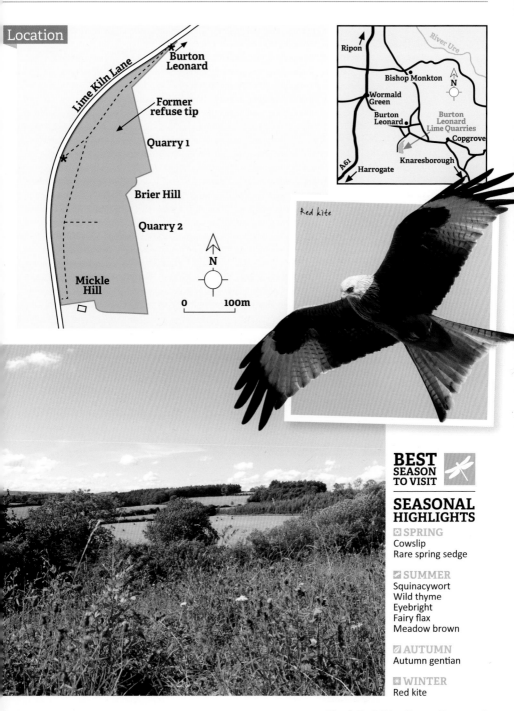

Red kite

BEST SEASON TO VISIT

SEASONAL HIGHLIGHTS

✚ SPRING
Cowslip
Rare spring sedge

◪ SUMMER
Squinacywort
Wild thyme
Eyebright
Fairy flax
Meadow brown

◪ AUTUMN
Autumn gentian

✚ WINTER
Red kite

BURTON RIGGS

NEAREST POSTCODE
YO12 4QE

NEAREST TOWN
Seamer

GRID REFERENCE
TA 029 832

PUBLIC TRANSPORT
Regular bus and train services run to Scarborough, with local buses stopping nearby in Eastfield and Crossgates and trains stopping at Seamer station, ½ a mile to the north.

DIRECTIONS
The lakes are to the east of the A64 Scarborough road, with a car park lying just west of the roundabout. Follow the path south under the A64 bridge and on to the nature reserve.

OTHER INFORMATION
Size: 14 ha

TOP TIP A visit early on a May morning will reveal a wealth of flowers, butterflies and some migrant birds.

The large, open lakes at Burton Riggs make it a good place to watch wildfowl and wading birds, particularly during autumn migration and over the winter months.

Tufted duck

An unusual habitat in the Ryedale area, Burton Riggs is a 14 hectare site primarily consisting of clean freshwater lakes with some scrub, woodland and grassland.

An early morning walk in spring can reveal summer migrant birds in the scrub such as whitethroat, blackcap and chiffchaff, with the occasional garden warbler. Grey herons and the occasional little egret are seen. During the winter months when the site is a little quieter, ducks including pochard and tufted duck gather.

The ponds surrounding the lakes have been home to great crested newt for a number of years.

Burton Riggs is bounded mainly by industrial land and housing, which makes it a valuable oasis for wildlife and local people alike. As an artificial site created by gravel quarrying in the 1970s for the construction of the adjacent A64, it is relatively young in wildlife terms, but already has a rich mix of habitats and species to its name. A public footpath runs through part of the nature reserve underneath the A64 road bridge and out into the industrial area to the east. Permissive paths run around the entirety of the site, with one route around the smaller lake specially designed for disabled access and the route around the larger lake being a rougher track with steps and boardwalks surmounting boggy and hilly parts.

Wildlife management includes keeping ponds clear from silting up, rotational coppicing of willow around the lakes and increasing the area of woodland so that there is a step-up from two to three patches around the site. The scrub is a vital habitat for small birds and mammals, and is retained as much as possible, only being cut back along the footpaths.

Common darter

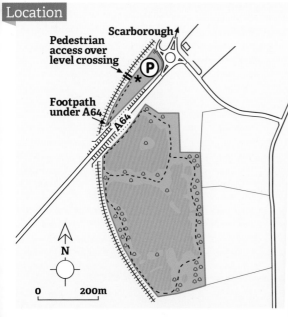

Scarborough↑

Pedestrian
access over
level crossing

P

Footpath
under A64

A64

N

0   200m

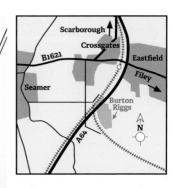

Scarborough↑

Crossgates

B1621   Eastfield

Seamer   Filey

Burton
Riggs

A64

N

Sedge warbler

BEST SEASON TO VISIT

SEASONAL HIGHLIGHTS

⊞ SPRING
Willow warbler
Sedge warbler
Cowslip

⊠ SUMMER
Common darter
Gatekeeper

⊠ AUTUMN
Green sandpiper
Grey heron

⊞ WINTER
Tufted duck
Pochard
Goldeneye
Short-eared owl

CALI HEATH

NEAREST POSTCODE
YO41 5PF

NEAREST TOWN
Pocklington

GRID REFERENCE
SE 751 496

PUBLIC TRANSPORT
Regular bus services run between Hull and York and stop at the Steer Inn opposite the nature reserve.

DIRECTIONS
On the north side of the A1079 Hull to York road, approximately 6¾ miles east of the A64/A1079 junction. The entrance to the site is almost opposite the Steer Inn. Please park carefully on the lane behind the pub and cross the A1079 to enter the site.

OTHER INFORMATION
Size: 11 ha

Dogs on leads permitted on the public footpath only.

TOP TIP Visit in mid-summer equipped with a hand lens or small magnifying glass to appreciate the tiny grassland flowers in full bloom. Crouching down you may also spot battalions of ants busy working or some of the beautiful mosses.

On a walk round Cali Heath you'll soon discover it is not your typical nature reserve, but a diamond in the rough. On close inspection you will be delighted by the detail of tiny flowering plants in the short rabbit-grazed sandy grasslands, or the numbers of common butterflies feeding on flowering grass and willowherb heads in the old allotments.

Cali Heath is an area of grassy heath – a habitat rare in Yorkshire. Tiny flowering plants can be seen in the grassland including bird's-foot trefoil, dove's-foot cranesbill and common stork's-bill – all typical of these sandy soils. Hare's-foot clover is worth looking out for, named for its fluffy-looking flower heads. Shepherd's cress, recorded in only three other places in Yorkshire, also grows here.

Parts of the site support rough grassland which is valuable for a huge number of insects. Over 370 fly species alone have been recorded here and the site is also important for beetles and bugs too. One fly species, *Hilara gallica*, was thought to be extinct in Britain until it was found here recently: the nature reserve is now its UK stronghold. Also, look out for green woodpeckers feeding on ants.

There are small areas of oak woodland in the drier parts of the site, with alders and willow fringing the ditches and in some of the wetter spots rushes and yellow flag iris grow.

At the time of the gold rush in America, when people travelled west to California to make their fortune, the heath was granted to the poor of Barmby Moor by a local Trust – so the people here similarly travelled west to make their fortune – hence the area became known as California Heath and shortened to Cali Heath. When Yorkshire Wildlife Trust took on the nature reserve in 2003 parts of the site were agricultural set-aside. Since then restoration of the acidic grassland habitat has been key, with grazing by rare breed cattle and sheep, and removal of invading scrub, bracken and bramble. The two fields which had been previously farmed were re-seeded to recreate the natural grasslands. The site is a true success story, as restoration is really working, with one of the restored grasslands now species-rich.

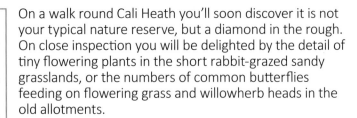

Minotaur beetle

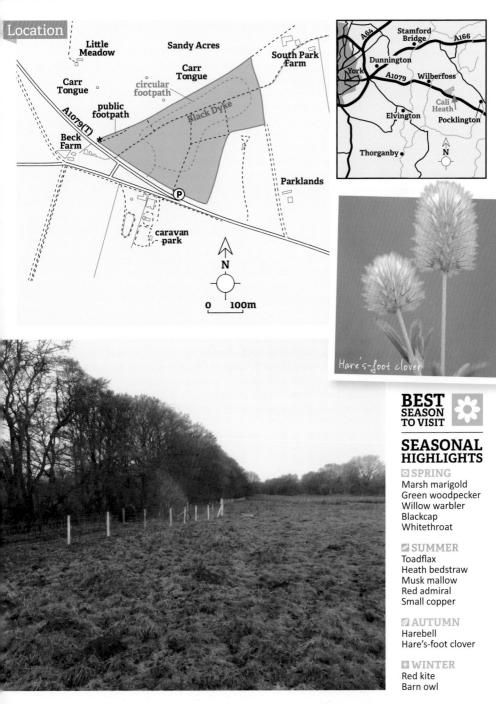

Location

Little Meadow

Sandy Acres

Carr Tongue

South Park Farm

Carr Tongue

circular footpath

Carr Tongue

A1079(T)

public footpath

Black Dyke

Beck Farm

Parklands

P

caravan park

N

0   100m

Stamford Bridge

A64

A166

Dunnington

A1079

Wilberfoss

York

Cali Heath

Elvington

Pocklington

Thorganby

N

Hare's-foot clover

BEST SEASON TO VISIT

SEASONAL HIGHLIGHTS

⊞ SPRING
Marsh marigold
Green woodpecker
Willow warbler
Blackcap
Whitethroat

▨ SUMMER
Toadflax
Heath bedstraw
Musk mallow
Red admiral
Small copper

▨ AUTUMN
Harebell
Hare's-foot clover

▧ WINTER
Red kite
Barn owl

CARBROOK RAVINE

NEAREST POSTCODE
S13 8FA

NEAREST TOWN
Sheffield

GRID REFERENCE
SK 393 857

PUBLIC TRANSPORT
Buses between Sheffield
and Woodhouse stop on
Castlebeck Avenue.

DIRECTIONS
Take Junction 34 off the
M1 and travel south on the
A6102. Cross over the A57
and then turn right onto
Castlebeck Avenue. There
is street parking nearby.

**OTHER
INFORMATION**
Contact information:
0114 263 4335
Size: 11 ha

Sheffield &
Rotherham

TOP TIP Visit early on a
calm May morning to savour
the aural delights of a superb
dawn chorus.

This narrow valley used to form part of an extensive 2,500 acre deer park for the gentry of Sheffield. Although there are no deer now there is plenty of wildlife about.

Sycamore

Carbrook Ravine lies in the southeast of Sheffield, near the Manor Estate. This small nature reserve is home to a wide variety of species like song thrush and bluebells, as well as skylark, which has significantly declined in recent years. The locally rare golden male fern also grows in this nationally important wet woodland area, while ash, maple, aspen, sycamore and hazel can be found in the species-rich northwest of the site.

The vast grassed areas are home to mice, voles and shrews, which make for tasty pickings for the local tawny owl and kestrel populations, while the large number of small woodland birds attract sparrowhawk.

The nature reserve is also important to the local community, providing a beautiful contrast to the predominantly manmade landscape around it. It is a great place to relax, explore and enjoy!

Sparrowhawk

Blackcap

Recreation Ground

Bowden Housteads wood

Daneshill Estate

Danewood

Castlebeck Avenue

Castlebeck Drive

Woodthorpe Estate

Spinkhill Avenue

Wainwright Avenue

Spinkhill Drive

Fishpond Road

A57

N

0   500m

Castlebeck

A57

A6102

Sheffield

N

Carbrook Ravine

Richmond →

B6065

Song thrush

BEST SEASON TO VISIT

SEASONAL HIGHLIGHTS

❁ SPRING
Bluebell
Skylark
Song thrush
Blackcap
Chiffchaff

❂ SUMMER
Golden male fern

❂ AUTUMN
Sparrowhawk

❁ WINTER
Aspen
Tawny owl

CARLTON MARSH

NEAREST POSTCODE
S71 3HL

NEAREST TOWN
Barnsley

GRID REFERENCE
SE 379 103

PUBLIC TRANSPORT
Buses from Barnsley Interchange to Royston or the Barnsley to Wakefield route. The bus stops at the top of Shaw Lane and the nature reserve is a ½ mile walk away on the right hand side.

DIRECTIONS
From Barnsley town centre, follow the A628 Pontefract Road towards Cudworth. At Cudworth take the third exit, the Cudworth bypass. Follow this for one mile and at the next roundabout take the first exit, Wheatshaw lane. Carlton Marsh is ¾ mile down on the left.

OTHER INFORMATION
Site designation:
Local Wildlife Site
Size: 18 ha

TOP TIP Tiny purple hairstreak butterflies can be seen flying in the tops of large oak trees on warm summer days. Occasionally they descend to bramble and other flowers seeking nectar.

A glorious mix of reedbed, fen, scrapes, marsh, meadows and wet-woodland makes Carlton Marsh is a great place to relax and enjoy some birding.

A core wildlife site of the Dearne Valley, Carlton Marsh hugs the Cudworth Dyke and is best viewed from the footpath on the old railway line running the length of the site.

It is incredible to think that Cudworth Dike, that feeds the Carlton Marsh, recently had the infamy of being classified as one of the most polluted water body in South Yorkshire. A major scheme involving Barnsley Council and the combined Dearne Valley Green Heart Partnership have worked together to restore the site.

Carlton Marsh benefitted from major habitat improvements in 2015. The dry reedbed was rejuvenated by excavating channels and pools making it a magnet for wildfowl and wading birds. There are well over 110 species of bird recorded annually at Carlton Marsh.

A wetland nature lover's delight, with gadwall, teal, mallard, shoveler, little grebes and greylag geese all enjoying the open water. Secretive water rails can sometimes be seen, along with more noticeable grey herons and little egrets, whilst equally-shy bitterns feed in the reedbed channels. Grasshopper warblers can be heard reeling from the brambles along the river in late spring and summer. Lapwings, redshanks and green sandpipers can be found on the open grassland and wader scrape at the southern end. Cudworth Dike winds around the site and creates a wet-woodland fringe which together with the delightful scrub makes this a core refuge for the nationally endangered willow tit with several territories on site. Carlton Marsh has an abundance of wildflowers throughout the seasons, including field scabious, devil's-bit scabious, weld, yellow archangel, ox-eye daisy to name but a few.

The marsh is also great for butterflies with small skipper, purple hairstreak and small heath amongst the species recorded.

The majority of the habitat management and recording is carried out in partnership with the vital Friends of Carlton Marsh volunteers. Self-set willows always require removing from the marsh to keep its open aspect so attractive to wetland birds and invertebrates.

Yorkshire wildlife Trust manage the park in partnership with Barnsley Council for the benefit of local people and wildlife.

Green sandpiper

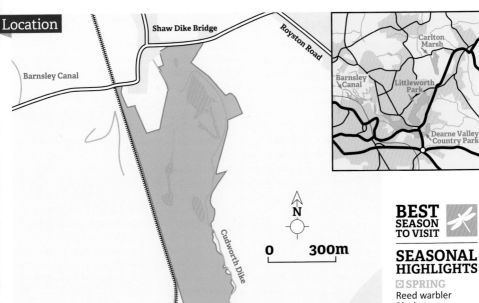

Shaw Dike Bridge

Royston Road

Barnsley Canal

Cudworth Dike

Cudworth

N

0   300m

Carlton Marsh

Barnsley Canal

Littleworth Park

Dearne Valley Country Park

BEST SEASON TO VISIT

SEASONAL HIGHLIGHTS

✦ SPRING
Reed warbler
Blackcap
Willow warbler
Redshank
Lapwing
Cuckoo
Ragged robin
Bird's-foot trefoil

✦ SUMMER
Little egret
Green sandpiper
Kingfisher
Swallow
House martin
Ox-eye daisy
Field scabious
Purple loosestrife

✦ AUTUMN
Shoveler
Tufted duck
Teal
Gadwall
Reed bunting
Willow tit
Goldfinch
Bullfinch

✦ WINTER
Bittern
Water rail
Buzzard
Great spotted
woodpecker
Fieldfare
Redwing

CARR HOUSE MEADOWS

NEAREST POSTCODE
S35 0DE

NEAREST TOWN
Sheffield

GRID REFERENCE
SK 282 954

PUBLIC TRANSPORT
A bus runs between
Sheffield and Stocksbridge,
which is 4½ miles from the
nature reserve.

DIRECTIONS
Take Junction 36 from the
M1 onto the A616. Turn
left onto Manchester Road
(A6102) for about four
miles. Take Brightholmlee
Lane and travel towards
More Hall Reservoir. The
nature reserve is off Carr
House Lane; please park
considerately in the village.

**OTHER
INFORMATION**
Contact information:
0114 263 4335
Site designation: LNR
Size: 16 ha

**Sheffield &
Rotherham**

Visit Carr House Meadows to experience
the old English style meadows, which
have been maintained here and which
create a lovely, peaceful setting.

Badger

The Carr House
Meadows are a
rare example of the
flower-rich fields that were
once a common sight in
England. They abound with
colour throughout the spring
and summer: bluebells,
yellow rattle and swathes
of red and white clover
can be seen early in the
season. Later in the year, field scabious and orchids bloom, as well
as bright pink ragged robin, a rarity in the Sheffield area. In turn,
butterflies are plentiful with ringlets and meadow browns being
particularly numerous.

Cattle are used to manage the meadows – grazing gives more
delicate wildflowers the space to grow. They churn up the ground
with their hooves creating niches for wet-loving plants to seed and
create an ideal habitat for insects.

Many insects thrive in the rich foliage, including species which are
indicators of good quality ancient meadow, such as the scorpion fly
Panorpa communis. The hedgerows and dry stone walls are home
to still more insects, plus a dense population of songbirds including
chiffchaff, willow warbler, bullfinch and goldfinch.

TOP TIP Enjoy a stroll
on a sunny June afternoon
to experience the wildflower
meadows at their best.

Ragged robin

White clover

Location

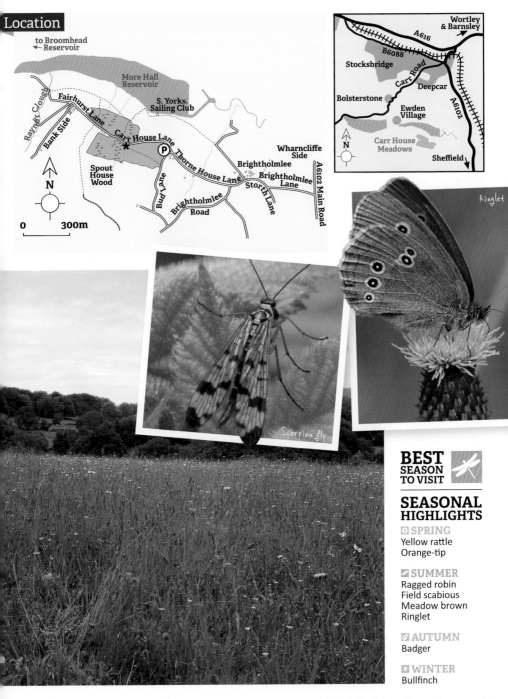

to Broomhead
← Reservoir

More Hall
Reservoir

S. Yorks.
Sailing Club

Fairhurst Lane

Rayney Clough

Bank Side

Carr House Lane

P

Thorne House Lane

Spout
House
Wood

Bud Lane

Brightholmlee
Road

Storth Lane

Wharncliffe
Side

Brightholmlee

Brightholmlee
Lane

A6102 Main Road

N

0   300m

Wortley
& Barnsley

A616

B6088

Stocksbridge

Carr Road

Deepcar

Bolsterstone

Ewden
Village

A6102

N

Carr House
Meadows

Sheffield

Ringlet

Scorpian fly

BEST SEASON TO VISIT

SEASONAL HIGHLIGHTS

SPRING
Yellow rattle
Orange-tip

SUMMER
Ragged robin
Field scabious
Meadow brown
Ringlet

AUTUMN
Badger

WINTER
Bullfinch

CENTENARY RIVERSIDE

NEAREST POSTCODE
S35 0DE

NEAREST TOWN
Rotherham

GRID REFERENCE
SK 282 954

PUBLIC TRANSPORT
Buses run from Sheffield Interchange to Meadow Bank Road/Psalter Lane. Train, tram or bus runs between Sheffield Interchange/Station to Meadowhall.

DIRECTIONS
Take the A6178 from the M1 into Rotherham city centre. The nature reserve is off Sheffield Road. Off road parking is available in Rotherham town centre and there is limited parking on Riverside Way.

OTHER INFORMATION
Contact information:
0114 263 4335
Site designation: LNR
Size: 5 ha

TOP TIP Enjoy the peace early in the morning and spot the wildlife living in this inner city haven.

Sheffield & Rotherham

Since opening in 2009 a programme of planting and construction works has transformed this former steel works site into a magical urban wetland and haven for wildlife.

Moorhen

On site, footpaths and ponds have been created, trees, grassland and wildflowers planted and seats, signage and sculptures installed. Eventually, it is hoped that many native species including otters will recolonise the area.

The huge relics of the site's industrial past have been retained, and used with the sculpture 'Steel Henge', on the flood defence bank. The concrete foundations have been adapted to create wildlife habitats, whilst the giant deckchair sculptures reflect the increasing use of the River Don for leisure.

As well as looking to the past, the Centenary Riverside will contribute to the area's economic future. An important part of Rotherham's flood defences, this unique flood storage wetland means that adjacent land is protected.

The site is a great place to visit and unwind from the hustle and bustle of the city.

Reed bunting

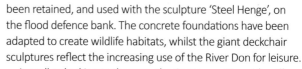

Purple loosestrife

Location

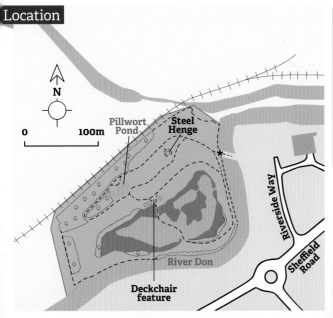

Pillwort Pond

Steel Henge

0   100m

N

River Don

Deckchair feature

Riverside Way

Sheffield Road

Rotherham

Main Street

N

Centenary Riverside

River Don

Centenary Way

Sheffield Road

Sheffield

Yellow flag iris

Footbridge across the main lake at Centenary Riverside

BEST SEASON TO VISIT

SEASONAL HIGHLIGHTS

SPRING
Yellow flag iris
Sedge warbler
Moorhen

SUMMER
Purple loosestrife
Kingfisher

AUTUMN
Common darter
Migrant hawker

WINTER
Reed bunting

CHAFER WOOD

NEAREST POSTCODE
YO13 9PA

NEAREST TOWN
Pickering

GRID REFERENCE
SE 899 832

PUBLIC TRANSPORT
The Scarborough to Helmsley bus runs along the A170 and stops nearby in Ebberston.

DIRECTIONS
From Pickering head east on the A170 to Ebberston. Pass The Grapes Inn and then turn left, north up a narrow lane. The nature reserve is found a short way up the lane on the left, with spaces to park alongside.

OTHER INFORMATION
Size: 28 ha

TOP TIP Visit early on a May morning for a chance of hearing singing redstarts.

Fox

Bluebells, ramsons and other woodland plants offer a tapestry of colour in this idyllic mixed broadleaved woodland nature reserve. The sounds of twigs snapping during an early morning stroll through the peaceful valley may alert you to passing roe deer. The views from the top of the wood are stunning.

Chafer Wood supports an interesting variety of habitats, home to a wide range of plants and birds.

The shaded lower parts of the valley are rarely exposed to sunlight and are therefore covered in delicate ferns and mosses. By the stream running through the nature reserve, woodland plants such as bluebells, baneberry, goldilocks buttercup and leopard's bane can be found, whilst a carpet of wild garlic (ramsons) fills the air with a distinctive fragrance during the spring.

Roe deer are very much in evidence on the site and may well be encountered on a quiet stroll. Rare species of cranefly also thrive, as conditions in the valley bottom create the perfect habitat in which to breed. Birds you might come across include nuthatch, green and great spotted woodpeckers, whilst in spring and summer redstarts, blackcaps and other warblers are present.

In addition to the woodland there are areas of limestone grassland that form small open glades within the trees which have a carpet of yellow cowslips in spring.

Before Yorkshire Wildlife Trust took ownership of the site in 1992, some areas had been used as a plantation, evident by small populations of introduced trees like sycamore and larch. Management by the Trust is focussed on removing these introduced tree species and replanting with native species which are then protected from deer and rabbit damage. Bracken is managed by cutting so it does not encroach and shade out other plants, whilst the open areas of limestone grassland are cut once or twice a year with the cuttings raked up to create habitat piles for insects to use.

Some historical interest remains on the site, including an ancient pinfold near the entrance which has been restored by the Trust. A two hundered-year-old structure, known as King Alfred's Cairn, also exists, at the top of a glade overlooking the Vale of Pickering, although excavation in the 1950s of the cave beneath revealed human remains dating back to Neolithic times.

Location

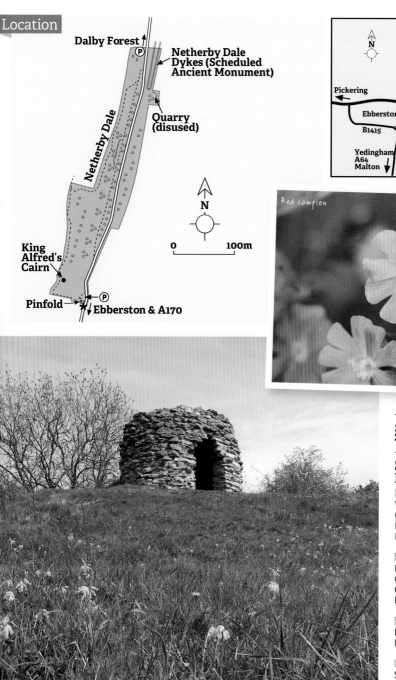

Dalby Forest

Netherby Dale Dykes (Scheduled Ancient Monument)

Quarry (disused)

Netherby Dale

King Alfred's Cairn

Pinfold

Ebberston & A170

N

0   100m

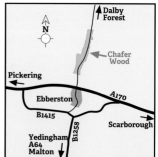

Dalby Forest

N

Chafer Wood

Pickering

Ebberston

A170

B1415

Scarborough

Yedingham A64 Malton

B1258

Red campion

BEST SEASON TO VISIT

SEASONAL HIGHLIGHTS

⊞ SPRING
Wild cherry
Cowslip
Bluebell
Redstart

◪ SUMMER
Pyramidal orchid
Green woodpecker
Craneflies
Rock-rose

◪ AUTUMN
Roe deer
Fox

⊞ WINTER
Sparrowhawk
Treecreeper

CRABTREE PONDS

Set in the middle of an urban area surrounded by roads, this handsome nature reserve provides some much needed greenspace for people and wildlife alike.

Sheffield & Rotherham

NEAREST POSTCODE
S5 7BJ

NEAREST TOWN
Sheffield

GRID REFERENCE
SK 361 899

PUBLIC TRANSPORT
The nearest train station is in Sheffield. Frequent buses run to the city centre.

DIRECTIONS
The nature reserve is off the Barnsley Road (A6135) in Sheffield city centre.

OTHER INFORMATION
Contact information:
0114 263 4335
Size: 1 ha

TOP TIP Visit at dusk on a summer evening to watch Daubenton's bats skimming low over the water like small hovercrafts and watch larger high-flying Leisler's bats seeking airborne insects.

C rabtree Ponds is part of a larger nature reserve, which is mainly used for recreational purposes, or as a cut-through by local residents. The site started out life in the nineteenth century as an ornamental pond for Crabtree Lodge, but today is a large area of standing water hosting abundant aquatic life, including several species of fish, such as rudd, roach, perch, crucian carp, three-spined stickleback and eels. Several local conservation priority species, such as smooth and palmate newts, frogs and toads can also be found here. The dense shrub layer provides an ideal habitat for fungi with 27 different species recorded on site. It also provides shelter perfect for hedgehogs and an ideal home for many insects. Common pipistrelle, Daubenton's and Leisler's bats all fly over from roosts in nearby Roe Woods to feed on insects at the pond.

In the woods sycamore, poplar and ash all flourish. Many birds breed here including treecreeper, great spotted woodpecker and several species of tits, some of which take advantage of the nest boxes which have been erected.

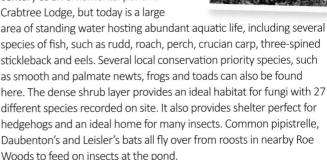

Palmate newt

BEST SEASON TO VISIT

SEASONAL HIGHLIGHTS

SPRING
Common frog
Palmate newt
Smooth newt

SUMMER
Common blue damselfly
Leisler's bat
Common pipistrelle
Daubenton's bat

AUTUMN
Common darter

WINTER
Moorhen

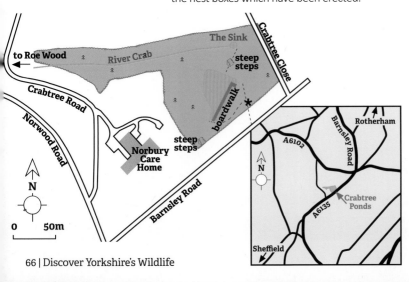

Your Yorkshire, Your Wildlife, **Your Lasting Legacy**

Gifts in Wills are vital, funding one in four of our nature reserves, enabling us to purchase and restore new nature reserves like Skerne Wetlands and helping us inspire the next generation by part-funding the new classroom at the Living Seas Centre. If you would like more information about gifts in Wills then please contact Jessica Thompson in confidence on **jessica.thompson@ywt.org.uk** or by calling **01904 659570**.

Yorkshire Wildlife Trust

DEARNE VALLEY COUNTRY PARK

This wildlife haven is less than a mile from Barnsley Town Centre and extends for two miles along the river Dearne from Hoyle Mill on the A61 to the Trans-Pennine Trail viaduct at Lundwood.

NEAREST POSTCODE
S71 1HS

NEAREST TOWN
Barnsley

GRID REFERENCE
SE 362 066

PUBLIC TRANSPORT
The fantastic Trans-Pennine Trail connects Dearne Valley Country Park into the regional cycling and walking network. Many regular bus services from Barnsley Town Centre stop at the bus stop at the main car park entrance on Pontefract Road. It's a 15 minute walk from the Barnsley railway station.

DIRECTIONS
From Barnsley Town Centre follow Pontefract Road towards Lundwood. The main car park is on your left a few hundred metres after the Hoyle Mill Inn.

OTHER INFORMATION
Site designation:
Cliffe Wood in Dearne Valley Country Park is a Local Wildlife Site (LWS)
Size: 80 ha

TOP TIP A brilliant place for a family picnic, dog-walk or to chill and watch the ducks !

Dearne Valley country park brings wildlife into the heart of Barnsley. This spectacular 80 hectare park includes the Cliffe Wood, a Local Wildlife Site, canal and riverside habitats, wet-woodland and grassland. There is an extensive network of paths for exploring the whole area. The park is used for dog walking, the Hoyle Mill Angling Club fish the beautiful main lake and there is even a skatepark and play area.

The site of the park was once an industrial waste, criss-crossed with mining infrastructure, roads, hardstanding, spoil heaps and the canals and bridges that served the coal industry. Although clues to its heritage can be found in hidden corners of the park it is now a vast 80 hectare haven for people and wildlife in an urban setting.

At the centre of the park is the River Dearne, now so full of life that this is one of the best places to see kingfishers in the valley at any time of year. Scores of wildfowl cruise the river with the ever-busy grey wagtails flitting from shore to shore.

There are two main lakes in the park. The largest lake forms the focal point for the park with many visitors taking the pleasant circular route for a dog walk, a family stroll or cycle ride. There are ample picnic benches in the park if you like to eat outdoors!

Upstream of the fishing lake is the wildlife lake that emerges from the wet woodland. One of the few stretches of the Barnsley Canal, still in water can be found at the west end of the Park. This is also a place to see kingfishers, frogs galore and the odd basking pike can be seen in the summer months.

We work with Barnsley Council to ensure that the grass is cut to leave a mosaic of different sward heights for invertebrates to forage, feed and breed, which in turn feeds birds and bats. We have also been removing rubbish from the wildlife-rich river.

Yorkshire wildlife Trust manage the park in partnership with Barnsley Council for the benefit of local people and wildlife.

Location

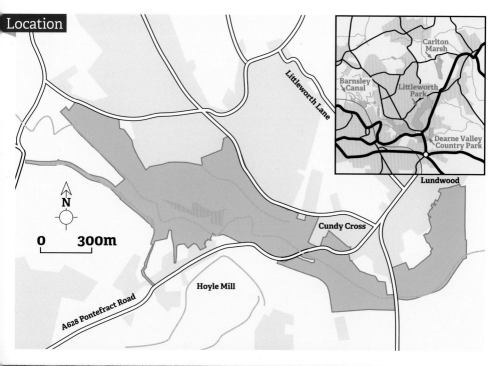

Littleworth Lane

Carlton Marsh

Barnsley Canal

Littleworth Park

Dearne Valley Country Park

Lundwood

N

0   300m

Cundy Cross

Hoyle Mill

A628 Pontefract Road

BEST SEASON TO VISIT

SEASONAL HIGHLIGHTS

✿ SPRING
Willow tit
Frog and toad colony
Great spotted woodpecker
Bluebell

☀ SUMMER
Kingfisher
Brown hawker
Grey wagtail
Pike

🍂 AUTUMN
Scarlet elf cap
Teal

❄ WINTER
Tawny owl
Goldcrest
Treecreeper
Bullfinch

DENABY INGS

NEAREST POSTCODE	S64 0JJ
NEAREST TOWN	Doncaster
GRID REFERENCE	SE 496 008
PUBLIC TRANSPORT	Train to Conisbrough or Mexborough from Doncaster and then a 30 minute walk.

DIRECTIONS

Denaby Ings lies north east of Mexborough. From Mexborough, take the A6023 and turn left down Pastures Road on the outskirts of the town. Follow this north east for 1 mile and then turn right into the car park shortly after crossing the River Dearne.

OTHER INFORMATION

Site designation: SSSI
Size: 23 ha

TOP TIP August and September can be a good time to see dragonflies and migrant wading birds, particularly if muddy edges are exposed by falling water levels.

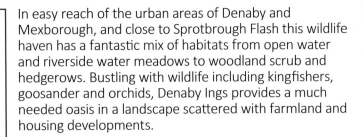

In easy reach of the urban areas of Denaby and Mexborough, and close to Sprotbrough Flash this wildlife haven has a fantastic mix of habitats from open water and riverside water meadows to woodland scrub and hedgerows. Bustling with wildlife including kingfishers, goosander and orchids, Denaby Ings provides a much needed oasis in a landscape scattered with farmland and housing developments.

Riverside meadows, dry meadows, open water, woodland scrub and hedgerow habitats are all found at Denaby Ings and support a diverse range of species. Grey herons sit by the river waiting to strike while parties of handsome goosander loaf during the winter months. In the meadows butterflies are abundant during the summer, visiting the assorted wildflowers, whereas winter sees flocks of migrant birds including fieldfare and lesser redpoll.

To catch sight of the wondrous wildlife here spend time in the two hides which overlook the main marsh and provide excellent sights over the open water of the Ings and the river valley to the wooded crags in the distance. Occasional rarities are seen including great white egret, spoonbill and garganey in recent years. Follow the raised embankment of the old Dearne Valley Railway to reach them. The railway, which was once used to transport coal from the local mines, is now full of the sound of birdsong during the spring and summer – perfect for a dawn chorus walk.

Close to the River Dearne, in times of flood, water can be diverted down the old course of the river into the flash. After the peak of the flood has passed, large iron gates allow water to escape. This storing of water on site provides vital flood relief for the area.

The Trust and local volunteers work to maintain the path and to keep open areas free from scrub. The marsh and meadows are regularly mown and grazed to maintain the habitat for a diversity of plants and insects. The water levels in the Ings are monitored and controlled to provide a mix of muddy shoreline and reedbeds attractive to birds such as avocet, greenshank and green sandpiper. This site has a long and varied history which can be traced as far back as Roman times, although more recently farming and coal mining has shaped the area. Mining subsidence has caused permanent open water areas to form where the River Dearne once flowed and these are now rich in aquatic life.

Spoonbill

Location

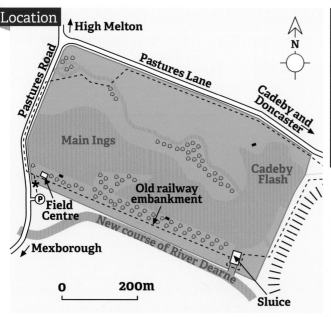

High Melton

Pastures Road

Pastures Lane

N

Cadeby and Doncaster

Main Ings

Cadeby Flash

Old railway embankment

P Field Centre

Mexborough

New course of River Dearne

0   200m

Sluice

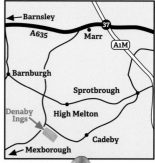

Barnsley

A635

37

Marr

A1M

Barnburgh

Sprotbrough

Denaby Ings

High Melton

Mexborough

Cadeby

Bee orchid

BEST SEASON TO VISIT

SEASONAL HIGHLIGHTS

✤ SPRING
Avocet
Sand martin
Sedge warbler
Grasshopper warbler

✿ SUMMER
Bee orchid
Pyramidal orchid
Common spotted orchid
Grass snake

✿ AUTUMN
Little egret
Common sandpiper
Green sandpiper
Wood sandpiper
Redshank
Greenshank
Black-tailed godwit

❄ WINTER
Bittern
Goosander
Siskin

ELLERBURN BANK

NEAREST POSTCODE
YO18 7LU

NEAREST TOWN
Pickering

GRID REFERENCE
SE 853 860

PUBLIC TRANSPORT
The nearest train station
is in Malton. Buses run to
Thornton-le-Dale and the
site is just over 2 miles
north of the village.

DIRECTIONS
From Thornton-le-Dale
take the Whitby road for
1½ miles and then turn
right into Forest Drive.
Two tracks lead to the site.
The first passes a sawmill
and the second is just
past the entrance gate to
Forest Drive. There is no
parking by the entrance
to the sawmill and there
is an admission charge to
enter Forest Drive.

**OTHER
INFORMATION**
Site designation: SSSI
Size: 3 ha

TOP TIP Visit in June for
best views of the fly orchids.

Hebridean sheep

A warm sunny day brings this small limestone grassland
to life, with colourful butterflies such as small copper and
day-flying moths including six-spot burnet fluttering
between vibrantly-coloured meadow flowers. Rare and
exquisite fly orchids can be found with careful searching.

Goshawk

This excellent example of
limestone grassland has
never been farmed or
worked in any way. Its thin, free-
draining soils support species such
as rock-rose, cowslip and quaking
grass. A few rarities can also be
found here including fly orchid
and greater butterfly orchid.

The meadows are generally at their most picturesque in June and
July, an impressive sight for such a small nature reserve. Rabbits, foxes,
badgers and roe deer are frequent visitors that leave tell-tale signs, and
some lucky visitors may even catch a glimpse of a stoat. Adders and
slow worms are seen occasionally around the drystone wall. Butterflies
breeding here include small copper and small skipper.

The field contains small amounts of hawthorn and gorse scrub and is
bounded by woodland on two sides. The bushes and trees surrounding
the site host willow warblers, bullfinches and yellowhammers. Buzzards
breed nearby and there is always the chance of an overflying goshawk
or crossbill, both of which breed in the forest. Situated on the shoulder
of Pexton Moor the nature reserve slopes down into the valley towards
Dalby Beck. Along the western edge of the site is an ancient earthwork
that is thought to be a late Bronze Age double bank and ditch. This is a
Scheduled Ancient Monument on which management is limited.

Winter grazing using Hebridean sheep keeps young
scrub in check and the grassland healthy, allowing it to
flower and seed throughout the summer. The patches
of scrub that do not get grazed sufficiently by the sheep
are mechanically managed to prevent it spreading into
the pasture. The northern boundary is drystone wall and
is maintained by Trust staff and contractors. Hedges are
kept in good condition by 'gapping up' with mixed tree
saplings that are protected from grazing by guards.

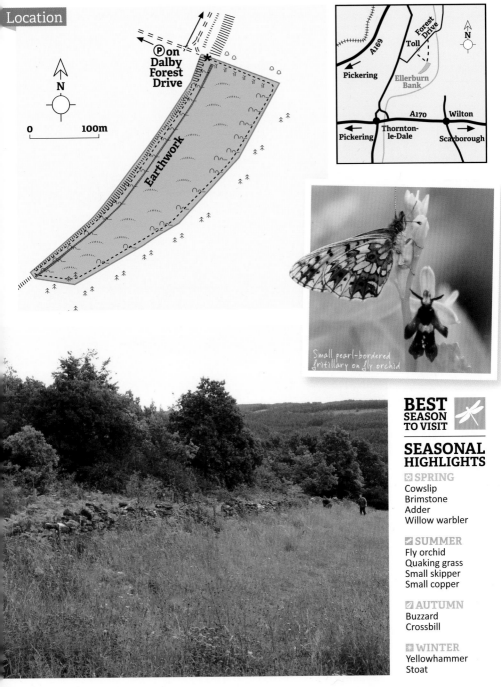

P on Dalby Forest Drive

N

0   100m

Earthwork

A169

Forest Drive

Toll

Pickering

Ellerburn Bank

A170   Wilton

Thornton-le-Dale

Pickering   Scarborough

N

Small pearl-bordered fritillary on fly orchid

BEST SEASON TO VISIT

SEASONAL HIGHLIGHTS

SPRING
Cowslip
Brimstone
Adder
Willow warbler

SUMMER
Fly orchid
Quaking grass
Small skipper
Small copper

AUTUMN
Buzzard
Crossbill

WINTER
Yellowhammer
Stoat

FEN BOG

NEAREST POSTCODE
YO18 7NT

NEAREST TOWN
Sleights

GRID REFERENCE
SE 857 982

PUBLIC TRANSPORT
Nearest railway station is
at Sleights. Buses run along
the A169 from Pickering
to Whitby.

DIRECTIONS
Adjacent to the A169
between Whitby and
Pickering just north of RAF
Fylingdales and south of
the Ellerbeck Bridge and
the turn off to Goathland.
There is room for several
cars on the track next to the
field gate – please
park considerately.

**OTHER
INFORMATION**
Size: 19 ha

TOP TIP The first half of
June is a great time to see both
small pearl-bordered fritillaries,
large heath butterflies and
whinchats.

Combining stunning views of the North York Moors
landscape with a terrific range of exciting plants,
insects and upland birds, Fen Bog is a delightful nature
reserve lying next to the Pickering to Whitby road.

Fen Bog is set in the stunning location of the North York Moors,
situated between the picturesque summits of Tom Cross Rigg
and Crag Stone Rigg. Bounded at both ends by moorland
streams, this long curving piece of land has two main sections: the
main valley mire and the higher ground leading down to it from
the parking area, which is primarily wet heath and moorland and is
separately fenced from the rest of the site.

The land here is dependent on regional rainfall and appropriate
levels of drainage to keep the mire in peak condition. Through
consistent and careful management by the Trust over the years some
of the most unusual species of sphagnum moss in the region have
survived and flourished in the mire bottom.

Besides controlling bracken by hand, the site is grazed by sheep
from neighbouring common land. This is beneficial in keeping down
coarse grasses that may threaten some of the plant species present
such as heather and hard ferns. Some of the more interesting plants
are round-leaved sundew, cranberry, common butterwort, heath
spotted orchid, marsh violet and bog asphodel which are all located
within the mire. In the upper areas there is a population of chickweed
wintergreen that benefits from being in one of the few areas that left
ungrazed on the moor. Tiny piebald small argent-and-sable moths can
be found among drifts of heath bedstraw above the stream. Some
flowers more typical of chalk grassland such as common spotted
orchid, can be found along the main track where crushed limestone
has influenced the soil.

The site is good for butterflies and dragonflies. Look for small pearl-
bordered and dark green fritillaries on the heath close to the car
park, and large heath, keeled skimmer and the majestic golden-
ringed dragonfly on the mire. Bog bush-crickets have recently
been found here. Curlew can be heard calling from the surrounding
moors and whinchat, wheatear and meadow pipit all breed.

If you time your visit well you may also see a steam train pass
down the Pickering railway line adjacent to the nature reserve.
Fen Bog was gifted to the Trust in 1964 by Air Marshal Sir John
Baldwin and Major CL Baldwin in memory of their son and
nephew respectively who were killed in action in World War II.

Common butterwort

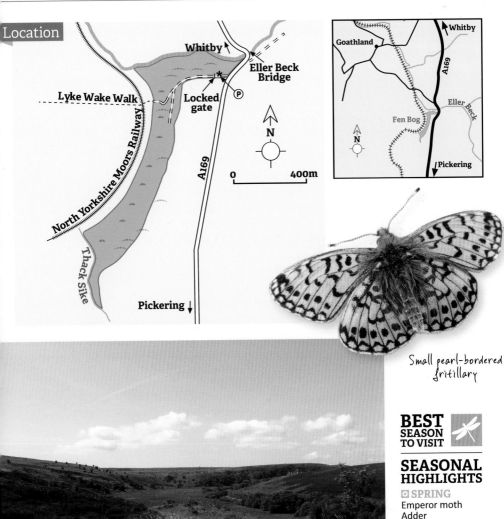

Location

Whitby

Eller Beck Bridge

Lyke Wake Walk

Locked gate

North Yorkshire Moors Railway

Thack Sike

Pickering

A169

P

N

0   400m

Goathland

Whitby

A169

Fen Bog

Eller Beck

Pickering

N

Small pearl-bordered fritillary

BEST SEASON TO VISIT

SEASONAL HIGHLIGHTS

✽ SPRING
Emperor moth
Adder
Whinchat
Meadow pipit

☀ SUMMER
Heath spotted orchid
Keeled skimmer
Small pearl-bordered fritillary
Large heath

🍂 AUTUMN
Merlin
Stonechat

❄ WINTER
Red grouse
Short-eared owl

FEN CARR

NEAREST POSTCODE
DN7 5LU (covers a large area so do not rely on Sat Nav).

NEAREST TOWN
Thorne

GRID REFERENCE
SE 657 156

PUBLIC TRANSPORT
Nearest train station is Hatfield and Stainforth, which have connecting services to Doncaster. Bus services run from Doncaster town centre.

DIRECTIONS
A mile after the hamlet of Fosterhouses the road turns sharply to the right. On the bend, an unsigned dirt track leads off to the left (Carr Head Lane). Parking is available on the lane but please be considerate of farm machinery requiring access. The nature reserve is about 200m up the lane on the right hand side.

OTHER INFORMATION
Size: 4 ha

TOP TIP With an abundance of wildflowers, this nature reserve provides a real treat when visiting in late spring or early summer.

Fen Carr is a hidden gem surrounded by a traditional farming landscape of small hedgerow-bounded fields. These traditional hay meadows contain locally rare and nationally declining species and form a vital stepping stone in the landscape.

S ympathetically farmed for nearly half-a-century by a local tenant farmer, Fen Carr comprises two traditional hay meadows that form part of the rural landscape.

Due to the 1925 Hatfield, Thorne and Fishlake Enclosure Award the owner of Fen Carr is required by Parliament to maintain 'forever' some of the hedgerows bordering the site. The Award also decrees that the two little brick bridges at the entrances be maintained and goes as far as to specify the depths and widths of all the ditches. These ditches are an important feature, as the high water table here supports much of the wildlife on the site.

The nature reserve is of botanical importance, containing over 70 plant species of which many are locally rare, as well as nationally declining. Sneezewort, sweet vernal grass and pepper saxifrage all grow at Fen Carr. These and others support a healthy population of butterfly and moth species including a number of browns, blues, coppers and hairstreaks, whites and the occasional skipper. Of the birds that visit, of particular interest are curlew and green woodpecker.

To manage this site a late hay cut is taken after the wildflowers have shed their seeds. Following this the land is grazed, usually by cattle. Yorkshire Wildlife Trust are also restoring hedgerows in addition to those recognised as important by the 1825 Award.

Pepper saxifrage

Common blue

Location

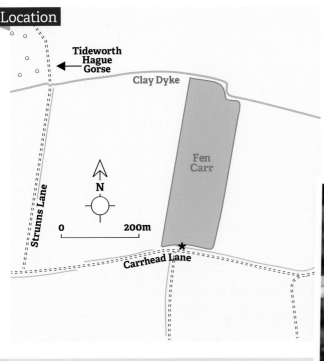

Tideworth Hague Gorse

Clay Dyke

Strunns Lane

Fen Carr

N

0   200m

★

Carrhead Lane

Fen Carr

A614

N

Sour Lane

M18

River Don

Sneezewort

BEST SEASON TO VISIT

SEASONAL HIGHLIGHTS

✴ SPRING
Green hairstreak
Curlew
Green woodpecker

☀ SUMMER
Pepper saxifrage
Sneezewort
Sweet vernal grass
Large skipper
Common blue

🍂 AUTUMN
Grassland fungi

❄ WINTER
Roe deer

FILEY DAMS

NEAREST POSTCODE
YO14 0DG

NEAREST TOWN
Filey

GRID REFERENCE
TA 106 807

PUBLIC TRANSPORT
Regular buses and trains serve Filey from Scarborough.

DIRECTIONS
From the roundabout on the A165, head into Filey and turn left at Wharfedale. Follow this road round to the left to the very end and drop down into the small car park. It is a ten minute walk from Filey railway station: turn right down Wharfedale and follow the long crescent round to the left and then along to the end.

OTHER INFORMATION
Size: 6 ha

TOP TIP Visit in August and September when dropping water levels reveals muddy edges, providing great feeding areas for migrant wading birds.

The last remaining freshwater marsh of any size in the area, Filey Dams is a magnet for migratory birds but is also a haven for plants, small mammals and amphibians.

This quiet gem consists of large freshwater lagoons surrounded by marsh and grassland grazed with cattle. Soft rush dominates, joined in the shallow water by toad rush, bottle sedge and branched bur-reed and the distinctive yellow flag iris, which flowers in early summer. A short walk from the car park is the Main Hide which overlooks the western end of the site. This is a great spot to watch for wading birds and ducks.

To explore further, return to the car park and follow the path through a small copse with nestboxes used by tree sparrows, along a boardwalk to a pond-dipping platform at the edge of a quiet pool. Here dragonflies skim the water settling on the mat of amphibious bistort; the fortunate might see a water vole but are more likely to hear them crunching their way through the soft stalks of water forget-me-not. Smooth, palmate and great crested newts all live here, the latter species in nationally important numbers.

Walk further along the boardwalk and arrive at the East Pool Hide where close views can be had of water birds such as little grebe and migratory wading birds such as greenshank, green and wood sandpipers in the autumn. Look out for water rails along the edge of the pool; they have bred occasionally. Across the pool the barn owl box may be occupied, the male often sitting nearby when displaced by his family. Moth trapping sessions have revealed healthy populations of a variety of moths, including small rufous and old lady. In turn many of these provide food for bats which include Nathusius' pipistrelle and Daubenton's bat.

The nature reserve is leased from Scarborough Borough Council and is managed in partnership with Filey Brigg Ornithological Group, who record the species of the area and carry out routine maintenance. The group own East Lea, another area of wetland just next to the site. East Lea is accessible to members of the group only.

Broad-bodied chaser

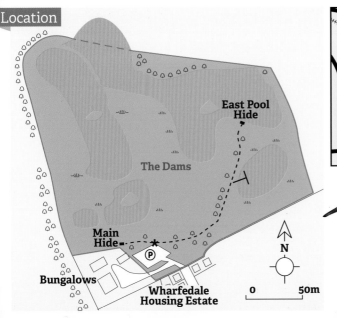

East Pool
Hide

The Dams

Main
Hide

Bungalows

Wharfedale
Housing Estate

N

0   50m

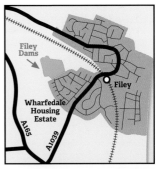

Filey
Dams

Filey

Wharfedale
Housing
Estate

A165

A1039

Ruff

BEST
SEASON
TO VISIT

SEASONAL
HIGHLIGHTS

⊡ SPRING
Broad-bodied chaser
Willow warbler
Sedge warbler
Water vole

⊠ SUMMER
Great crested newt
Green sandpiper
Wood sandpiper
Nathusius' pipistrelle
Daubenton's bat

⊠ AUTUMN
Common darter
Ruff
Greenshank
Dunlin

⊞ WINTER
Teal
Water rail
Tree sparrow

FLAMBOROUGH CLIFFS

NEAREST POSTCODE
YO15 1BJ

NEAREST TOWN
Flamborough

GRID REFERENCE
TA 239 720

PUBLIC TRANSPORT
Nearest train station is at Bridlington. Regular bus services run between Bridlington and Flamborough, some of which stop at Thornwick.

DIRECTIONS
The nature reserve can be accessed by walking along the clifftop footpath northwest from Flamborough Head lighthouse or by following the B1265 from Flamborough village to North Landing, where a large private car park and café exists. There is a small car park at Thornwick which has an admission charge.

OTHER INFORMATION
Site designation: SSSI, SAC, SPA, Flamborough Head Heritage Coast
Size: 36 ha

TOP TIP For best views of the seabirds, take a boat trip from North Landing. You can book at the Living Seas Centre at South Landing – see map.

Flamborough Head has one of the most important seabird colonies in Europe and is the best place to see puffins in mainland Britain. In summer the cliffs are packed with tens of thousands of breeding auks, gannets and gulls creating a memorable experience. Beautiful plants and interesting insects make their home in the chalk grassland along the the clifftops and at Holmes Gut.

Flamborough Cliffs Nature Reserve consists of three sections, Breil, Holmes and Thornwick, each with their own character but all-important for the seabird colonies nesting on the 100-foot high sheer chalk cliffs. Mid-May to mid-July the cliffs host internationally important numbers of breeding seabirds including fulmars, herring gulls, kittiwakes, guillemots and razorbills. Excellent views of nesting puffins can be seen from the top of the cliffs.

A small number of shags also breed while gannets, nesting nearby at Bempton Cliffs, can be seen close by, flying past at eye height in straggly lines. A small colony of house martins breed on the cliffs here and rock pipits can be seen on the beach. Landward of the clifftop footpath are grassland fields which host nesting skylark and meadow pipit whose numbers have increased as grazing has improved the habitat.

In Holmes Gut there is an area of gorse scrub which attracts breeding linnet and yellowhammer and provides shelter for significant numbers of migrant birds. At Thornwick the two reedbeds, though small, host reed warbler, sedge warbler and reed bunting.

Both the base of the steps into Holmes Gut and near Thornwick cottages are fantastic spots for wildflowers. Growing here in the chalk grassland is bird's-foot trefoil, cowslip, common spotted orchids and pyramidal orchids. Along the cliff edge there is a beautiful show of delicate pink thrift and northern marsh orchids that bloom in profusion in June.

A number of butterflies are attracted to these flowers including wall, small skipper and painted lady. The nature reserve is also home to the scarce burnet companion moth.

Flamborough is renowned as a great place for witnessing bird migration. Out at sea, large numbers of terns, skuas and shearwaters move past in early autumn, followed by flocks of wildfowl later in the year. With poor weather and northeasterly winds large 'falls' of migrants occur in the autumn, which at times can be spectacular, with thousands of blackbirds, fieldfares, redwings and goldcrests coming in off the sea, with the occasional woodcock, long-eared owl or great grey shrike thrown in for good measure. In spring, migrants can arrive in good numbers but never quite matching the autumn movements. Every day can bring something new, with black redstarts flitting around the buildings at Thornwick, wheatears along the fencelines and various warblers in the bushes.

Puffin

Sea thrift

FLAMBOROUGH CLIFFS

LIVING SEAS CENTRE

Just down the way from Flamborough Cliffs Nature Reserve is the Trust's Living Seas Centre, which is dedicated to the North Sea's amazing marine wildlife. Find out what to look out for on the coast along with the latest bird, whale and dolphin sightings, as well as the ever changing children's arts and crafts activities. The event programme is the centre's key attraction – join the expert marine team for guided walks and Seashore Safaris which run regularly at weekends and throughout school holidays – see www.ywt.org.uk for details. The Living Seas Centre is open daily from February to November and every Sunday year round. Our Discovery Room is open to the public every weekend between February and November; every Sunday year round; and every day during Yorkshire school holidays (except Christmas holiday). On weekdays during term time the Discovery Room is reserved for education groups. Our opening times are 10am – 5pm (4pm October half-term to Easter). Visiting the Living Seas Centre is free but we welcome donations. Parking is in a Council pay & display car park. Light refreshments are available from the centre.

Rockpooling

Living Seas Centre

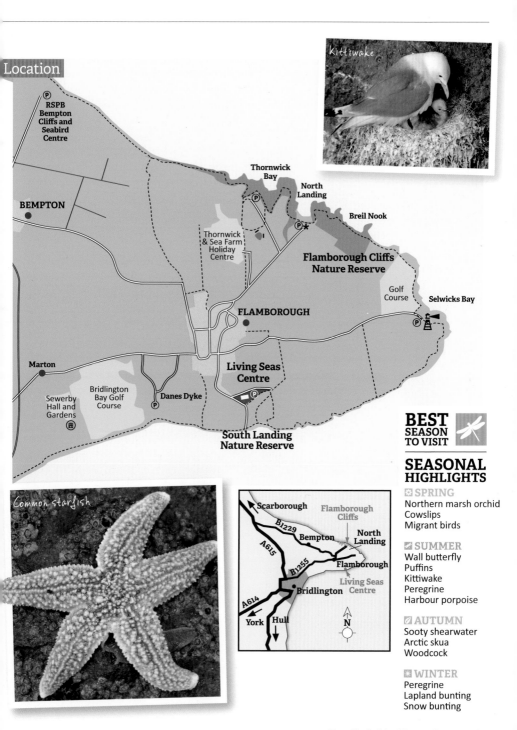

Kittiwake

RSPB
Bempton
Cliffs and
Seabird
Centre

BEMPTON

Thornwick
Bay

North
Landing

Breil Nook

Thornwick
& Sea Farm
Holiday
Centre

Flamborough Cliffs
Nature Reserve

Golf
Course

Selwicks Bay

FLAMBOROUGH

Living Seas
Centre

Marton

Sewerby
Hall and
Gardens

Bridlington
Bay Golf
Course

Danes Dyke

South Landing
Nature Reserve

Common starfish

BEST
SEASON
TO VISIT

SEASONAL HIGHLIGHTS

SPRING
Northern marsh orchid
Cowslips
Migrant birds

SUMMER
Wall butterfly
Puffins
Kittiwake
Peregrine
Harbour porpoise

AUTUMN
Sooty shearwater
Arctic skua
Woodcock

WINTER
Peregrine
Lapland bunting
Snow bunting

Scarborough
Flamborough
Cliffs
B1229
Bempton
North
Landing
A615
B1255
Flamborough
Living Seas
Centre
Bridlington
A614
York
Hull
N

FOX HAGG

NEAREST POSTCODE
S10 4LW

NEAREST TOWN
Sheffield

GRID REFERENCE
SK 288 865

PUBLIC TRANSPORT
Buses run from Sheffield
to Bakewell and Castleton.
Alight on Rivelin Valley
Road and walk just under a
mile to the nature reserve.

DIRECTIONS
From Sheffield city
centre take the
Manchester Road (A57)
out of the city. At Rivelin
take Lodge Lane. Parking
is available on Lodge Lane
or at Rivelin Dams.

**OTHER
INFORMATION**
Contact information:
0114 263 4335
Site designation: LNR
Size: 23 ha

**Sheffield &
Rotherham**

Perched high on a hillside overlooking
Rivelin Valley is one of Sheffield Wildlife
Trust's newly extended nature reserves.

F ox Hagg Nature Reserve is notable for its peaceful atmosphere
and spectacular views over the Rivelin Dams and the woods
of Wyming Brook further up the valley. The site's own varied
and dramatic scenery is as stunning as the view, with its patchwork
of bilberry and heather moorland, silver birch woodland and
scrubby areas.

The range of upland habitats attract a wide variety of birds
including the resident meadow pipits and its close relative, the tree
pipit, which is a summer visitor to the nature reserve. Both species
perform parachuting song flights in spring, with the dive made by a
tree pipit leading to the top of a tree or a bush, whereas a meadow
pipit habitually lands on the ground. A flash of red in the trees could
indicate the presence of a redstart with its fiery-coloured rump,
one of the most attractive summer migrant birds here. Less visually
attractive, but with beautiful songs are the range of warblers that can
be heard singing from the scrub and woodland, including willow and
wood warbler, blackcap and whitethroat. Linnets can be seen all year
round feeding on heather and other seeds.

Once managed as a holly hagg, when the soft spikeless upper
leaves of holly were cut for winter fodder for sheep and cattle, Fox
Hagg is now managed for its wildlife. Small areas of scrub are cut on
a five year cycle, and bracken is controlled to allow heather to grow.
Remnants of holly can still be seen in the gulley
around the stream known as Allen Syke and along
the northern edge of the nature reserve.

TOP TIP Visit after a rain
shower in the summer when
the scents of the moorland
flowers are at their strongest.

Meadow pipit

Bell heather

Location

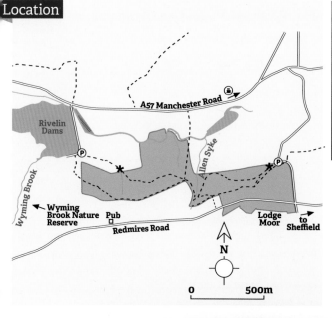

A57 Manchester Road

Rivelin Dams

Wyming Brook

Allen Syke

Wyming Brook Nature Reserve

Pub

Redmires Road

Lodge Moor

to Sheffield

N

0   500m

Damflask Reservoir

N

Wyming Brook

Rivelin Dams

A6101

Fox Hagg

Sheffield

Redmires Reservoirs

Wood warbler

BEST SEASON TO VISIT

SEASONAL HIGHLIGHTS

SPRING
Meadow pipit
Blackcap
Willow warbler
Wood warbler

SUMMER
Heather
Tree pipit
Redstart
Whitethroat

AUTUMN
Linnet

WINTER
Holly

GARBUTT WOOD

The dramatic Whitestone Cliff towers above the wood and shines out from the southern end of the Hambleton Hills across the Vale of Mowbray to the Dales. A walk around the wood at any time of the year gives you fantastic views as well as a variety of habitats to explore.

NEAREST POSTCODE
YO7 2EH

NEAREST TOWN
Thirsk

GRID REFERENCE
SE 506 835

PUBLIC TRANSPORT
Buses from Thirsk stop at the Sutton Bank Visitor Centre.

DIRECTIONS
Take the A170 Thirsk to Scarborough road. Climb the steep Sutton Bank and park in the visitor centre car park on the left shortly after reaching the top of the climb. There is a parking charge. From the car park, follow the Cleveland Way footpath north and then look for a footpath left off the track. This footpath is rocky and descends steeply down through the site to Lake Gormire.

OTHER INFORMATION
Site designation: SSSI
Size: 24 ha

Toilets and a café are available at Sutton Bank National Park Centre.

TOP TIP A walk at any time of the year is invigorating due to the nature of the terrain, but you are best rewarded by a visit in late April/early May when the bluebells are in full bloom and the wood is alive with bird song.

I nteresting for both its biological and geological features, this impressive nature reserve with a variety of habitats is home to good numbers of breeding birds, beautiful flowering plants, and oak and birch woodland.

From 305m above sea level on the cliff top, the nature reserve tumbles 150m to its western boundary just above Lake Gormire. At the eastern edge the notable cliff face of Whitestone Cliff towers an impressive 15-21m. Rockfalls have been known in the past here, but the last major incident was several centuries back, recorded in the 1775 diary of Methodist John Wesley who was preaching in the area.

Above the cliff you will find bilberry and heather moor, whereas below the boulder-strewn scree many micro-habitats have established ideal for lichens, mosses and ferns. Here you will also find evidence of man's activity as the sandstone from the cliff was quarried until 1840 and shaped into square sleepers for use on the railways. The main area of woodland is acidic consisting mainly of birch, oak and holly, but pockets of other tree species occur including aspen, ash, sweet chestnut and sycamore, whereas the more open areas of the nature reserve are covered with bracken and scrub. Tree pipits breed here in summer and can be heard singing on warm summer days. In the northwest corner of the site where springs have made it too wet for the bracken, remnants of the plants that once existed survive. Common fleabane, ragged robin and common spotted orchid are amongst the flowers that flourish.

Established as a nature reserve in 1966, the wood forms part of Gormire SSSI and is part of a network of woodland and forestry plantations that stretches for some distance along the Hambleton Hills. The earliest reference to the woodland is from Tudor times.

Currently Yorkshire Wildlife Trust leases the land from the Forestry Commission; the Trust's main management focus is the control of sycamore. Bracken is also controlled in some areas by pulling, bashing or tree planting.

Redstart

Location

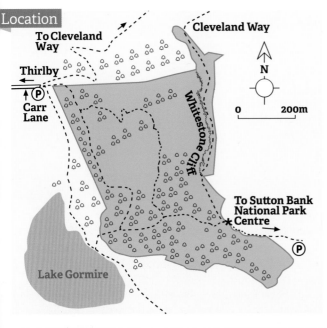

To Cleveland Way

Cleveland Way

Thirlby

Carr Lane

P

Whitestone Cliff

N

0   200m

To Sutton Bank National Park Centre

P

Lake Gormire

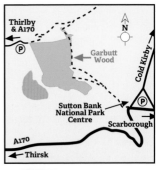

Thirlby & A170

P

Garbutt Wood

Cold Kirby

N

Sutton Bank National Park Centre

P

Scarborough

A170

Thirsk

Wood sorrel

BEST
SEASON
TO VISIT

SEASONAL
HIGHLIGHTS

SPRING
Wood sorrel
Moschatel
Redstart
Tree pipit
Blackcap

SUMMER
Common spotted orchid
Common valerian
Meadow sweet
Ringlet
Meadow brown

AUTUMN
Fly agaric
Milk cap

WINTER
Sparrowhawk
Bullfinch

GLOBEFLOWER WOOD

TOP TIP Take a peek
in June or July when the
globeflowers are in full bloom.

Situated towards the edge of the Malham Tarn basin,
Globeflower Wood come late spring is a bright spot in
a generally bleak and open upland landscape.

Globeflower

Despite its small size, Globeflower
Wood is of great interest due to the
high concentration of globeflowers
and other tall herbs. The golden yellow
globeflowers create a wonderful display,
blooming alongside great burnet, water avens,
meadowsweet and melancholy thistle. There
are some large sycamores in the drier eastern corner
of the nature reserve, whilst willow scrub with some hazel, alder
and birch has developed in the wet area. One of the Trust's smallest
nature reserves, Globeflower Wood is also one of the Trust's oldest,
having been acquired in 1963. The farmer at the time had kept the
area ungrazed because he liked the globeflowers and upon selling the
farm, he wanted the flowers to be protected. The nature reserve is a
triangular limestone walled enclosure largely composed of ungrazed,
damp meadow fringed by various small willows. Due to its small size
and dampness, the nature reserve is a fragile site and while there
is a step stile in the wall, there is no public access. Fortunately, the
globeflowers and other plants can be viewed easily by looking over the
wall. Management is essentially to help this small area remain frozen
in time, ready for the opportunity for the flowers
to spread back into the surrounding area. Walls
are kept stock proof, the willows are kept in check
and invasive species such as stinging nettle and
rosebay willowherb are controlled.

**BEST
SEASON
TO VISIT**

SEASONAL
HIGHLIGHTS

⊞ **SPRING**
Water avens
Willow warbler

⊞ **SUMMER**
Wood cranesbill
Melancholy thistle
Globeflower
Meadowsweet

⊞ **AUTUMN**
Migrant hawker
Chaffinch

⊞ **WINTER**
Robin

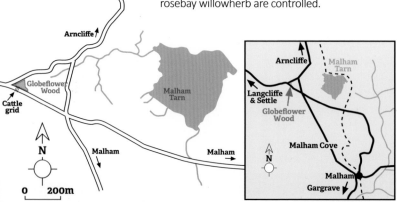

Arncliffe

Globeflower
Wood

Cattle
grid

N

0   200m

Malham

Malham
Tarn

Malham

Arncliffe

Malham
Tarn

Langcliffe
& Settle

Globeflower
Wood

N

Malham Cove

Malham

Gargrave

GET INVOLVED
with Yorkshire Wildlife Trust!

Help wildlife ● Learn new skills ● Make new friends

Email **volunteering@ywt.org.uk**
or visit **www.ywt.org.uk/volunteer**

GRASS WOOD (& WEYBECKS PASTURE)

NEAREST POSTCODE
BD23 5NE

NEAREST TOWN
Grassington

GRID REFERENCE
SD 985 655

PUBLIC TRANSPORT
Nearest railway station is at Skipton. Buses from Skipton stop in Grassington, a one mile walk away.

DIRECTIONS
From the B6265 in Grassington, head north up Wood Lane towards Conistone. The site lies on the right hand side of the road about a mile north of the village.

OTHER INFORMATION
Site designation: SSSI
Size: 78 ha

TOP TIP The timber extraction track into the wood from the gate furthest from Grassington gives superb views over Wharfedale.

Grass Wood is one of the largest areas of broadleaved woodland in the Dales. It is a wildlife-rich ash woodland occupying an area of carboniferous limestone on the north side of Wharfedale.

Grass Wood's importance lies mainly in its extremely rich and varied plant life. It is located on a series of limestone terraces, with much exposed rock and, therefore, open areas. This mix of habitats has a varied flora which includes plants such as lily-of-the-valley, lady's-mantle, melancholy thistle and rock rose.

Alongside the many interesting and attractive plants are a whole range of other, sometimes nationally uncommon wildlife. A diminutive butterfly, the northern brown argus, can be found in the grassy areas – here it is at the southern edge of its British range. Resident birds include tawny owl, the familiar chaffinch and the brightly coloured green woodpecker. An early morning visit in May and June can reveal a wealth of singing birds including the spectacular wood warbler which literally vibrates when singing its high-pitched metallic trill. Other migrants to look out for include the handsome pied flycatcher, the more subdued spotted flycatcher and the fiery-tailed redstart.

The continued existence of the diverse wildlife on the site relies on the persistence of the light and airy conditions found underneath upland ash. Underplanting with conifers and the removal of native trees in the middle of the last century was detrimental to the site, and current management aims to extend the area of mature ash woodland by addressing these issues. The Trust originally became involved in managing the wood when, in the 1960s, it leased a small portion from the Forestry Commission. Over the years it became more involved, finally completing purchase of the whole wood in 1983, since which date it has gradually increased active management, ably supported by an enthusiastic team of volunteers.

The Trust also owns nearby Weybecks Pasture (3ha, Grid Ref. SD 968 691, postcode BD23 5PT). Come late spring this small, yet superb limestone grassland site is home to an excellent wildflower display, particularly along the stream. Look out for species including pignut and bird's-eye primrose. Grazed by a tenant farmer, cattle are sometimes on site. There is limited parking for one car.

Puffballs

Wood anemones

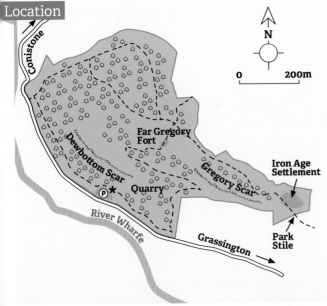

Pied flycatcher

BEST SEASON TO VISIT

SEASONAL HIGHLIGHTS

✿ SPRING
Pied flycatcher
Bluebell
Primrose
Lily-of-the-valley
Spotted flycatcher

☀ SUMMER
Dropwort
Bloody cranesbill
Northern brown argus

🍂 AUTUMN
Common puffball
Milkcap
Brittlegills
Clouded funnel cap
Roe deer

❄ WINTER
Tawny owl
Nuthatch
Treecreeper

GRENO WOODS

Sheffield & Rotherham

NEAREST POSTCODE
S35 7DS

NEAREST TOWN
Sheffield

GRID REFERENCE
SK 328 954

PUBLIC TRANSPORT
Buses from Sheffield and Rotherham call at Hillsborough, Grenoside, High Green, Chapeltown, and Thorpe Hesley.

DIRECTIONS
From Sheffield city centre take the A625 until Hanover Way. Follow the A61 across three roundabouts. Turn left at Salt Box Lane, then right at Main Street. Continue onto Woodhead Road. The Forestry Commission car park is opposite Greno Woods on the left of Woodhead Road.

OTHER INFORMATION
Site designation: LNR
Size: 169 ha

TOP TIP Visit on a summer evening to watch roding woodcocks, bats and dusk flying moths such as the northern spinach.

Covering an area of 169 hectares, Greno Woods is a beautiful ancient woodland rich in wildlife, with records dating back as far as the Middle Ages.

Below the canopy of 30 tree species a wide range of characteristic wildflowers can be found including carpets of bluebells in May, followed later by more unusual species such as common cow-wheat and goldilocks buttercup. Heather and bilberry grow in open patches, where the influence of the sandstone creates more acidic conditions. This diverse plantlife in turn attracts many insects — moths are particularly noticeable, with species including dusky brocade.

Over 60 species of birds have been recorded including breeding spotted flycatcher, exquisite wood warblers and all three woodpeckers, including the diminutive lesser spotted. In the heathland areas nightjar breed and the evocative churring of these birds can be heard from the end of May on warm, still evenings. Visitors may see woodcock roding along the edge of clearings, flying at treetop height. This unusual wading bird nests in the woods and males defend their territories by flying around the boundaries at dawn and dusk, uttering a sharp squeak and peculiar grunting sounds. At other times, particularly during the winter, woodcock are sometimes flushed from underfoot in damp wooded areas, where they fly up rapidly on arched, rufous wings, twisting away through the trees.

Greno and the surrounding woodlands were managed as coppices from at least as early as medieval times until the late 19th Century, with larger standard trees in 20 to 30 year cycles. Timber from the standards was used as building material and underwood for charcoal, clog soles, brush heads and baskets. Two soaking ponds survive today from these activities. The purchase of the woods by Sheffield and Rotherham Wildlife Trust in 2012 means that in the future sustainable management techniques will be employed including timely thinning, removal of some of the non-native conifers, track maintenance and footpath creation.

Common cow-wheat

Location

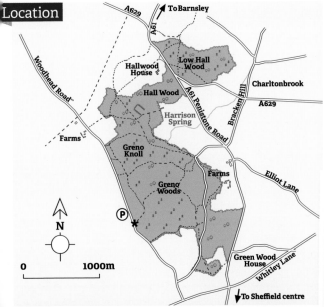

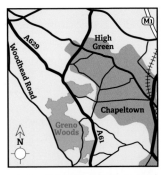

Nightjar

BEST SEASON TO VISIT

SEASONAL HIGHLIGHTS

✿ SPRING
Bluebell
Wood anemone
Adder
Lesser spotted woodpecker
Brown hare

☀ SUMMER
Common cow-wheat
Grass snake

🍂 AUTUMN
Willow tit
Nuthatch

❄ WINTER
Woodcock
Bullfinch
Roe deer

HAMMOND'S FIELD

NEAREST POSTCODE
S10 4QZ

NEAREST TOWN
Sheffield

GRID REFERENCE
SK 263 859

PUBLIC TRANSPORT
A bus service runs to nearby Lodge Moor. The nearest railway station is in Sheffield.

DIRECTIONS
On the western outskirts of Sheffield near Redmires Reservoirs, 1½ miles west of Lodge Moor. From Sheffield, take the A57 turning left at Crosspool. Alternatively, at Rivelin Mill Bridge, take Lodge Lane uphill to Lodge Moor, turning right at Redmires Reservoirs. Access is along the conduit path opposite the upper reservoir. The car park is 200m beyond the conduit path at the corner of the reservoir. There is a small layby for vehicles with disabled passengers.

OTHER INFORMATION
Site designation: SPA, SSSI
Size: 4 ha

wildlife TRUSTS
Sheffield & Rotherham

One of the few remaining areas of unimproved farmland around the moorland fringe, Hammond's Field is a small part of the South Pennine Moors Special Protected Area.

Rich in wildlife, this semi-improved wet pasture has an interesting mosaic of habitats enclosed by traditional drystone walls. Hammond's Field is generally very wet in winter as evidenced by large areas of soft rush and smaller clumps of sphagnum moss. Field wood-rush and grasses such as Yorkshire fog, common bent and marsh foxtail are commonly found. Other species include creeping buttercup, cuckooflower, heath bedstraw and tormentil. The field is important for wading birds such as curlew, snipe, redshank and lapwing, both in the breeding and winter seasons. A scrape has been excavated for their use. A large number of common toads and smooth newts have been found hibernating in the old dry-stone wall on the southern boundary. It is thought they spawn in the adjacent drainage ditch along with breeding insects including the large common hawker dragonfly. Management is focused around the control of soft rush, with work mostly taking place during autumn when there is least disturbance to breeding birds and ground flora. The Trust uses cattle grazing in summer to give the wildflowers a helping hand. There is no access to the field but a viewing area has been created in the south west corner by the permissive approach track. Whilst currently managed by Yorkshire Wildlife Trust, this site is in the process of being transferred to Sheffield and Rotherham Wildlife Trust due to its proximity to them.

TOP TIP April is a great time to see a fine display of cuckooflowers whilst wading birds are busy setting up their territories.

BEST SEASON TO VISIT

SEASONAL HIGHLIGHTS

SPRING
Common toad

SUMMER
Common hawker
Snipe
Redshank
Lapwing
Tormentil

AUTUMN
Common hawker

WINTER
Lapwing

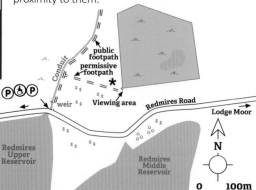

HARLAND MOUNT

Set on a steep hill ascending out of Scarborough, this rough acid pasture and scrub woodland nature reserve offers beautiful views across the town and over the sea.

I n the past this acid grassland has seen some agricultural improvement but now the pasture at Harland Mount Nature Reserve is managed by traditional methods to restore it to the species-rich grassland it once would have been. There are currently few rarities

Ox-eye daisy

on site, but interesting and attractive species including ox-eye daisy and common knapweed flourish. The nature reserve is worth a visit simply for its unspoilt nature, as well as to take in the magnificent views over Scarborough to the north. The steeply-sloping woodland bisects the meadows and is primarily a dense mix of ash, oak, elder and hawthorn where the song of willow warblers can be heard. Yorkshire Wildlife Trust currently thins out the woodland to allow ferns and other flora to colonise more of the ground making the most of the newly created lighter conditions. Bluebell, primrose and dog violet grow on the banks below the woodland. The fields here are grazed in spring and autumn to maintain a healthy sward and to allow flowering plants to seed. There is a small dew pond in the upper field that has long been dry and offers potential for restoration in the future.

NEAREST POSTCODE
YO12 5NL

NEAREST TOWN
Scarborough

GRID REFERENCE
TA 021 871

PUBLIC TRANSPORT
Nearest train station is Scarborough. Buses run from Scarborough to Jacobs Mount next to the site.

DIRECTIONS
As the A170 Pickering road descends into Scarborough, you pass the Jacobs Mount Caravan Park on the right. Descend through the wood and then pull into House Cliff Lane on the right just past the first house. There is room for a couple of cars here, but please do not block the lane. Follow the lane to access the site.

OTHER INFORMATION
Size: 8 ha

TOP TIP Climb up the mount on a clear spring day for wonderful views over Scarborough to the North Sea beyond.

BEST SEASON TO VISIT

SEASONAL HIGHLIGHTS

✦ SPRING
Bluebell
Primrose
Whitethroat
Willow warbler

☀ SUMMER
Dog violet
Ox-eye daisy
Grasshoppers

☘ AUTUMN
Fungi

❄ WINTER
Roe deer

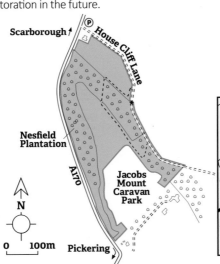

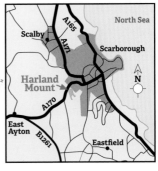

HETCHELL WOOD

A mix of woodland, species-rich grassland and wet flushes, Hetchell Wood provides a tranquil retreat on the edge of the conurbation of Leeds. The variety of habitats provide refuge for rare species which were once widespread in the local landscape. The path network allows visitors to explore each of the habitats in turn, along with other significant features such as the imposing rocky crags.

NEAREST POSTCODE
LS23 6NA

NEAREST TOWN
Wetherby

GRID REFERENCE
SE 380 423

PUBLIC TRANSPORT
A bus runs via Bardsey; alight here and walk approximately one mile to the nature reserve.

DIRECTIONS
The nature reserve is seven miles north east of Leeds. If approaching from Wetherby via the A58 Leeds-Wetherby road, to reach the main entrance on Milner Lane take the left turn signposted Thorner at The New Inn pub crossroads at Scarcroft. Keep left at a triangular intersection and the nature reserve entrance is on the left ½ mile further on. Park in the roadside layby. There is also a public footpath and parking for a few cars from the side of the A58 at Bardsey.

OTHER INFORMATION
Site designation: LNR, SSSI
Size: 12 ha

TOP TIP Hetchell Wood provides contrasting views throughout the seasons. In spring the site is alive with woodland flowers, whilst come summer the meadow follows suit. Autumn has a wonderful rustic feel as the leaves change colour, whilst winter gives visitors a chance to spot wildlife hiding in the undergrowth.

When visiting Hetchell Wood for the first time you soon become enthralled by its beauty and awakened to a landscape that appears locked in times gone by. Walking through the woodland evidence of historical coppicing of hazel for firewood is all around. The multi-stemmed hazel stools grow back with vigour and the recent re-establishment of this ancient management practice lets in valuable light to the woodland floor, allowing wildflowers to flourish and promoting tree regeneration.

Visitors to the site will strike upon an attractive strip of limestone grassland at the centre of the nature reserve which is full of cowslips in spring – a showcase for the surrounding pastures in time gone by when untouched by intensive agricultural practices. Picture-perfect images are created year-round with a stream, the Bardsey Beck, running through the bottom of the site, meandering slowly amongst the trees and rocky outcrops jutting out alongside the bridleway. There are fantastic views across the local valley from the top of the crags, whilst the beech trees provide dappled shade along the pathway through the woodland. In early summer, look carefully at the hazel stools and you may find the unusual toothwort which parasitises hazel. A carpet of bluebells and wild garlic provides a lovely sight, interspersed with yellow archangel, greater stitchwort and early purple orchids.

Yellow archangel

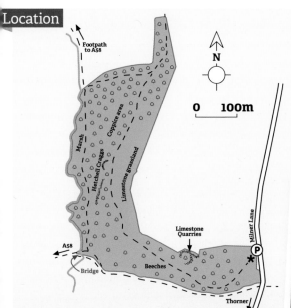

Footpath to A58

N

0   100m

Marsh

Coppice area

Hetchell Craggs

Limestone grassland

A58

Bridge

Beeches

Limestone Quarries

Milner Lane

P

Thorner

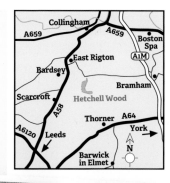

Collingham

A659

A659

Boston Spa

A1M

East Rigton

Bardsey

Bramham

Scarcroft

Hetchell Wood

A58

Thorner

A64

A6120

Leeds

York

N

Barwick in Elmet

Toothwort

BEST SEASON TO VISIT

SEASONAL HIGHLIGHTS

❄ SPRING
Bluebell
Early purple orchid
Wood anemone
Greater stitchwort
Toothwort

☀ SUMMER
Thistle broomrape
Yellow archangel
Blackcap
Dyers greenweed

🍂 AUTUMN
Fungi
Treecreeper
Jay
Devil's-bit scabious

❄ WINTER
Tawny owl
Nuthatch
Roe deer

HODGSON'S FIELDS

NEAREST POSTCODE
HU12 0UU

NEAREST TOWN
Hull

GRID REFERENCE
TA 376 205

PUBLIC TRANSPORT
A bus service passes
Skeffling on the way to
Easington. The nearest
railway station is at Hull.

DIRECTIONS
From Hull take the
A1033 Withernsea road
to Patrington, then take
the B1445 Easington
road. At the eastern end
of Skeffling village, turn
left down Out Newton
Road. The road dissects
the nature reserve after
a mile.

**OTHER
INFORMATION**
Size: 45 ha

Dogs are allowed on leads
on the public rights of way
in the western part of the
nature reserve only.

TOP TIP For a peaceful
walk, visit as the sun goes
down on a summer evening.
Yellowhammers call from the
hedgerows and barn owls
hunt in the fields.

Vivid cerise marsh orchids grow within grassy glades
surrounded by hawthorn scrub and whilst large
pastured fields that attract whimbrel during
migration are surrounded by mature hedgerows,
home to farmland birds and butterflies.

Hodgson's Fields is an oasis of grassland and scrub within the
mainly arable landscape of South Holderness. This extensive
patch of rough grassland habitat is rare here as although
once farmed it was not intensive, which is unusual in the locality. As a
result the site is a haven for wildlife.

The 45 hectare nature reserve supports grassland in which plants
including yarrow, wild angelica, self-heal and meadow vetchling
thrive. An impressive display of southern and northern marsh orchids
bloom during June and July. The tussocky grassland is ideal for small
mammals, and barn owls and kestrels can regularly be seen hunting
for them throughout the year. Whimbrel also frequently drop into
feed in the fields on their autumn migration.

Some areas support scattered bushy-scrub of varying age and
structure. This, along with mature hedgerows of hawthorn, rose,
blackthorn and bramble, are excellent sources of food and shelter for
many birds. Farmland birds such as linnet, yellowhammer and tree
sparrow are commonly seen and heard. Scrub also provides shelter
for insects and butterflies such as large skipper, meadow brown,
ringlet and small heath. A small farm pond provides a hunting ground
for migrant hawker dragonflies.

The site is a great spot for mammals including brown hare,
harvest mouse and field vole – look out for the white rumps of
roe deer bobbing along the hedgerow as you walk along. A visit
at dusk may well reward you with the
sight of several species of bat feeding in
the sheltered flight lines between scrub
patches and hedgerows.

Management here focuses on rotational
hedgerow management, maintenance
of scrub of different ages, as well as
traditional meadow management and
grazing by traditional or rare breed cattle
to keep the areas of grassland open.

Small tortoiseshell

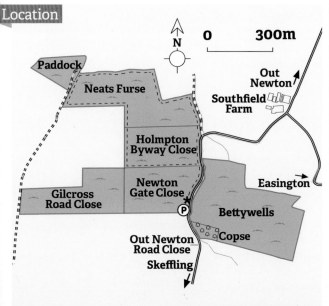

N

0   300m

Paddock
Neats Furse
Out Newton
Southfield Farm
Holmpton Byway Close
Newton Gate Close
Easington
Gilcross Road Close
Bettywells
Out Newton Road Close
Copse
Skeffling
P

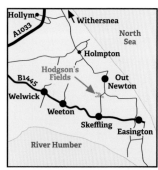

Hollym
Withersnea
North Sea
A1033
Holmpton
Hodgson's Fields
Out Newton
B1445
Welwick
Weeton
Skeffling
Easington
River Humber

Whimbrel

Brown hare

BEST SEASON TO VISIT

SEASONAL HIGHLIGHTS

✿ SPRING
Whitethroat
Grasshopper warbler
Brown hare

✿ SUMMER
Marsh orchids
Large skipper
Ringlet
Small tortoiseshell

✿ AUTUMN
Whimbrel
Barn owl
Yellowhammer
Linnet

✿ WINTER
Redwing
Fieldfare
Roe deer

HOLLINHURST WOOD

NEAREST POSTCODE
LS26 8AW

NEAREST TOWN
Leeds

GRID REFERENCE
SE 403 289

PUBLIC TRANSPORT
The nearest train station is at Woodlesford, which is three miles away. Buses run from Leeds Rail Station to Leeds Road in Great Preston, which is a short walk away.

DIRECTIONS
From the north leave the M1 South at Junction 46 onto the A63 (Selby road). Take the second right onto the A642 (Wakefield road), then a left in Swillington onto Astley Lane. Carry on this road for just over a mile, then take Wood Lane on your left. Park in the lay by at the side of the road.

OTHER INFORMATION
Site designation: SEGI
Size: 10 ha

TOP TIP Visit in summer to see the meadow at its best, with many wildflowers in bloom and pollinators buzzing around.

Home to a diverse number of plants and trees, Hollinhurst Wood bursts forth with colour and sweet scents come summer as the meadow wildflowers come into full bloom.

Meadowsweet

H ollinhurst Wood is home to a variety of species including oak, wych elm, hazel and of course holly from which Hollinhurst gets its name. Other tree species include crab apple, hawthorn, blackthorn and guelder rose, which offer up a bountiful autumn harvest to birds and small mammals. Before the woodland canopy returns to full leaf in summer, bluebells make the most of the sunlight reaching the forest floor, providing an impressive display not to be missed for the sweet smell alone.

Also home to meadow habitat, this nature reserve allows us a peek back in time as there is evidence of the medieval ridge and furrow. This has created a striped vegetation effect as in the damp furrows you'll find meadowsweet, wild angelica, devil's-bit scabious and sneezewort, whilst in the drier ridges species such as sheep's sorrel, harebell and tormentil can be found.

This stand of semi-natural woodland provides a haven for nesting birds who also use the nearby St Aiden's wetland. On the western side there is an area of meadow and scrub, which is being managed to provide a diverse structure and supports a range of wildflowers, small mammals and insects.

Hollinhurst Wood is owned by Leeds City Council and managed in partnership with Yorkshire Wildlife Trust. One of the practices carried out by the Trust and a group of loyal volunteers is the cutting and raking of the meadow in September; this allows late flowering plants time to set seed. Many small footpaths criss-cross this relatively small site, allowing a wanderer to get lost under the tree canopy then find themselves basking with butterflies on the meadow shortly after.

Location

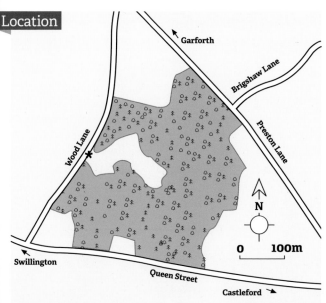

Garforth
Brigshaw Lane
Preston Lane
Wood Lane
Swillington
Queen Street
Castleford

N

0   100m

A642
Kippax
Great Preston
N
Hollinhurst Wood
A656
Allerton Bywater

Holly

BEST SEASON TO VISIT

SEASONAL HIGHLIGHTS

⊞ SPRING
Wood anemone
Blackcap
Chiffchaff
Bluebells

☑ SUMMER
Devil's-bit scabious
Sneezewort
Harebells

☑ AUTUMN
Guelder rose
Crab apple

⊞ WINTER
Great spotted woodpecker
Treecreeper
Wood mouse

HOPYARD MEADOW

NEAREST POSTCODE	DN8 5GS

NEAREST TOWN
Doncaster

GRID REFERENCE
SE 663 109

PUBLIC TRANSPORT
Train link available to
Hatfield and Stainforth
from Doncaster railway
station. Bus services
available from Doncaster
town centre.

DIRECTIONS
From Hatfield village
(NE of Doncaster) follow
Cuckoo Lane north past
St Lawrence Church and
the church primary school
on your right. Carry on
out of the village, then
turn left onto Guile Carr
Lane, approximately 20
yards prior to the Pumping
Station. The nature reserve
is on the right where the
lane bends.

**OTHER
INFORMATION**
Site designation: Local
Wildlife Site
Size: 2 ha

TOP TIP Visit in June or
July to see the wildflowers and
butterflies at their best.

Hopyard Hay Meadow is home to a glorious mix of
wildflowers surrounded by ancient hedgerows.

The hedgerows that line this small meadow are mentioned in
the Hatfield, Throne and Fishlake Enclosure Award of 1825
which shows that this site has been grassland for hundreds of
years. There is a list of over 70 plant species, including sweet vernal-
grass, pignut, great burnet, pepper saxifrage and goldilocks buttercup.
The ratio of meadow foxtail to great burnet suggests a flood meadow
of a rare grassland type.

Butterfly and moth species include the chimney sweeper moth,
a good indicator of old grassland, plus good numbers of butterflies
including common blues, small coppers, whites, skippers and recent
records of purple hairstreak. Birds recorded include green woodpecker,
little owl and large numbers of wintering finches, some of which breed.
The Trust is in the process of trying to enhance the floral diversity of the
site through native seed translocation and by carrying out annual hay
cuts in late summer. The old wild service tree that was there died some
years ago (formally the largest in South Yorkshire), but a young tree
near the old one will hopefully replace it.

OWSTON MEADOW

Eight miles west of Hopyard is Owston Meadows,
a SSSI and a truly stunning example of a
traditional hay meadow. This nature reserve has
no public access to prevent trampling of fragile
plant species. The fields have traditionally been
managed for hay with autumn grazing resulting in
a rich assemblage of plants with over 90 species
recorded, including meadow rue, common
twayblade and adder's-tongue fern.

**BEST
SEASON
TO VISIT**

**SEASONAL
HIGHLIGHTS**

SPRING
Snake's-head fritillary

SUMMER
Pignut
Great burnet
Pepper-saxifrage
Meadow foxtail
Purple hairstreak

AUTUMN
Green woodpecker

WINTER
Little owl

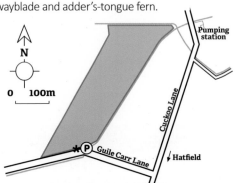

Yorkshire's wildlife faces what could be the most critical period in its history. Join our Wildlife Guardians scheme and make a commitment to halting the decline of Yorkshire's wildlife.

For more information email info@ywt.org.uk or visit www.ywt.org.uk/wildlifeguardians.

JEFFRY BOG (& KIRKHAM WOOD)

Jeffry Bog lies in the tranquil setting of Kirkham Gorge and offers a range of habitats, with an impressive range of wildflowers, including early purple orchid, bogbean and betony.

Lying on the banks of the River Derwent, Jeffry Bog is a relic wet pasture with an important lowland marsh that is embraced by the Howardian Hills Area of Outstanding Natural Beauty. Despite its small size, the range of different habitats make this an interesting place to visit, particularly during the spring and summer. In spring the grasslands are yellow with the flowers of cowslip and primrose, whilst in the wetter areas the large glossy heads of marsh marigolds can be seen. Other notable plants early in the season include early purple orchid. Adjacent to the nature reserve, areas of wet woodland known as alder carr are to be found.

By summer the cocoons of spiders and moths can be found among the tall grasses. The grasslands thrive with betony, great and salad burnet, and common spotted orchid. In the marsh, blunt-flowered rush, oval and brown sedges, and marsh arrowgrass can be found among the cream sprays of meadowsweet, cerise ragged robin and prominent yellow flag iris. At ground level, some spiders can be seen carrying parcels of young whilst others guard territories. Damselflies and day-flying moths can be seen in abundance on warm, sunny days.

Visitors should keep an eye overhead as buzzards are a regular sight. Look along the riverbank as signs of otters are frequent, though this shy mammal is only rarely seen. Barn owls can be seen at any time of the year hunting for field voles, though are most active when feeding young in summer. Kingfishers are a regular sight along the river, joined in summer by an occasional common tern and in winter by goosanders. There is historical evidence of farming on site, with remnants of ridge and furrow to be seen in the grassland. Today, Yorkshire Wildlife Trust grazes the nature reserve with cattle to bring back the wildflowers to the ridge and furrow fields. The Trust also owns nearby Kirkham Wood (0.25 ha; Grid Ref. SE 734 656).

Betony

River Derwent

Centenary Way

Jeffry Bog Plantation

Ant hills

Ridge and furrow

Ditch

River Derwent

Jeffry Bog

Malton

A64 & Kirkham

Church Farm

Westow

N

0   100m

Limited parking (take care not to block farm tracks)

P

Marsh marigold

Goosander

BEST SEASON TO VISIT

SEASONAL HIGHLIGHTS

⊞ SPRING
Early purple orchid
Cowslip
Primrose
Marsh marigold

☑ SUMMER
Marsh valerian
Betony
Banded demoiselle
Yellow meadow ant

☑ AUTUMN
Buzzard

⊞ WINTER
Goosander
Barn owl

NEAREST POSTCODE
HU17 8UL

NEAREST TOWN
Beverley

GRID REFERENCE
TA 034 386

PUBLIC TRANSPORT
The nearest train station is Beverley, from which it is a 20 minute walk to the nature reserve.

DIRECTIONS
Access is off Lincoln Way in the southern suburbs of Beverley. Park in the lay by at the northern end of the road, just before it meets Woodmansey Mile and walk across the grass to the woodland.

OTHER INFORMATION
Size: 0.5ha

TOP TIP A great place to listen to the dawn chorus early on a May day.

Step back in time with a visit to Keldmarsh, a remnant of the kind of habitat that would have once covered this area.

Clear chalk springs bubble up in pools and flow through this secluded wet woodland. The name Keldmarsh is derived from the Scandinavian word 'kelda', meaning spring. This aptly describes the nature reserve, which in wet years sees several springs emerging, forming pools and streams of clear water. This water is fed by underground streams that run through the chalk bedrock.

The site is covered by woodland which, due to changing ground conditions, appears to be making a transition itself. Crack willow and alder, trees fond of getting their roots wet, are giving way to young ash which survive better in the drier conditions. Some venerable ancient willows lie fallen, but their twisted trunks and stems still provide homes for wildlife in their nooks and crannies. Elder, hawthorn and blackthorn provide scrubby areas of cover and birds breeding on site include chiffchaff, blackcap and dunnock. Some of the rarest species found at Keldmarsh are slime moulds. These strange 'growths' look like lichen or fungi, but are actually colonies of very tiny, primitive creatures, that act as one organism. Often found on wet, dead timber they can be seen to move if observed over several days. Wetland plants such as fool's water-cress, yellow flag iris and marsh marigold are found in and around the wet pools and common frogs are a regular sight.

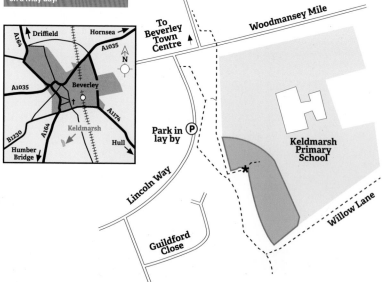

BEST SEASON TO VISIT

SEASONAL HIGHLIGHTS

SPRING
Dog's mercury
Herb-robert
Common frog

SUMMER
Yellow flag iris
Marsh marigold
Red admiral
Small white
Orange-tip

AUTUMN
Song thrush

WINTER
Long-tailed tit

KILNSEA WETLANDS

NEAREST POSTCODE
HU12 0UB

NEAREST TOWN
Withernsea

GRID REFERENCE
TA 405 167

PUBLIC TRANSPORT
Buses stop at Easington, a two mile walk from Kilnsea Wetlands.

DIRECTIONS
From Easington, follow the signs for Spurn. Shortly before entering Kilnsea, the straight road goes over a bank and round a bend. Just after this the nature reserve car park is on the left.

OTHER INFORMATION
Size: 35 ha

TOP TIP Flocks of sandwich terns gather in late summer and at this time some of the newly-arrived arctic wading birds look fabulous in their breeding colours.

Created in 2012 by the Environment Agency, this new wetland has been designed to compensate for habitat being lost nearby on the eroding Holderness coastline.

Kilnsea Wetlands is intended to provide refuge for passage and wintering wading birds that leave the adjacent Humber mudflats at high tide to roost. Large flocks of knot, dunlin and redshank gather at high tide and provide a spectacular sight as they fly into the wetlands. A variety of habitats are being developed to support these birds, but it will take a number of years for them to reach their full potential. Freshwater and saline pools with islands and spits, plus wet grassland with seasonal scrapes will provide this site with roosting and feeding locations, but also hopefully the right conditions in the spring for breeding birds.

The nature reserve is managed in a sustainable way using local livestock. The grazing animals keep the site open and free from scrub, the grass short and the edges of the lagoons muddy. This location is one of the driest parts of the UK, and as there is no ability to bring water onto the site from surrounding areas, the functionality of the lagoons relies on rainfall and groundwater levels.

In spring and autumn, small migrant birds such as wheatears and whinchats can be seen around the site, feeding in the open areas. In time, the grassland should become established and we hope this will provide some botanical value and interest, in turn supporting a host of insects including dragonflies. Salt-tolerant plant species such as spiral tassel weed may well find a home here too.

Dunlin

Greenshank

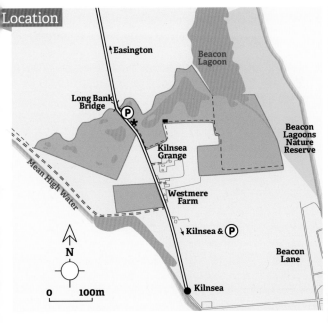

↑ Easington

Beacon Lagoon

Long Bank Bridge

Ⓟ

Kilnsea Grange

Beacon Lagoons Nature Reserve

Mean High Water

Westmere Farm

↓ Kilnsea & Ⓟ

Beacon Lane

N

0   100m

● Kilnsea

A165

Hornsea

North Sea

Hull

● Hedon

B1242

Withernsea

A1033

Easington

Patrington

B1445

River Humber

Welwick

Welwick Saltmarsh

Kilnsea

N

Kilnsea Wetlands

Grimsby

Spurn

Golden plover

BEST SEASON TO VISIT

SEASONAL HIGHLIGHTS

✿ SPRING
Avocet
Little ringed plover
Oystercatcher
Tree sparrow

☀ SUMMER
Clouded yellow
Wall butterfly
Ox-eye daisy

🍂 AUTUMN
Greenshank
Grey plover
Green sandpiper
Yellow wagtail

❄ WINTER
Brent goose
Golden plover
Lapwing
Dunlin
Merlin

KIPLINGCOTES CHALK PIT

NEAREST POSTCODE
YO43 3NA

NEAREST TOWN
Market Weighton

GRID REFERENCE
SE 913 433

PUBLIC TRANSPORT
The nearest train station is at Beverley, nine miles east.

DIRECTIONS
The nature reserve is 2½ miles northeast of Market Weighton. From Market Weighton take the road signposted Kiplingcotes. Use the car park on the old railway line and walk 300m northeast along the line – enter the nature reserve via a kissing gate on your left. Access is down some steep steps.

OTHER INFORMATION
Site designation: SSSI
Size: 4 ha

TOP TIP Don't miss the amazing show of flowering plants in late June and early July, when the orchid spikes are at their most numerous. On a warm day, clouds of butterflies may also greet you.

A wander through Kiplingcotes Chalk Pit in high summer will reveal a riot of colour, with dozens of butterflies fluttering around an explosion of wildflowers in some of the sheltered spots and farmland birds such as yellowhammers singing from the scrub. A walk to the top of this old quarry will give lovely views back along the valley.

Nestled in a narrow Wolds valley Kiplingcotes Chalk Pit provides a haven for chalk-loving plant and animal species. As vegetation colonises the bare chalk, different wildlife communities spring up over time. The first 'pioneers' are mosses and lichens, which colonise the quarry face, whilst short turfed grassland develops on the thin soils of the quarry floor. These soils support wild pansy, wild thyme and mouse-ear hawkweed, whereas the more established soils on the quarry top support common and greater knapweed, field scabious and burnet saxifrage.

Ant hills built by yellow meadow ants are scattered across the nature reserve and are characterised by being covered in springy beds of wild thyme – fragrant when crushed. Some of these anthills can be decades old and in the wider countryside are only found in areas that are not damaged by ploughing or mechanical cutting.

The nationally scarce red hemp-nettle is found here, as is a large population of basil thyme, which has undergone a huge decline in the UK. Butterflies typical of chalky soils occur in good numbers on the nature reserve including marbled white. Blackcap, bullfinch and linnet can be found in the scrub, whereas in winter migrant birds pass through feeding on berries. Little owls are present in the hedgerows.

Quarried until 1902 the site was used to supply chalk during the building of the embankment of the Beverley to Market Weighton railway line, which opened in 1865. Nature then took over and the Trust has managed the site since 1965. Management has concentrated on keeping the grassland in good condition, with autumn and winter grazing by Hebridean sheep and Exmoor ponies helping keep some of the rough, competitive grasses in check, allowing finer grasses and flowering plants to thrive. Scrub and weed control is carried out, and cutting and hedgelaying takes place to manage the hedgerow on the northern boundary.

Greater knapweed

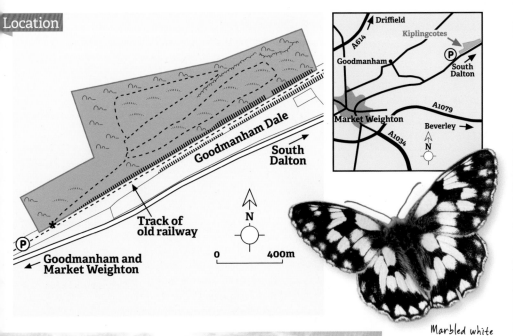

Goodmanham Dale

South Dalton

Track of old railway

Goodmanham and Market Weighton

N

0   400m

Driffield
Kiplingcotes
A614
Goodmanham
South Dalton
Market Weighton
A1079
A1034
Beverley
N

Marbled white

BEST SEASON TO VISIT

SEASONAL HIGHLIGHTS

✿ SPRING
Cowslip
Willow warbler
Brimstone
Yellowhammer

✿ SUMMER
Pyramidal orchid
Common spotted orchid
Common twayblade
Dingy skipper
Marbled white

✿ AUTUMN
Autumn gentian
Redwing
Fieldfare
Little owl

✿ WINTER
Buzzard
Red kite
Grey partridge

East Yorkshire Nature Reserves | 111

KIPPAX MEADOWS

NEAREST POSTCODE
LS25 7QQ

NEAREST TOWN
Garforth

GRID REFERENCE
SE 414 298

PUBLIC TRANSPORT
Buses run between Leeds and Castleford, stopping at Kippax.

DIRECTIONS
From the north leave the M1 South at Junction 46 onto the A63 (Selby road). Take a right turn onto the A656, then a right to Kippax on the B6137. Take the first exit on the roundabout down Butt Hill, then bear left onto Brigshaw Lane. Parking is either on the roadside or in the bowling club car park. Reserve access off Cromwell Rise.

OTHER INFORMATION
Site designation: SEGIs
Size: 8 ha

TOP TIP Visit in June to see enjoy the orchids at their best.

A green oasis for locals, this site is nestled in among houses and provides a sizeable patch of grass for birds, butterflies and other insects.

Kippax Meadows consists of a mosaic of species-rich grassland and scrub habitat tucked away on the edge of Kippax. The neutral and calcareous grassland supports a number of notable species including common spotted, bee and southern marsh orchid. The underlying geology is predominantly Pennine middle coal measures, but the northern edge of the site has an outcrop of magnesian limestone which has the potential to be excellent for wildflowers with correct management.

A range of breeding birds can be found here amongst the scrub, whilst butterflies take advantage of the grassland flowers including small tortoiseshell and peacock.

This area was saved from development by locals so that it could be kept as a recreational greenspace. There are accessible surfaced paths throughout the site making this an excellent spot for a short morning walk. Kippax Meadows is owned by Leeds City Council and managed in partnership with the Trust.

BEST SEASON TO VISIT

SEASONAL HIGHLIGHTS

❊ SPRING
Chiffchaff
Bullfinch
Yellowhammer

☀ SUMMER
Common spotted orchid
Bee orchid
Southern marsh orchid
Common blue
Small skipper

❂ AUTUMN
Redwing
Fieldfare

❄ WINTER
Linnet

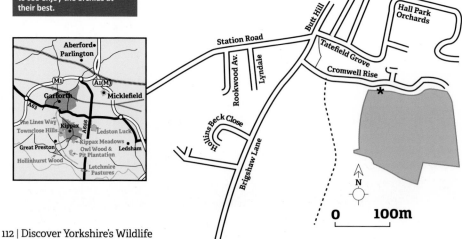

 **Yorkshire**
Wildlife Trust

POTTERIC CARR

South Yorkshire's biggest and best wetland nature reserve. Open daily 9am to 5pm*

- **WARM WELCOME!**
- **MILES OF NATURE TRAILS**
- **ACTIVITIES FOR ALL THE FAMILY**
- **LOCALLY-SOURCED FOOD AND DRINK**
- **CAR PARKING**

*except Christmas Day and Boxing Day. Check website for Christmas closures

KIRKSTALL VALLEY

NEAREST TOWN
Leeds

GRID REFERENCE
SE 268 345

PUBLIC TRANSPORT
Regular buses from Leeds
City Centre run down
Kirkstall Road. Alight at
Redcote Lane. The nearest
train station is Burley Park.

DIRECTIONS
Access the nature reserve
from the end of Redcote
Lane, just off Kirkstall
Road. To reach the nature
reserve gates pass Fitness
First and City Golf. Parking
is to the right, just in
front of the railway
bridge. Please do not
block the gateway.

**OTHER
INFORMATION**
Size: 10 ha

TOP TIP Cycle or walk
down the Leeds-Liverpool canal
towpath and make a day of it
by combining a visit to Kirkstall
Abbey and Rodley Nature
Reserve on an autumnal day to
see the colours at their best.

Only two miles from the bustling city centre of Leeds and surrounded by residential and commercial development, Kirkstall Valley Nature Reserve is a surprisingly green, quiet and relatively undisturbed mix of wetland, meadow and young woodland copse with great views of the River Aire.

On the site of the former Kirkstall Power Station, the nature reserve today supports large areas of wildflower meadow and wetland areas of pond, bog and reedbed. A large tree planting exercise has seen 15,000 trees planted to complement the existing oak, birch and willow on site with an understorey of fruiting shrubs such as guelder rose, blackthorn and sea buckthorn. The area, once noted for orchards in medieval times, also supports a number of fruit trees including medlar, quince and five apple varieties.

Over 180 plant species have been recorded on site along with 65 species of birds including grey partridge and a number of mammals such as foxes and badgers as well as pipistrelle, noctule and Daubenton's bats. Otters may be seen by the old ford, which is generally impassable for most of the year. Six dragonfly and 16 butterfly species including comma and small copper have also been recorded.

Much of the site is raised above the floor of the Aire Valley as it rests on a plateau formed by the deposition of fly ash from the power station, which was demolished in the late 1970s. The area was then used for landfill until the early 1990s when it was capped and seeded with native wildflower mixes, which is the basis of today's meadows.

Yorkshire Wildlife Trust manages the meadows by cutting and raking in late summer after seed dispersal. The woodland is lightly coppiced and thinned in the winter.

Guelder rose

Grey partridge

Location

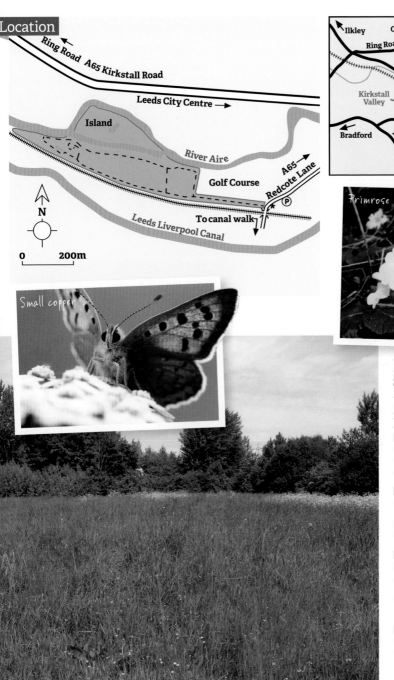

Ring Road A65 Kirkstall Road

Leeds City Centre →

Island

River Aire

Golf Course

A65
Redcote Lane

P

To canal walk

Leeds Liverpool Canal

N

0   200m

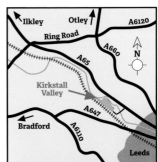

↖Ilkley   Otley↑   A6120

Ring Road   A660

A65

N

Kirkstall
Valley

A647

Bradford   A6110

Leeds

Primrose

Small copper

BEST SEASON TO VISIT

SEASONAL HIGHLIGHTS

SPRING
Cowslip
Primrose
Apple tree blossom

SUMMER
Ox-eye daisy
Meadow vetchling
Small copper
Common toad

AUTUMN
Sloe
Apple
Pear
Quince
Medlar

WINTER
Goosander
Grey heron
Kingfisher
Bullfinch
Reed bunting

West Yorkshire Nature Reserves | 115

LEDSHAM BANK

NEAREST POSTCODE	LS25 5LL
NEAREST TOWN	Castleford
GRID REFERENCE	SE 461 300
PUBLIC TRANSPORT	A bus runs between Castleford and Ledsham.

DIRECTIONS

Take Junction 42 off the A1(M) towards Ledsham/Kippax. Cross the first roundabout and take the first exit onto the A1246 on the second roundabout. Take the first right onto Holyrood Lane, after approximately 800 metres park in the layby on the left. Access to the site is across the road a little further along.

OTHER INFORMATION

Size: 5 ha

TOP TIP **Come during the height of summer to see the wildflower blooms at their best.**

A botanist's dream come midsummer, Ledsham Bank is alive with colour from fantastic displays of wildflowers.

Centaury

Situated in a north-south running valley the nature reserve supports a range of plants characteristic of the magnesian limestone soil. In spring, a carpet of pale yellow cowslips can be found, followed by the vivid spikes of pyramidal and common spotted orchids, which create an amazing show in June and July.

Other typical limestone-loving plants here include hoary plantain, yellow-wort and impressive stands of bright yellow dyer's greenweed, which is rare in Yorkshire. Field scabious and common knapweed attract lots of marbled white butterflies from late June until the end of July, and many other butterflies have been recorded, including commas, small and large skippers, common and holly blues.

A mature hedgerow runs down the west side of the nature reserve, providing food and shelter for winter finches and thrushes. Listen out for nuthatches calling from the woodland that borders the eastern edge of the nature reserve. Little owls are present and are sometimes seen at dusk. Cattle and sheep graze the site at certain times of the year to help keep the grassland in optimum condition.

BEST SEASON TO VISIT

SEASONAL HIGHLIGHTS

🟦 **SPRING**
Cowslip
Holly blue

🟨 **SUMMER**
Centaury
Large skipper
Common blue
Dyer's greenweed

🟫 **AUTUMN**
Little owl
Nuthatch

🟦 **WINTER**
Redwing
Fieldfare
Siskin

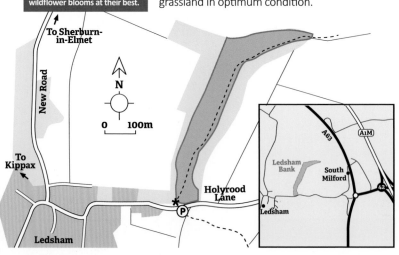

Fieldfare

LEDSTON LUCK

A hidden paradise, this once industrial site might not look much on first glance, but on entry bursts forth with wildflowers and butterflies. Come summer orchids are abundant and the pond teems with life.

NEAREST POSTCODE
LS25 7BF

NEAREST TOWN
Leeds

GRID REFERENCE
SE 432 309

PUBLIC TRANSPORT
Buses run between Leeds and Castleford, stopping on Ridge Road.

DIRECTIONS
From the north leave the M1 South at Junction 47. Take the first exit onto A656. Head straight over at the roundabout and continue on the A63. Turn left into the Enterprise Park car park.

OTHER INFORMATION
Size: 18 ha

TOP TIP Enjoy the true spectacle of over 4,000 orchids in bloom at once by visiting in June.

I t is easy to drive right past Ledston Luck, but then you would be missing a truly peaceful haven. The car park at Ledston Luck Enterprise Park (housed in former colliery buildings) is a stark reminder that this nature reserve was once a pit stack.

Ledston Luck coal pit was sunk in the 1870s and became part of the linked 'superpit' around Selby. The pit closed in 1986 and a range of wildlife habitats have since sprung up and are thriving. Some have developed naturally, although much of the woodland, ponds and some areas of meadow were created in the early 1990s as part of a landscape improvement scheme.

During the summer the main pond buzzes with activity: emerald damselfly, emperor dragonfly, large red damselfly and four-spotted chasers are just some of the many species you can see here.

The grasslands also burst into life with a variety of wildflowers, including a staggering 4,000 orchids which are prospering on the nutrient poor soils. However, there is an aspiration to graze with rare breed cattle. This will ensure scrub and rank grasses do not outcompete the orchids and other wildflowers, so that they stay for years to come.

The woodland and scrub are home to breeding birds such as grasshopper warblers and yellowhammers, whilst fieldfares and redwing can be spotted in the autumn. Selective thinning of the plantation will reduce the number of non-native tree species and create more space for natives to flourish, increase deadwood habitat and provide openings for ground flora.

By taking the informal footpaths through the site you can enjoy the different habitats which have transformed this post-industrial site into something quite special. Ledston Luck is owned by Leeds City Council and managed in partnership with the Trust.

Yellowhammer

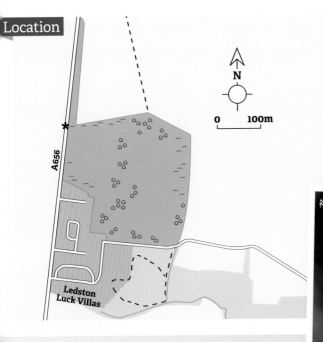

N

0   100m

A656

Ledston
Luck Villas

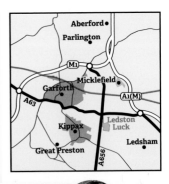

Aberford
Parlington
M1
Micklefield
Garforth
A63
A1(M)
Kippax
Ledston
Luck
Great Preston
Ledsham
A656

Redwing

BEST SEASON TO VISIT

SEASONAL HIGHLIGHTS

✤ SPRING
Brimstone
Large red damselfly
Broad-bodied chaser
Willow warbler
Sedge warbler

✤ SUMMER
Common spotted orchid
Bee orchid
Four-spotted chaser
Grasshopper warbler

✤ AUTUMN
Fieldfare
Redwing

✤ WINTER
Grey heron
Yellowhammer

LETCHMIRE PASTURES

NEAREST POSTCODE	WF10 2BW
NEAREST TOWN	Castleford
GRID REFERENCE	SE 424 274
PUBLIC TRANSPORT	Regular buses run from Leeds City Centre to Allerton Bywater. Alight on Station Road.
DIRECTIONS	Take the A656 north out of Castleford and turn left into Allerton Bywater on Station Road. Letchmire Pastures is along this road on left. Parking is on the roadside only.
OTHER INFORMATION	**Site designation:** LNR **Size:** 12 ha

TOP TIP Come during the height of summer to see the masses of dragon and damselflies.

When the sun begins to shine and the days get longer delicate bee orchids bloom in this wild, reclaimed former colliery site, where meadows and a young woodland thrive.

Transformed through landscaping by Leeds City Council in 1996 and 1997, Letchmire Pastures comprises a number of water features, wet grassland, acidic and neutral grassland, scrub and hedgerows. Its history as a receptor site for coal mined immediately to the north of Station Road, is now a distant memory as nature takes over. Soil and vegetation was translocated from Stourton Marsh, a wetland site to the south east of Leeds to create this new wilderness, meaning some regionally rare plants including grass vetchling, wood small-reed and many orchids now grow here. Located on low-lying land near to the River Aire, the site has subsided following the mining activity in the area, resulting in a series of small, shallow ings (pools of water that form when rivers flood). Recent landscaping has further enhanced the ings, meaning that a number of ponds of different sizes and depths now exist attracting some water birds.

BEST SEASON TO VISIT

SEASONAL HIGHLIGHTS

SPRING
Broad-bodied chaser
Lapwing

SUMMER
Bee orchid
Grass vetchling
Stork's-bill
Wood small-reed

AUTUMN
Reed bunting

WINTER
Snipe

N

0   100m

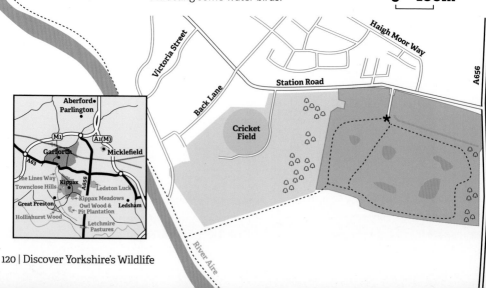

Lapwing

LEYBURN OLD GLEBE

NEAREST POSTCODE
YO62 5LE

NEAREST TOWN
Leyburn

GRID REFERENCE
SE 568 845

PUBLIC TRANSPORT
Buses running between
Leyburn and Hawes stop
in Wensley half a mile
away.

DIRECTIONS
From Hawes take the A6108
to Wensley, then turn left
onto Low Lane. The nature
reserve is on the right hand
side of this road half a mile
east of the village. There
is a small parking spot
by the entrance gate, or
alternatively drive a little bit
further and park on the lay
by on the right hand side of
the road, and walk back to
the nature reserve.

**OTHER
INFORMATION**
Site designation: SSSI
Size: 3 ha

TOP TIP Visit in May or
June for the best display of
wildflowers or tie in a trip with
a visit to the local pub, the
Three Horseshoes in Wensley,
for a hearty fire and pint of ale!

A traditional hay meadow, Leyburn Old Glebe is the
richest remaining fragment of Ellershaw, a district
well-known to naturalists since the 19th Century.

Eyebright

Leyburn Old Glebe is a rare jewel in an area where so many fields are regularly fertilized and cut for silage. This small wildflower meadow is situated on a gently sloping bank above the River Ure in the lower reaches of Wensleydale, with fine views across the dale to Penhill and to the ridge above Coverdale which rises towards Great Whernside. To the north is the wooded limestone scar of Leyburn Shawl.

The site is a fine example of the type of species-rich flower meadow that would have been common in the Yorkshire Dales before agricultural intensification resulted in the improvement of grasslands.

Over 80 plants have been recorded in recent surveys, many of which are typical of calcareous grassland. They thrive here on the thin soil of the south-facing slope of the nature reserve. Eleven species of grass, including common bent, heath grass and quaking grass grow here. Flowers include an abundance of salad burnet and wild thyme as well as a range of other species such as cowslip, fairy flax, eyebright and orchids, including green-winged orchids in May, followed by spectacular burnt-tip orchids in June.

Once belonging to the local church, the field was never ploughed or reseeded, which has allowed it to retain its integrity. Yorkshire Wildlife Trust acquired the site in 1983 and has continued to manage it as a traditional hay meadow. The wildflowers are left to grow and set seed before being cut for hay in July. The field is then usually grazed with a few sheep over winter. The nature reserve is entered through a field gate, which was erected in memory of Cherrill Ingram, a former Honorary Secretary to Yorkshire Wildlife Trust. The nature reserve is a small fragile site susceptible to damage through trampling of the sward and flower picking, so please take care when visiting.

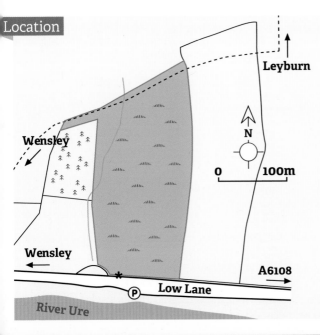

Leyburn

Wensley

Wensley

N

0 | 100m

A6108

P Low Lane

River Ure

Leyburn Old Glebe

Leyburn

N

Wensley

A684

River Ure

A1 →

Hawes

A6108

Middleham

Ripon

Cowslip and burnt-tip orchid

BEST SEASON TO VISIT

SEASONAL HIGHLIGHTS

⊞ SPRING
Cowslip
Salad burnet
Green-winged orchid
Burnt-tip orchid

⊞ SUMMER
Eyebright
Fairy flax
Common blue

⊞ AUTUMN
Yellowhammer

⊞ WINTER
Stoat

LITTLEBECK WOOD

NEAREST POSTCODE
YO22 5HA

NEAREST TOWN
Whitby

GRID REFERENCE
NZ 879 049

PUBLIC TRANSPORT
Nearest train station is at Sleights.

DIRECTIONS
Turn off the A169 Whitby to Pickering road just south of Sleights to the village of Littlebeck. The entrance to the nature reserve is just before the ford. Park considerately in the village.

OTHER INFORMATION
Site designation: SSSI
Size: 26 ha

TOP TIP Visit in April when the spring flowers are blooming and the trees have not yet cast complete shade.

Littlebeck Wood is a glorious mix of oak, ash, alder and cherry under the canopies of which lives a wealth of plants, mammals and insects.

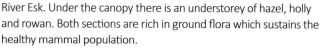

Moschat

Primarily broadleaved woodland with a small pasture at the southern end, the site avoids the worst of the North York Moors weather being situated in a secluded position at the bottom of the valley.

The nature reserve is split into two by the Little Beck as it makes its way down to the River Esk. Under the canopy there is an understorey of hazel, holly and rowan. Both sections are rich in ground flora which sustains the healthy mammal population.

In the spring and early summer wood anemone, bluebell, primrose, yellow pimpernell and early purple orchid are in full flower, whilst ferns dominate the shadier areas. Opposite-leaved golden saxifrage grows on the banks of the streams and hart's-tongue fern is common. Badger scrapes may be discovered around dense areas of bluebells, whilst deer tracks might be seen in the damp sections of the path and rodent holes in the banks around the site. Sightings of birds are commonplace, including the secretive treecreeper, with dippers and grey wagtails along the river. Dead wood provides an important food source for insects, several of which are rare and listed in the Red Data Book. These attract great spotted woodpeckers which actively dig out the larvae of some of these insects from the rotting wood.

Yorkshire Wildlife Trust has worked to maintain the woodland since taking over the lease in 1970 from the Forestry Commission and then later purchasing it in 1986. Bird boxes provide vital breeding spaces for nuthatches, tits and owls. Tree health is also a primary concern, with any diseased or damaged trees made safe with regards to the public and left as dead wood where possible. The understorey is also managed to retain tree health, with the thinning of holly and coppicing of hazel. The pasture is cut for hay and grazed by neighbouring farmers' livestock.

Early purple orchid

Location

Littlebeck
Sleights
B1416
Village Hall
Ford
Old Alum Works
Shale cliffs
Swindseydale Beck
Little Beck

N

0   200m

Whitby
Sneaton
Sleights
Pickering   A169
Little Beck Wood   B1416
Scarborough →
N

Marsh tit

Wood anemone

BEST SEASON TO VISIT

SEASONAL HIGHLIGHTS

❋ SPRING
Bluebell
Wood anemone
Primrose
Early purple orchid
Dog violet

❋ SUMMER
Moschatel
Great spotted woodpecker
Spotted flycatcher

❋ AUTUMN
Fungi
Dipper

❋ WINTER
Grey wagtail
Treecreeper

LITTLEWORTH PARK

NEAREST POSTCODE
S71 5RL

NEAREST TOWN
Barnsley

GRID REFERENCE
SE 368 072

PUBLIC TRANSPORT
From Barnsley interchange buses stop at Pontefract Road, Lundwood. Get off the bus at the junction with Littleworth Lane in Lundwood and follow the lane up the hill. Littleworth Park is on your right hand side.

DIRECTIONS
From Barnsley town centre, take the A628 Pontefract Road, cross a mini-roundabout at Lundwood and continue to the next traffic lights. Turn left onto Littleworth Lane. After 200 meters, there is a car park on your right, or continue up Littleworth Lane and park in a small car park opposite Kitson Drive.

OTHER INFORMATION
Site designation:
Local Wildlife Site
Size: 38 ha

TOP TIP To enjoy the heather at its purple best, visit in August. On warm days, it can be buzzing with bumblebees and other nectaring insects.

Littleworth Park never ceases to surprise. Surrounded by housing, nature is taking back control of this former colliery and it is quickly reverting to lowland heath and grassland with stunning blooms of heather and wildflowers.

This park has been created on an old colliery spoil heap and landfill site. It is now covered with species-rich grassland interspersed with wooded copses. An extensive site that's great for a stroll or dogwalk or for burying your head amongst the wildflowers.

Originally the routes of the Barnsley canal and a railway ran through the site. They are long gone but to the south of the site the old towpath and railway line form a perfect wildlife corridor and path joining Littleworth Park to nearby Dearne Valley Country Park.

The extensive grassland is ablaze with yellow bird's-foot trefoil in the spring and summer making Littleworth a butterfly-spotting heaven with 24 species recorded. Bees and other invertebrates also abound making the most of the nectar source.

To the northern end of the site is the most extensive heather colony, which makes a splash of purple in late summer. New self-set colonies are springing up across the site.

Littleworth is a place where you can really appreciate the value of good scrub habitat with willow warblers and lesser redpolls a couple of the beneficiaries you can find. Drainage ditches on the edge of the site have become valuable habitats for smooth newts, common frogs and toads, as well as dragonflies and other wetland insects.

The site is a great example of how lowland heath can be recreated on old mineral workings. In order to protect the heather and help it colonise the site we remove birch trees that would shade it out and ensure that the contract grass-cutting does not destroy any of the newly-colonising heather plants.

We are creating new ponds on the site to attract a larger colony of amphibians, invertebrates and birds.

Yorkshire wildlife Trust manages the park in partnership with Barnsley Council for the benefit of local people and wildlife.

Smooth newt

Fish Dam Lane

Monk
Bretton

Burton Road

Pontefract Road

Littleworth Lane

Lundwood

N

0   300m

Carlton
Marsh

Barnsley
Canal

Littleworth
Park

Dearne Valley
Country Park

Goldcrest

BEST SEASON TO VISIT

SEASONAL HIGHLIGHTS

◼ SPRING
Smooth newt
Hedgehog
Willow warbler
Lesser redpoll

◼ SUMMER
Bird's-foot trefoil
Bee orchid
Common centaury
Heather

◼ AUTUMN
Six-spot burnet
Bullfinch
Rabbit
Fox

◼ WINTER
Fieldfare
Redwing
Goldcrest
Goldfinch

LOW WOOD

NEAREST POSTCODE
BD20 5QN

NEAREST TOWN
Keighley

GRID REFERENCE
SE 056 439

PUBLIC TRANSPORT
A bus service runs
between Bradford and
Keighley, stopping on
Grange Road in Riddlesden
– a short walk away. The
nearest train station is
at Keighley. Cycle and
footpath access is gained
by following the towpath
of the Leeds-Liverpool
canal going northwards to
Booth's Bridge.

DIRECTIONS
Take the B6265 to
Riddlesden and turn left
onto Bar Lane, followed
by another left onto Scott
Lane. Follow the unmade
track as far as Riddlesden
Golf Course club house
(¾ mile), then turn by the
Leeds-Liverpool canal,
where this a small area for
parking on the roadside at
the site entrance. Access
is gained by a small gate,
which is signed Private
Scout Activity Centre.
Keeping to the path, pass
through the Scout wood to
the nature reserve beyond.

**OTHER
INFORMATION**
Size: 3 ha

TOP TIP Escape the hustle
and bustle of urban life in this
secluded woodland retreat –
don't miss the bluebells and visit
at dusk for badgers or in spring
to enjoy the dawn chorus.

Low Wood is an attractive, secluded woodland which is notable for its beautiful spring displays of bluebell, a wide range of woodland birds, coupled with occasional sightings of badger and roe deer.

Beside the canal, Low Wood provides a pleasant oasis away from the busy and noisy urban landscape of Keighley. Beautifully carpeted with bluebells in spring, this broadleaved woodland is also home to a wide range of fungi, with over 36 species recorded, as well as the usual range of birds and plants you might expect to find in our traditional woodlands.

Blackcap, great spotted woodpecker, tawny owl, treecreeper and nuthatch are just some of the birds you might be lucky enough to encounter on a visit here. At least three species of bat also make this nature reserve their home. The small pond within the site is used by amphibians, including common frogs, which congregate in early spring.

The woodland is steeply sloping with evidence of glacial meltwater erosion of the millstone grit forming cliffs towards the top. A footpath encircles the wood, but these upper parts are steep and require both energy and care when climbing. The views from the top are well worth the effort though.

Volunteers are involved in much of the management of the site, and over the last eight years self-seeded sycamore have been removed from the wood to allow native species like oak, birch and rowan to flourish in the canopy and holly, hawthorn and hazel in the understorey. Glades, or clearings, have been created within the wood to allow light through and encourage butterflies such as speckled wood. Bracken is also controlled to allow the successful re-establishment of native woodland plants.

Speckled wood

Location

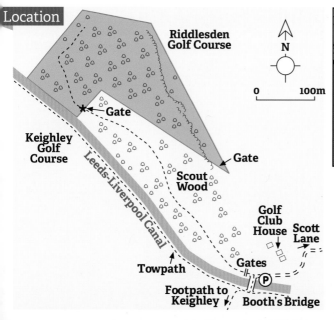

Riddlesden Golf Course

N

0   100m

Keighley Golf Course

Leeds-Liverpool Canal

Gate

Scout Wood

Gate

Golf Club House

Scott Lane

Towpath

Gates

P

Footpath to Keighley

Booth's Bridge

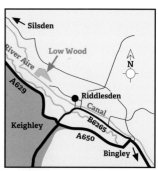

Silsden

River Aire

Low Wood

N

A629

Riddlesden

Canal

B6265

Keighley

A650

Bingley

Wall of water

  BEST SEASON TO VISIT

SEASONAL HIGHLIGHTS

✦ SPRING
Bluebell
Nuthatch
Treecreeper

☀ SUMMER
Foxglove
Badger
Speckled wood
Pipistrelle bat

🍂 AUTUMN
Woodland fungi
Tawny owl

❄ WINTER
Roe deer

MALTBY LOW COMMON

Rich in wildflowers and grasses, including the delicate grass-of-Parnassus, this nature reserve is a joy to behold come early summer, whilst the varied geology is clearly visible, reflected in a change of vegetation from one side to the other.

Maltby Low Common has a wide variety of soil types giving rise to dry grassland and fen meadows, providing an excellent home for both wildflowers and insects. The south part of the site sits on limestone, and the grassland here is typical of this soil, with an impressive display of grass-of-Parnassus, field scabious and small scabious. The flat area below the bank includes species more typical of fen meadow like glaucous sedge.

Other plants to look out for include marsh valerian, mat grass, tufted hair-grass, heather, pepper saxifrage, meadow thistle, sneezewort, lousewort and aspen. Oval and carnation sedges also grow here. Beautiful common spotted orchids can be found flowering in abundance from early June. Rich in insects, the site has over 400 species recorded, with various butterfly and moth species including brimstone, orange-tip, small copper, wall, heath, cinnabar and silver-Y among them. Birds regularly seen include buzzard, kestrel, whitethroat and garden warbler, and come winter parties of foraging tits and thrushes, including redwings and fieldfares.

Leased from the Earl of Scarborough, the nature reserve is part of a much larger site managed by the Sandbeck Estate. This small patch was opened as a nature reserve in 1971 and management since then has focused on improving the grassland habitat for the plants and insects that rely on them. In recent times work has included the laying of hedges that bound the site, to increase habitat for nesting birds.

Glaucous sedge

Silver-Y

Location

Sports Ground

B6427

P

Birk Holt
Housing
Estate

×

N

0   100m

B6376

Doncaster

N

Maltby

A631

B6427

Rotherham

A634

Tickhill

Blyth

Maltby Low
Common

Grass-of-Parnassus

BEST SEASON TO VISIT

SEASONAL HIGHLIGHTS

SPRING
Whitethroat
Orange-tip

SUMMER
Grass-of-Parnassus
Tufted hair-grass
Pepper saxifrage
Meadow thistle
Sneezewort

AUTUMN
Fungi

WINTER
Long-tailed tit

MOORLANDS

NEAREST POSTCODE
YO32 2RE

NEAREST TOWN
York

GRID REFERENCE
SE 579 587

PUBLIC TRANSPORT
Buses run between York and Skelton.

DIRECTIONS
Moorlands is approximately five and a half miles north of York. From York take the A19 Thirsk Road for about three and a half miles to Skelton. Turn right off the A19, continue through the village and the nature reserve is another two miles further on the left. Parking is permitted on the verge near the entrance gate.

OTHER INFORMATION
Size: 7 ha

TOP TIP This popular nature reserve is perfect for any age, with a level path and seating dotted all about the site.

This small woodland garden, originally part of the ancient Forest of Galtres, is ablaze with colour in spring. Snowdrops, daffodils, wood sorrel, bluebells and foxgloves form the backdrop to a succession of mature rhododendrons, azaleas and maples, some of which are very old, large and uncommon.

Rhododendro[n]

The trees here are a source of great pleasure with mature native species growing alongside the more unusual snake-bark maple, two dawn redwoods, magnolias and some magnificent conifers. A downloadable tree trail around the site gives guidance to some of these.

The wealth of trees and flowering plants in turn attract many species of birds and mammals. A number of bat boxes have been successfully used by common pipistrelle and brown long-eared bats, with soprano pipistrelle, Brandt's and Daubenton's bats having also been recorded within the nature reserve.

From the tree hide a great variety of woodland birds, including great spotted woodpecker, nuthatch and a variety of tits can be observed visiting the feeders. Woodcock are occasionally seen during autumn, which is also an ideal time to find amazing fungi during a stroll through the leaf litter.

There are two small ponds, the first of which encourages families with nets to the large dipping platform. A third, secluded pond helps to feed to other ponds via a dyke.

Mr Edward Grosvenor Tew bought Moorlands House in 1909 and transformed the estate by planting a great variety of trees, rhododendrons, azaleas and daffodils. In 1940 the estate was acquired by the Retreat in York for use as a hospital. In 1955 the Yorkshire Naturalists' Trust, now Yorkshire Wildlife Trust, bought 17 acres and Moorlands became its second nature reserve.

Management of the site aims to preserve both the special character of this Edwardian woodland garden and to encourage native wildlife within the nature reserve. Wooden sculptures and a nature trail, with waymarkers depicting the species found in the woodland can be enjoyed by families visiting the site.

Shaggy inkcap

Fly agaric

Location

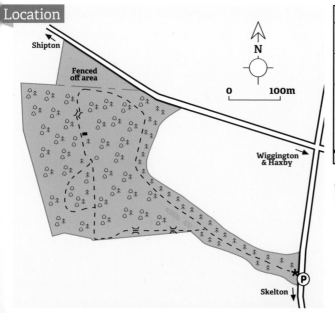

Wood carving

BEST SEASON TO VISIT

SEASONAL HIGHLIGHTS

✿ SPRING
Primrose
Cuckooflower
Marsh marigold
Rhododendrons
Azaleas

☀ SUMMER
Woodland ferns
Foxglove
Common blue damselfly
Speckled wood
Brown long-eared bat

🍂 AUTUMN
Fungi
Maple
Nuthatch

❄ WINTER
Woodcock
Great spotted woodpecker

MOSS VALLEY

NEAREST POSTCODE
S8 8BG

NEAREST TOWN
Sheffield

GRID REFERENCE
SK 376 805

PUBLIC TRANSPORT
Buses run from Sheffield city centre.

DIRECTIONS
Follow the Sheffield Ring Road (A6102). At the Norton roundabout turn onto Lightwood Lane and continue for one mile. Park in the layby.

OTHER INFORMATION
Contact information:
0114 263 4335
Site designation: LNR
Size: 26 ha

TOP TIP A visit in May is essential to see one of the best bluebell displays in South Yorkshire.

THE wildlife TRUSTS

Sheffield & Rotherham

Moss Valley Nature Reserve is a wonderful, quiet and peaceful woodland oasis, which is home to a great diversity of wildlife, including butterflies which feed and seek shelter in the coppiced Bridle Road Wood.

Moss Valley encompasses several woodlands including Coal Pit Wood which is filled with oaks, occasional horse chestnuts and sycamores, Newfield Spring Wood and Long Wood, where oak and beech dominate, and Bridle Road Wood. Wildflowers, including bluebells, yellow pimpernel, St John's-wort, wood speedwell and sweet woodruff, all indicate areas of ancient woodland throughout this complex. Thanks to its south-facing aspect, unimproved soils and wide variety of plants, the Dowey Lumb meadow is teeming with insects. Many species of moth and butterfly can be found including the elusive white-letter hairstreak around the remnant elms.

Brown trout and the extremely rare native white-clawed crayfish have been found in the two streams which run through the nature reserve. Increasingly scarce birds such as linnet, song thrush and bullfinch are frequently found in the woods and open areas, grey wagtail and kingfishers may be seen by the streams and tawny owls and sparrowhawks hunt small birds and mammals.

Adders, slow-worms and great crested newts have all been spotted, as have larger animals like badgers, brown hare and roe deer.

Great crested newt

Linnet

Location

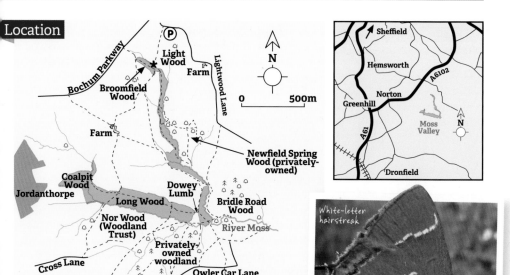

Light Wood
P
Farm
Bochum Parkway
Broomfield Wood
Lightwood Lane
N
0   500m
Farm
Newfield Spring Wood (privately-owned)
Coalpit Wood
Jordanthorpe
Long Wood
Dowey Lumb
Bridle Road Wood
Nor Wood (Woodland Trust)
River Moss
Cross Lane
Privately-owned woodland
Owler Car Lane

Sheffield
Hemsworth
A6102
Norton
Greenhill
A61
Moss Valley
N
Dronfield

White-letter hairstreak

BEST SEASON TO VISIT

SEASONAL HIGHLIGHTS

⊞ SPRING
Brimstone
Bluebell
Bullfinch
Great crested newt
Adder

⊠ SUMMER
Yellow pimpernel
White-letter hairstreak
White-clawed crayfish
Slow-worm

⊠ AUTUMN
Roe deer

⊞ WINTER
Tawny owl
Badger

South Yorkshire Nature Reserves | 135

NEWBIGGIN PASTURES

An undiscovered gem in the Yorkshire Dales, Newbiggin Pastures Nature Reserve has stunning views of little visited Bishopdale and provides a taste of traditional farming practices in the Dales.

NEAREST POSTCODE
DL8 3TF

NEAREST TOWN
Leyburn

GRID REFERENCE
SD 987 850

PUBLIC TRANSPORT
The nearest village with a bus service is Worton, a 20–25 minute walk away. The nearest train station is at Garsdale which is 10¼ miles away.

DIRECTIONS
Turn off the A684 Leyburn to Hawes road onto the B6160/Ellers Lane. Continue on this road for 3¾ miles past West Burton and the Street Head Inn and caravan site. The nature reserve is on your left half a mile after passing the pub. Limited roadside parking. Enter the nature reserve through the field gate.

OTHER INFORMATION
Size: 28 ha

Dogs are not permitted on site.

TOP TIP It's a steep climb, so take a packed lunch to sit and enjoy whilst you appreciate the stunning views from the top. A visit can be turned into a strenuous circular walk by joining the public right of way at the top of the site and following it down into the village of Newbiggin, where another footpath returns you to the road at the bottom of the valley, where the Street Head Inn is conveniently located.

Set in Bishopdale, the nature reserve offers a mix of different habitats, from flower-rich meadows characteristic of the region, to the upland rough grassland of the high moors. Stretching from the valley bottom up to the edge of Wassett Fell, visitors will enjoy spectacular views across the stunning landscape of Bishopdale.

A work in progress, the Trust manages parts of the site as a traditional hay meadow with grazing by sheep in the autumn and a hay cut following the seeding of the wildflowers. The rough grassland at the upper end of the site is managed to provide a variety of habitats suitable for upland bird species including snipe, lapwing and curlew. With the help of volunteers the Trust recently planted six hectares of new woodland across the site including areas of sparse juniper woodland. This is the preferred habitat of black grouse and it is hoped as the woodland develops it will provide suitable habitat for this iconic upland bird. Ravens sometimes fly over the site.

The working agricultural landscape of the Yorkshire Dales can be appreciated from Newbiggin Pastures. The lower fields of the dale are small and enclosed by dry stone walls: these are the traditional hay meadows that would be cut for hay in the summer. Many of these fields have stone barns in which the hay would be stored and cattle housed over winter. Further up the slope the fields are larger and managed as rough grazing pasture. Higher still and the land changes to open moorland managed by light grazing often under commoners rights. Newbiggin Pastures is grazed by a local tenant, so we ask visitors to keep to field edges and not to disturb the livestock.

Raven

Corncockle

Location

Bishopdale Beck

To Newbiggin
Village and
Street Head
Inn

B6160

Bleacarr Sike

N

0   1000m

Howgill Gill

Floutgate Scar

River Ure Carperby Brunton Bank

A684

Aysgarth

N

West
Burton

Bishopdale Beck

Newbiggin

Newbiggin
Pastures

B6160

Walden Beck

Agrimony

BEST
SEASON
TO VISIT

SEASONAL
HIGHLIGHTS

✠ SPRING
Lapwing
Curlew
Wheatear

☑ SUMMER
Lady's mantle
Moschatel
Corncockle
Agrimony

☑ AUTUMN
Raven

✠ WINTER
Juniper

NORTH CAVE WETLANDS

NEAREST POSTCODE
HU15 2LY

NEAREST TOWN
Brough

GRID REFERENCE
SE 886 328

PUBLIC TRANSPORT
Buses stop in North Cave
village, half a mile away.

DIRECTIONS
Leave the M62/A63 at
junction 38 and take
the B1230 east to North
Cave village. At the first
crossroads, turn left on to
Townend Lane and follow
the brown signs. From the
A1079, turn south through
North Cliffe towards
North Cave, turning right
into the nature reserve
just before a sharp left
hand bend.

**OTHER
INFORMATION**
Size: 39 ha

Dogs on leads are
permitted on Dryham Lane
only. The privately-owned
Wild Bird Café is present
daily and toilets are
available by the entrance.

TOP TIP Look out for the
stiff-winged butterfly like
display of little ringed plovers
flying over the wetlands in April
and May.

North Cave Wetlands is a true example of a 21st Century nature reserve, developed in the footprint of a large sand and gravel quarry. A day spent here at any time of the year will reward visitors with close up views of a range of wetland wildlife. From spring avocets and common terns, summer dragonflies and flowers, to wintering flocks of wildfowl, this really is a super place.

A mixture of shallow and deep water lakes and reedbeds, North Cave Wetlands provides outstanding habitat for passage, breeding and wintering wildfowl, wading birds, terns and gulls. A 1¼ mile perimeter path gives access around the established nature reserve and four large hides are positioned to give excellent viewing over key areas for birdwatchers and photographers alike.

Shallow gravel islands have been created in some of the lakes to provide breeding grounds for little ringed and ringed plovers, avocet, oystercatcher, lapwing and common tern. A large breeding colony of black-headed gulls attracts Mediterranean gulls and it is worth

checking carefully for this handsome colonist. There is a resident population of tufted duck, gadwall, great crested and little grebe and sometimes shoveler. In spring and autumn small numbers of migrant wading birds pass through, with the occasional rarity, such as Temminck's stint or red-necked phalarope. Reed and sedge warblers and reed buntings are common in and around the reedbed and north side of the nature reserve. A feeding station by the viewpoint overlooking Village Lake attracts tree sparrows and siskins. Look out for water rails in the ditch alongside Dryham Lane in the winter months.

Butterflies, dragonflies and damselflies thrive on the grassy banks beside the perimeter path; watch out for four-spotted chasers and emperor dragonflies along the ditches and sometimes a water vole. There is a small colony of brown argus butterflies in the meadow between Main and Carp Lakes, access to which is opened in summer months.

Great crested grebe

NORTH CAVE WETLANDS

Emperor dragonfly

The original 40 hectare nature reserve was acquired in 2001 following quarrying activity. In the following three years 250,000 tonnes of material was moved in, out or around the site to create a suitable open wetland habitat, with established trees confined to the boundaries and to the western end. Six large lakes provide both deep and shallow water with wide margins and islands, connected underground to give control over winter and summer water levels.

Starting in 2008 and to finish 12 to 15 years thereafter an additional 100 ha of land to the immediate south and west is being quarried. This will be progressively restored with wildlife in mind before being gifted to Yorkshire Wildlife Trust. Temporary colonies of sand martins establish each spring in the neighbouring quarries and feed over the site, in turn attracting predatory hobbies. Dryham Ings, to the south of the lane was restored in 2012 and now hosts breeding waterfowl, avocets, little ringed plovers and common terns.

Brown argus

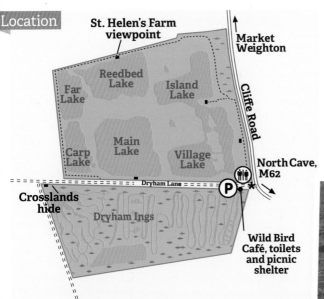

St. Helen's Farm viewpoint

Market Weighton

Reedbed Lake

Island Lake

Far Lake

Cliffe Road

Main Lake

Village Lake

North Cave, M62

Carp Lake

Dryham Lane

Crosslands hide

Dryham Ings

P

Wild Bird Café, toilets and picnic shelter

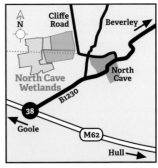

N
Cliffe Road
Beverley
North Cave Wetlands
North Cave
B1230
38
Goole
M62
Hull

Avocet

Water vole

BEST SEASON TO VISIT

SEASONAL HIGHLIGHTS

❉ SPRING
Litte ringed plover
Avocet
Redshank
Sand martin
Sedge warbler

☀ SUMMER
Brown argus
Emperor dragonfly
Four-spotted chaser
Common tern
Hobby

🍂 AUTUMN
Common darter
Migrant waders
Tree sparrow

❄ WINTER
Teal
Wigeon
Tufted duck
Water rail
Snipe

NORTH CLIFFE WOOD

NEAREST POSTCODE
YO43 4XE

NEAREST TOWN
Market Weighton

GRID REFERENCE
SE 860 374

PUBLIC TRANSPORT
Buses from Market
Weighton serve the
nearby North Cliffe village.

DIRECTIONS
From the A1079 at Market
Weighton, head south
towards North Cliffe. Turn
right after four miles down
Sand Lane. Park on the left
by the wood.

**OTHER
INFORMATION**
Size: 33 ha

TOP TIP Visit in late
April or early May to see the
bluebells at their best.

A lovely woodland nature reserve rich in wildlife. In spring, a lilac haze of bluebells stretches out beneath the vibrant green leaves of birch, while the songs of a host of warblers can be heard all around.

North Cliffe Wood is a woodland nature reserve lying on sandy soils. In spring a carpet of bluebells, greater stitchwort and other woodland flowers provide a beautiful sight. Up in the woodland canopy and bushes, migrant birds, including willow and garden warblers, plus chiffchaff and blackcap add their songs to the resident species, such as treecreeper, song thrush, chaffinch and green woodpecker. In recent years, woodlarks have occasionally bred and it is worth listening out for their beautiful, melodic song delivered from high in the sky.

North Cliffe Wood was drained in the late 19th Century and the mature trees clear-felled in 1921. Bracken and rabbits were then able to fully exploit the sandy soils and prevent the regeneration of trees until myxomatosis destroyed the rabbit population in 1954. Conditions were thus set for the rapid spread of birch and rowan, the seeds of which are readily distributed by wind and birds respectively. These two species are still the most common trees in the wood today, although over 20 species have been recorded. The site is quite varied, with the lower lying western areas flooding in most winters, providing suitable conditions for willow scrub. To the south of the main entrance there is an area of high oak forest, with a clump of multi-stemmed alders nearby, being evidence of coppicing activity that took place in the original forested landscape.

In the south west corner there is substantial clearing of lowland heathland that supports typical species including ling heather, heath rush and common cotton grass. Several pools within the woodland and heathland areas provide homes for damselflies and dragonflies and grassy clearings within the wood are a hive of activity for summer butterflies. Grass snakes can regularly be seen basking in the sun along paths and in open areas.

Brimstone

Location

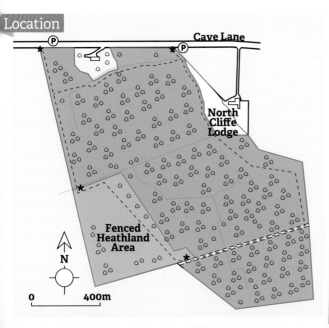

Cave Lane

North Cliffe Lodge

Fenced Heathland Area

N

0   400m

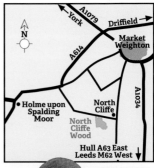

N

A1079 — York   Driffield →

Market Weighton

A614

A1034

• Holme upon Spalding Moor

North Cliffe

North Cliffe Wood

Hull A63 East
Leeds M62 West ↓

Willow warbler

BEST SEASON TO VISIT

SEASONAL HIGHLIGHTS

✕ SPRING
Bluebell
Greater stitchwort
Primrose
Grass snake
Chiffchaff

✕ SUMMER
Cotton grass
Speckled wood
Garden warbler
Blackcap

✕ AUTUMN
Fungi
Black darter
Common hawker
Siskin

✕ WINTER
Green woodpecker
Great spotted woodpecker
Redwing
Treecreeper

NEAREST POSTCODE
YO43 4SQ

NEAREST TOWN
Market Weighton

GRID REFERENCE
SE 917 371

PUBLIC TRANSPORT
Buses run from Market Weighton to North Newbald village.

DIRECTIONS
Just east of North Newbald alongside the Beverley road. Park considerately in the village and walk to the site. The nature reserve is on the right 300m, past Townend Road.

OTHER INFORMATION
Size: 2 ha

There are no marked footpaths on site and it is very wet most of the time. Wellies are recommended.

TOP TIP Visit in spring to witness the greatest variety and colour of marsh flowers. The marsh orchids flower later.

In spring a visual feast of marsh flowers can be enjoyed at this small spring-fed Yorkshire Wolds nature reserve, whilst in early summer marsh orchids abound.

N orth Newbald Becksies is fed by several clear chalk springs which are almost never known to dry up. The water remains at a remarkably constant temperature of 9°C throughout the year and can be seen steaming on cold winter mornings. The terrain of the nature reserve is fairly undulating and in most areas extremely wet, though there is a drier section at the north east corner.

By far the most interesting sections of the site are the open marshy areas which contain a good range of marsh plants including butter-yellow marsh marigolds and abundant marsh orchids, said to be a hybrid swarm of mainly *Dactylorhiza praetermissa*, though other species do occur. Another special plant is bogbean – a rarity in this part of Yorkshire. Grass-of-Parnassus was recorded as recently as the mid-1990s and may still be present. Moorhen are common and snipe occur in the wetter areas during the winter. Water shrews are present and there have been sightings of water voles on the stream.

The Trust looks after the nature reserve by removing scrub which encroaches on to the marsh and also reduces the abundance of greater willowherb and meadowsweet to allow other plants to prosper. The marsh was originally used for pasturing cattle from the village while they were waiting to be milked and as such is classed as common land. Today, a small number of rare breed cattle are used to assist with site management through summer grazing.

Lady's mantle

Marsh orchid

Location

N

0   100m

Becks Farm

Becks Cottages

Beverley →

← North Newbald

Beverley Road

Market Weighton

A1034

North Newbald Becksies

Beverley →

North Newbald

South Newbald

Brough

N

Bogbean

Snipe

BEST SEASON TO VISIT

SEASONAL HIGHLIGHTS

✢ SPRING
Marsh marigold
Cuckooflower
Water avens
Bogbean
Orange-tip

✤ SUMMER
Marsh orchids
Lady's mantle
Watercress
Fool's water-cress
Meadowsweet

✤ AUTUMN
Devil's-bit scabious

✤ WINTER
Snipe

East Yorkshire Nature Reserves | 145

OWL WOOD AND PIT PLANTATION

NEAREST POSTCODE
Garforth

GRID REFERENCE
SE 413 288

PUBLIC TRANSPORT
Regular buses run between Castleford and Allerton Bywater.

DIRECTIONS
On the M1 south take junction 47 for the A656/A642 exit to Castleford. At the roundabout take the first exit onto the A656. On the approach to Allerton Bywater take the right turn onto Park Lane, then at the roundabout take the second onto Leeds road. Take a right onto Doctors Lane and you will approach Owl Wood on your right.

OTHER INFORMATION
Size: 4 ha

TOP TIP Pick up a bat detector or join in with a guided event on a summer's evening to hear the calls of the various bats on site.

This attractive little woodland is popular with wildlife, with great displays of bluebells in late spring and a fascinating array of bats come summer.

These two neighbouring semi-mature woodlands are located just off the Lines Way in Allerton Bywater. More or less surrounded by arable farmland they offer a sheltered retreat, and former woodland management has meant there is plenty here for local wildlife. Owl Wood is dominated by sycamore, oak and silver birch, which has naturally regenerated on site relatively recently. This area is known to have been wooded since the end of the 18th Century. Spring bluebells carpet the ground among 18th Century bell pits and the crumbled field boundaries, which originally contained a smaller element of woodland that has gradually extended. Pit Plantation, as its name suggests, is of planted origin, primarily of beech, and was first documented in the 1913 map of the township of Allerton Bywater. Numerous bat boxes have been erected to ensure the survival of an impressive collection of bat species on site, including common pipistrelle, Natterer's and Daubenton's. Owl Wood and Pit Plantation are owned by Leeds City Council and managed in partnership with the Trust.

BEST SEASON TO VISIT

SEASONAL HIGHLIGHTS

SPRING
Bluebell
Song thrush

SUMMER
Bats
Hedgehog

AUTUMN
Beech

WINTER
Tawny owl

Common pipistrelle bat

Brigshaw School

The Lines Way

Owl Wood & Pit Plantation

Doctor's Lane

Aberford
Parlington
M1
A1(M)
Garforth
Mickdefield
A63
The Lines Way
Townclose Hills
Kippax
A656
Ledston Luck
Great Preston
Kippax Meadows
Owl Wood &
Pit Plantation
Ledsham
Hollinhurst Wood
Letchmire
Pastures

Bluebells

PAULL HOLME STRAYS

Paull Holme Strays lies alongside the mighty River Humber offering spectacular views across the south Holderness landscape which includes local historical features. The site is managed in partnership with the Environment Agency.

NEAREST POSTCODE
HU12 8AX

NEAREST TOWN
Hull

GRID REFERENCE
TA 376 205

PUBLIC TRANSPORT
Buses from Hull stop in Paull village.

DIRECTIONS
From the A1033 follow the signs for Fort Paull and then head south on Thorngumbald Road. The entrance to the car park is on the right just less than a mile after the entrance to Fort Paull.

OTHER INFORMATION
Site designation: Adjacent to the Humber Estuary SPA, Ramsar Site and SAC.
Size: 105 ha

TOP TIP Check tide times. If you visit in the winter a couple of hours before a large incoming tide then the wading birds spectacle can be simply stunning.

To see Paull Holme Strays at its spectacular best a visit during the winter months is a must. Thousands of wintering wading birds use the site to feed and roost, and this large gathering entices predators including peregrine and merlin. Many an hour can be passed watching the shimmering flocks of knot and golden plover swirling around. Other wading birds at this time include black and bar-tailed godwits, redshank, dunlin, lapwing and curlew. The surrounding ditches, grassland and farmland provides winter hunting grounds for short-eared owl, hen and marsh harriers along with regular sightings of roe deer, brown hare and stoat.

The summer is a quieter time for the site but still produces some great wildlife encounters. Water voles are present in the freshwater habitats along with a variety of dragon and damselflies, including common darter, broad-bodied and four-spotted chasers, migrant hawker and small red-eyed damselfly. The song of skylark is ever present along with little egret feeding on the fringes and the striking yellow wagtail along the banks. From mid-summer, numbers of returning wading birds start to build up on the mudflats.

Paull Holme Strays was the first major managed coastal flood realignment scheme on the River Humber and was breached by the Environment Agency in 2003. The site provides approximately 80 hectares of inter-tidal habitat to compensate for the loss of saltmarsh and mudflats in the area, and is fronted by the extensive Paull Holme Sands.

Dunlin and sanderling

Short-eared owl

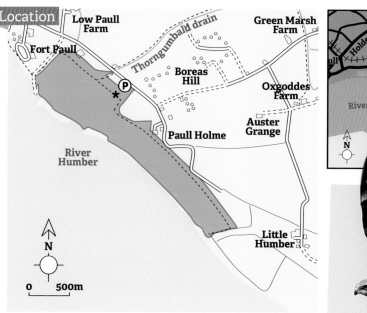

Low Paull Farm

Fort Paull

Thorngumbald drain

Green Marsh Farm

Boreas Hill

P

Oxgoddes Farm

Paull Holme

Auster Grange

River Humber

Little Humber

N

0   500m

Holderness Road

Marfleet

Preston

Hull Road

Hedon

River Humber

Paull Holme Strays

N

Marsh harrier

BEST SEASON TO VISIT

SEASONAL HIGHLIGHTS

◧ SPRING
Cuckoo
Yellow wagtail
Sedge warbler
Reed warbler

◩ SUMMER
Marsh harrier
Spotted redshank
Little stint
Curlew
Dragonflies

◪ AUTUMN
Avocet
Green sandpiper
Common sandpiper
Whimbrel

◧ WINTER
Merlin
Dunlin
Redshank
Bar-tailed godwit
Golden plover

PEARSON PARK WILDLIFE GARDEN

NEAREST POSTCODE
HU5 2TD

NEAREST TOWN
Hull

GRID REFERENCE
TA 083 430

PUBLIC TRANSPORT
Frequent buses run to
Princes Avenue, with the
nearest bus stop a one
minute walk away. The
nearest train station
is Hull.

DIRECTIONS
Pearson Park Wildlife
Garden is located just off
Princes Avenue in Hull,
opposite Westbourne
Avenue. On street car
parking is available in the
area with a short walk to
the garden.

**OTHER
INFORMATION**
Opening times: 9am till
5pm – 7days a week
Contact: 01482 441013
Size: 0.5 ha

TOP TIP Expect the
unexpected! This maybe a small
space but its unique location
and the active community that
support it means you never
know what might be happening
– events, plays, lantern parades.
Crammed with wildlife, spaces
for picnics, art and sculptures
and much more!

Pearson Park Wildlife Garden may be small in size but packs a punch with over 240 different species recorded on site, with the local community actively involved in its care.

Divided into different areas, the wildlife garden gives visitors a taste of the different habitats that can be created in a small space and is crammed with ideas and inspiration to help people make a difference for wildlife in their own patch.

Green shield bug

Although small, Pearson Park Wildlife Garden is perfectly formed with different areas of interest, including ponds, hedgerows, woodland and a meadow, as well as a fruit and vegetable patch. There is plenty of wildlife making the most of these varied habitats including garden birds like blue tits, long-tailed tits and robins, as well insects such as butterflies, shield bugs, ladybirds and solitary bees.

Wander through the meadow, sample the herbs from the herb garden and sit back and enjoy the wildlife on one of the many benches and seating areas dotted about the garden. At the back of the site there are two demonstration gardens to help those that have small yards – they help show that even if you don't have a lot of space you can still make room for wildlife. An amphitheatre area provides space for outdoor productions, whilst a cob pizza oven is excellent for events. Volunteers have also recently created a new fernery, a lovely addition the garden with some interesting species added – this is strategically placed to lead you seamlessly into the mini woodland.

The garden is maintained by a group of dedicated volunteers that meet every Friday , with new and enthusiastic people always welcome along. Trust staff also run a busy events programme throughout the school holidays and on weekends, with events suitable for families such as minibeast hunts to adult-themed events such as wreath making.

Location

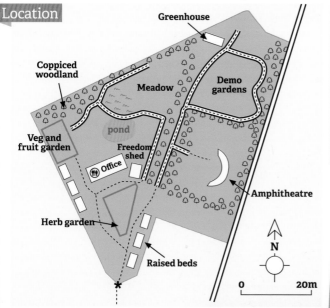

Greenhouse
Coppiced woodland
Meadow
Demo gardens
Veg and fruit garden
pond
Freedom shed
Office
Amphitheatre
Herb garden
Raised beds

N

0   20m

HULL

Buff-tailed bumblebee

BEST SEASON TO VISIT

SEASONAL HIGHLIGHTS

❄ SPRING
Smooth newt
Blue tit
Snowdrop
Bluebell
Chaffinch
Goldfinch

☀ SUMMER
Peacock butterfly
Green shield bug
Meadow cranesbill
Purple loosestrife
Migrant hawker

🍂 AUTUMN
Pipistrelle bat
Garden spider
Hazel

❄ WINTER
Long-tailed tit
Robin
Fox

POTTERIC CARR

NEAREST POSTCODE
DN4 8DB

NEAREST TOWN
Doncaster

GRID REFERENCE
SE 589 007

PUBLIC TRANSPORT
Regular buses run from the
Frenchgate Interchange in
Doncaster to Lakeside and
the White Rose Way. Alight
by B&Q, opposite OneCall
and cross the White Rose
Way at the traffic lights.
The nearest train station is
Doncaster.

DIRECTIONS
By Junction 35 of the
A1. From the M18 take
Junction 3 towards
Doncaster and follow signs
for the A6182 (White Rose
Way). At the first set of
lights you reach, turn right
onto Mallard Way. The car
park is 60 metres on your
right hand side.

**OTHER
INFORMATION**
Opening times:
9am – 5pm, 7 days a week.
No entry after 5pm. For
Christmas closures please
see the Trust's website.
Contact information:
01302 570077
Size: 240 ha

TOP TIP An afternoon
winter visit can be great for
spotting bittern – ask for latest
sightings at reception, wrap up
warm and wait. Starlings also
perform impressive aerobatics
over the lake at dusk in winter.

Famed for its wetland birds including bitterns, Potteric Carr has a network of paths and hides enabling visitors to explore the mosaic of habitats and enjoy stunning vistas. With excellent facilities including a fantastic new visitor centre overlooking a lake containing a shop, toilets and restaurant, it is perfect for a day out.

An area of low-lying land to the south east of Doncaster, Potteric Carr forms the floodplain of the River Torne. Renowned for birdwatching, there are many highlights amongst the 230 species of birds that have been recorded here, including breeding bitterns, black-necked grebes and marsh harriers.

Many of the lakes are fringed with reedbeds and this habitat has attracted wintering bitterns which in recent years have stayed on to breed. New areas are also due to be landscaped to the east and west of the existing site, adding a major extension that will be transformed into wildlife-rich habitat over the next couple of years.

Spring and autumn are an exciting time on the nature reserve, as resident bird populations are boosted by the arrival of migrant birds, which can turn up at any time. In summer the marshes support a wide range of plants providing a spectacle of colour as yellow flag iris and purple loosestrife bloom bright. Other plants visitors may stumble across include greater and lesser spearwort, water soldier, water violet and southern marsh orchid. The disued railway embankments that run throughout the site were constructed of magnesian limestone, which suits common spotted and bee orchids, and old man's beard – Britain's only wild clematis.

Great crested newts and palmate newts are present in some of the pools, and toads are common. Mammals here include water shrew, harvest mouse and roe deer, whilst recent surveys have

Hoverfly and clematis

Willow tit

POTTERIC CARR

shown promising signs of a healthy water vole population – a species that has seen huge declines in recent decades. The nature reserve is excellent for invertebrates too, with impressive lists of moths, spiders, beetles, bugs and hoverflies. Purple hairstreak and brown argus are among the 28 species of butterfly to be seen, whilst there have been 21 species of dragonfly noted.

In the 16th Century the area was a small part of the Hatfield Royal Deer Chase, but it eventually fell out of favour due to being continuously flooded. Over a period of 150 years various attempts were made at draining the area, the final successful attempt being in the 1760s. In the 1950s coal mines from Rossington Colliery penetrated under the area. Over the next 15 years, as subsidence occurred, the former fen conditions returned, and its corresponding wildlife.

In 1968 a small area (13 hectares) was declared a nature reserve by Yorkshire Wildlife Trust. Over time the site has gradually increased as parcels of land have been added in, with the most recent extension in 2015 taking the site to 240 hectares. The mosaic of habitats we see here today is largely due to recent management work by the Trust's staff and its hardworking volunteers.

An extensive education and events programme runs from this site, suitable for all ages and abilities. Visit the Trust's website for details.

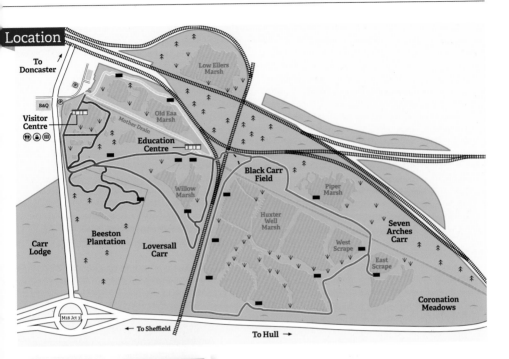

Location

To Doncaster

B&Q

Visitor Centre

Low Ellers Marsh

Old Eaa Marsh

Mother Drain

Education Centre

Willow Marsh

Black Carr Field

Piper Marsh

Huxter Well Marsh

Seven Arches Carr

Carr Lodge

Beeston Plantation

Loversall Carr

West Scrape

East Scrape

Coronation Meadows

M18 Jct 3

← To Sheffield

To Hull →

Little egret

Gadwall

Southern marsh orchid

A630 · A18 · A638 · B1396 · A6182 · Doncaster · A60 · M18 · Potteric Carr · A1(M) · River Torne · Rossington

N

BEST SEASON TO VISIT

SEASONAL HIGHLIGHTS

◰ SPRING
Colt's-foot
Black-necked grebe
Marsh harrier
Little ringed plover
Avocet

◰ SUMMER
Purple loosestrife
Southern marsh orchid
Banded demoiselle
Brown argus
Green sandpiper

◰ AUTUMN
Little egret
Teal
Gadwall
Willow tit
Roe deer

◰ WINTER
Bittern

PULFIN BOG

NEAREST TOWN
Beverley

GRID REFERENCE
TA 050 441

PUBLIC TRANSPORT
Buses from Beverley stop in Tickton.

DIRECTIONS
Pulfin Bog lies about two miles north east of Beverley. The nearest parking is at Hull Bridge, on the old part of the A1035. From Beverley take the A1035 eastwards and after crossing the River Hull, turn right for Tickton, then right again immediately afterwards. Park on the roadside near the footbridge over the river. Walk north along the public footpath on the east bank of the river for about 1½ miles until a large lake is reached. Turn left along the bank between the lake and the river, then right on reaching a row of trees. The nature reserve starts where the trees end.

OTHER INFORMATION
Site designation: SSSI
Size: 15 ha

TOP TIP Keep an eye on the sky as hobbies regularly hunt dragonflies during the summer.

In spring a visual feast of marsh flowers can be enjoyed at this small spring-fed River Hull Valley nature reserve, whilst in early summer marsh orchids abound.

Pulfin Bog is remnant of the extensive fens that once occupied the valley of the River Hull and probably owes its survival to the springs that emerge as pools on the surface.

The name Pulfin is believed to be a corruption of "pool fen", the name given to the site in a 14th Century document. The nature reserve is bounded on three sides by the River Hull and on the fourth side is an old flood bank, separating the site from High Eske Lake. When the nature reserve was acquired by the Trust a ditch was clearly visible dividing the site into northern and southern sections. The northern half, dominated by reed sweet-grass, was grazed until 1955. The southern half, in which the springs emerge, is dominated by common reed.

Pulfin Bog is very rich in plant life. Fenland plants such as common meadow-rue, common valerian and marsh woundwort can be found during the summer along with yellow and purple loosestrifes and the rare marsh pea. Patches of scrub occur, most of them dominated by grey willow, but bay willow is also present.

The opening of one of the springs has been greatly enlarged to form a pool providing habitat for aquatic plants. Here, water soldier and marsh fern grow secluded under the shade of the stands of willow. Both sedge and reed warblers regularly breed around the margins and water rail, kingfisher and reed bunting can be found throughout the year. Sixteen species of dragonfly have been seen, with large red damselfly and hairy dragonfly two of the first species to emerge in spring. A large variety of ducks can be seen on the adjacent High Eske Lake, along with occasional migrant terns and wading birds.

Common darter

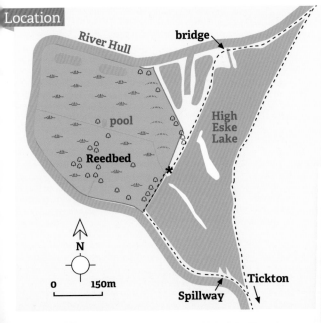

River Hull

bridge

pool

Reedbed

High Eske Lake

N

0   150m

Spillway

Tickton

Pulfin Bog

River Hull

N

Hull Bridge

A1035

Hornsea →

Tickton

Beverley

P

Yellow loosestrife

BEST SEASON TO VISIT

SEASONAL HIGHLIGHTS

✱ SPRING
Hairy dragonfly
Large red damselfly
Sedge warbler

✱ SUMMER
Yellow flag iris
Yellow loosestrife
Marsh pea
Water soldier
Brown hawker

✱ AUTUMN
Common darter
Migrant hawker
Snipe
Reed bunting

✱ WINTER
Kingfisher
Water rail
Otter

RIFLE BUTTS QUARRY

NEAREST POSTCODE
YO43 3JA

NEAREST TOWN
Market Weighton

GRID REFERENCE
SE 897 427

PUBLIC TRANSPORT
Market Weighton is served
by buses from York and
Goole via Holme-on-
Spalding-Moor. The Hudson
Way cycle route runs on
a disused railway line
between Market Weighton
and Beverley.

DIRECTIONS
After passing Market
Weighton Secondary
School, continue
straight on at the next
junction. A mile further
on take a sharp left
turn, go between the
embankments where
a bridge once took the
Market Weighton –
Beverley railway line over
the road. The site is on
the right hand side at the
end of the first field and
parking is on the wide
grass verge in front of the
nature reserve. Please
don't block the gate into
the field next to the site.

**OTHER
INFORMATION**
Site designation: SSSI
Size: 0.3 ha

TOP TIP In winter the
quarry sides provide shelter
from the winter wind and on a
sunny day it is possible to have
a picnic in mid-January.

A tiny nature reserve full of wildflowers and butterflies
in summer Rifle Butts Quarry provides an introduction
to the wildlife typical of the remaining natural areas of
the Yorkshire Wolds.

Rifle Butts Quarry was created to provide stone for the
construction of the railway line adjacent to the nature reserve.
The site was then used as a rifle range from the 1890s to
the First World War. Over 150 plants have been recorded on this site
including characteristic chalk species such as cowslip, marjoram, field
scabious and wild basil. The old target marker pit has been filled in with
topsoil and as a result winter aconite, comfrey, giant bellflower, sweet
cicely and leopard's bane were introduced to the site. Breeding birds
include willow warbler and yellowhammer. Ringlet and common blue
butterflies are a common sight with occasional marbled whites.

Of particular interest at this small nature reserve is the geological
feature exposed on the quarry face. The exposure, of national
importance, shows a Cretaceous unconformity, where sediments from
the Jurassic and Lower Cretaceous periods were eroded away. In the
late Cretaceous period the sea once again covered the area depositing
red and then white chalk. Compared to other areas in North Yorkshire
some 1000 metres of sedimentary rock is missing from the Rifle Butts
sequence. A shelter has been
constructed to protect the
quarry face from erosion.

The Trust works to protect
the rock exposure and the
chalk grassland. Hawthorn and
elder scrub is removed from
the most important grassland
areas and the site is grazed
with Hebridean sheep.

Clustered bellflower

Winter aconite

Location

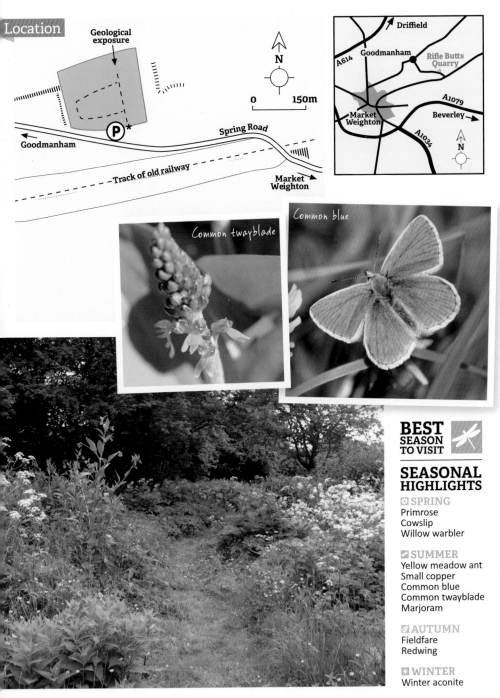

Geological exposure

N

0   150m

P *

Goodmanham

Spring Road

Track of old railway

Market Weighton

Driffield

Goodmanham

A614

Rifle Butts Quarry

A1079

Market Weighton

Beverley

A1034

N

Common twayblade

Common blue

BEST SEASON TO VISIT

SEASONAL HIGHLIGHTS

✿ SPRING
Primrose
Cowslip
Willow warbler

☀ SUMMER
Yellow meadow ant
Small copper
Common blue
Common twayblade
Marjoram

🍂 AUTUMN
Fieldfare
Redwing

❄ WINTER
Winter aconite

RIPON LOOP

This dynamic nature reserve lies within the largest meander of the River Ure and features rarities such as thistle broomrape and otters.

NEAREST POSTCODE
HG4 3HJ

NEAREST TOWN
Ripon

GRID REFERENCE
SE 317 737

PUBLIC TRANSPORT
Ripon to Masham buses stop on the A6108 at Ripon City Golf Club.

DIRECTIONS
Turn right at Ripon City Golf Club, ¾ miles north of Ripon on the A6108. Drive past the tennis club and driving range, past a right turn to a farm and take the next right (just after a no unauthorised entry sign) and drive to the end. A small parking area is available on the left just after the cattle grid at the entrance. Please do not park on the verge outside the nature reserve.

OTHER INFORMATION
Site designation: SSSI
Size: 41 ha

Pay particular attention to the river when visiting, making sure to avoid the floodplain when flooding threatens.

TOP TIP Visit in late June or July for your best chance of seeing the colony of thistle broomrape.

Thistle broomrape

On dry summer days the Ure loops tranquilly around the grassland and wet woods of Ripon Loop, whilst in times of flood the river changes course and cuts across the site. As floods recede water is held in pools and ditches, providing natural flood protection for areas downstream. Ripon Loop forms part of the Ripon Parks SSSI.

Kingfishers dart past and in winter large fish-eating goosanders are frequently seen along the river. Numbers increase if cold weather freezes over lakes and gravel pits in the area, forcing them to use the open water of the river. In summer, sand martins feed on insects overhead, breeding in the nature reserve's soft river banks. They are one of the earliest summer migrant birds to arrive and their buzzing calls can be heard from early March.

Thistle broomrape is a rare plant that grows on thistle in chalk or limestone only in Yorkshire. Though the plant flourishes on the site, the population is variable: in some years there are hundreds of the creamy-purple coloured flower spikes growing from the base of thistles, in other years, there are but a few. The dry woodlands host bluebells, primrose, sanicle and toothwort – another member of the broomrape family. Grassland restoration carried out in 2015 should see an increase in the botanical diversity of two of the fields, building on remnants of species-rich grassland found in banks and patches within those fields. Species include harebell, agrimony, bird's-foot trefoil, pignut, quaking grass, cuckooflower, goat's beard, mouse-ear hawkweed, cowslip, ladies bedstraw and angelica.

Dragonflies are common, with banded demoiselles abundant along the river. Butterflies abound in sheltered areas in summer, including meadow brown, ringlet, large and small skipper and wall.

Grassland areas are maintained by grazing with sheep and cattle, and with a traditional hay cut in some areas. Thistles are managed to prevent them becoming dominant, with a few left to maintain the colony of thistle broomrape. Invasive plants are also removed.

Location

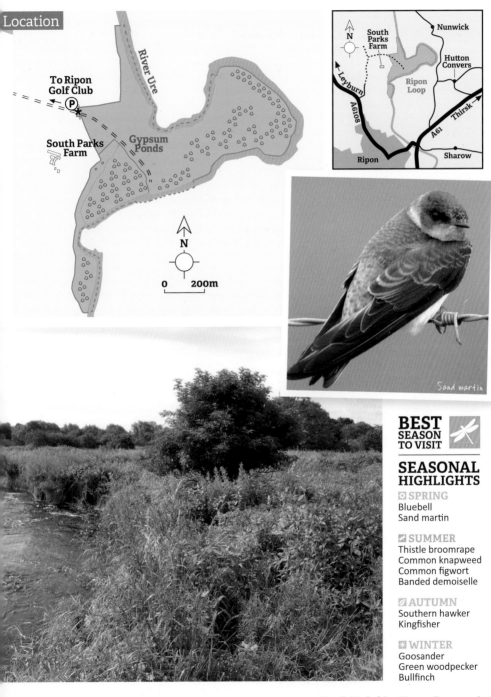

River Ure

To Ripon
Golf Club

South Parks
Farm

Gypsum
Ponds

N

0   200m

South
Parks
Farm

Nunwick

N

Hutton
Convers

Leyburn

A6108

Ripon
Loop

Thirsk →

A61

Ripon

Sharow

Sand martin

BEST
SEASON
TO VISIT

SEASONAL HIGHLIGHTS

SPRING
Bluebell
Sand martin

SUMMER
Thistle broomrape
Common knapweed
Common figwort
Banded demoiselle

AUTUMN
Southern hawker
Kingfisher

WINTER
Goosander
Green woodpecker
Bullfinch

ROTHWELL COUNTRY PARK

NEAREST POSTCODE
LS26 0JY

NEAREST TOWN
Rothwell

GRID REFERENCE
SE 353 296

PUBLIC TRANSPORT
Regular buses run between Leeds and Rothwell, stopping on Leeds Road.

DIRECTIONS
On the M1 south take Junction 44, and turn left onto the A639/ Leeds Road going south to Castleford. Follow this road to Rothwell and take a left onto First Avenue. Rothwell Country Park is at the end of the road. Roadside parking is available at the top of Bullough Lane.

OTHER INFORMATION
Size: 54 ha

TOP TIP The pond trail, which leads you around the 15 ponds, makes for a pleasant family visit on a sunny day!

A peaceful spot away from the hustle and bustle of urban West Yorkshire, this park offers the perfect weekend walk for families wanting time and space to breathe in the fresh air and take in the sights and sounds of nature.

Rothwell Country Park provides a much needed oasis for quiet recreation and enjoyment which is of value to wildlife and people alike.

The park lies in the south-eastern corner of the Leeds district, nestled between the northern flank of Rothwell town and the Aire and Calder Navigation Canal, making it easily accessible from the Trans-Pennine Cycle Way as well as other public footpaths.

The park was once occupied by Rothwell Colliery, but following its closure in 1983 it became a post-industrial wasteland, remnants of which are still visible today. Fortunately, in the mid 1990's a partnership was formed between local people, Leeds City Council and Groundwork Leeds, which saw great changes to the site. Over five years extensive landscaping allowed the land to be carefully reprofiled and tracts of wildflower meadow, woodland and wetlands were created.

Finally on the 24th June 2000 Rothwell Country Park was opened to the public. Since then wildlife has started to colonise the site, with several birds taking up residence and the pond buzzing with life during the summer months.

The park now boasts an extensive network of paths including a sculpture and pond trail. Follow the signpost to 'the summit' to enjoy 360 degree views over Leeds and West Yorkshire.

Rothwell Country Park is owned by Leeds City Council and managed in partnership with the Trust. A Friends of Rothwell Country Park group was set up in 2010 who help with this work, ensuring that the park is both people and wildlife-friendly.

Tree sparrow

Common toad

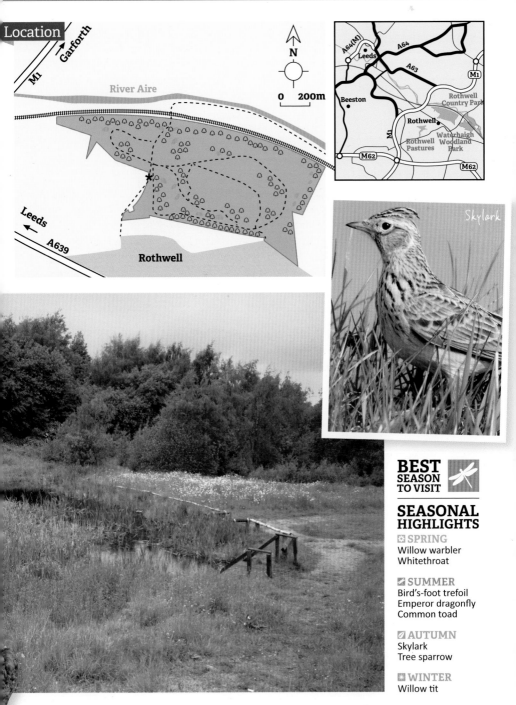

Garforth

M1

River Aire

N

0   200m

Leeds

A639

Rothwell

A64(M)

A64

Leeds

A63

M1

Beeston

Rothwell Country Park

Rothwell

M1

Rothwell Pastures

Waterhaigh Woodland Park

M62

M62

Skylark

BEST SEASON TO VISIT

SEASONAL HIGHLIGHTS

✚ SPRING
Willow warbler
Whitethroat

◪ SUMMER
Bird's-foot trefoil
Emperor dragonfly
Common toad

◪ AUTUMN
Skylark
Tree sparrow

✚ WINTER
Willow tit

ROTHWELL PASTURES

NEAREST POSTCODE
LS26 0QL

NEAREST TOWN
Rothwell

GRID REFERENCE
SE 340 283

PUBLIC TRANSPORT
Regular buses run
between Rothwell and
both Leeds and Castleford.

DIRECTIONS
Take the A639 from Leeds.
At the roundabout take
the second exit onto A61/
Leeds Road. Keep right
on the A61 and then take
the second left at the
next roundabout, above
the M1. Take the next
left onto Wood Lane and
follow this round until you
reach Church Street. There
is a small car park on your
right at the bottom of
the hill.

**OTHER
INFORMATION**
Site designation: Leeds
Nature Area
Size: 24 ha

TOP TIP Enjoy a walk in
summer looking for the various
butterflies and moths that feed
on the flowering plants.

Cinnabar

Based around a network of streams, meadows and a
disused railway line, Rothwell Pastures has a special
importance for both local history as well as wildlife,
which has gained it recognition as a Leeds Nature Area.

A site steeped in history, there was once a grand mansion
that was passed down over the centuries between various
landowners and even frequented by kings of the time. Today
all that remains is a stack of stones not far from the Church Street car
park, known locally as Rothwell Castle. As a result the significance of
this site as a former manorial hunting estate is often lost – with water
voles more likely seen than wild boar at large!

Around 1069 Rothwell Pastures was granted to Ilbert de Lacy by
William the Conqueror, and amongst the many changes that came
to be under the de Lacy family was that the vast woodland which
covered the district of 'Rothwell Haigh' became a hunting park. It is
thought that the park was rich in wildlife at the time, with wild boar
and deer regularly becoming part of the feast for the many lords and
ladies that frequented the manor house and grounds.

In fact, the area became a little too popular as ever more regal
guests visited including King John and Edward II. Come 1339, John
O'Gaunt reputedly killed the last wild boar. Following this the manor
house and buildings, which had been the administrative centre for
the district, fell out of favour and by the end of the 15th Century were
said to be in 'great ruyine and decay'.

Although the land was farmed until the late 1970s the buildings
were all but demolished, leaving Rothwell Castle as the last remnants
of the medieval manor house.

Rothwell Pastures is now a mix of scrub, hedgerows, ponds and
meadows, with each habitat home to a wealth of wildlife. Look for
ragwort, bladder campion and bird's-foot trefoil, which provide food
to butterflies like the common blue and moths including the striking
day-flying cinnabar. Watch the transformation of hawthorn, oak
and ash trees as nectar-producing blossoms become nut and berry
autumn larders for birds like yellowhammer and blackbird. Listen out
for woodpeckers as they drum holes in trees looking for grubs to eat
and keep eyes peeled for toads and frogs in the marshland.

The disused railway link to the west also connects a variety of smaller
habitats, providing an important corridor for wildlife and public access.

Rothwell Pastures is owned by Leeds City Council and managed in
partnership with the Trust.

Location

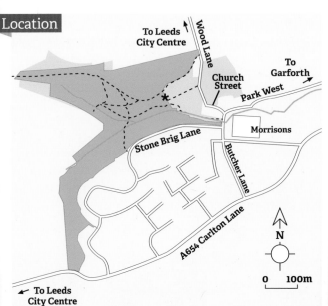

To Leeds City Centre

Wood Lane

Church Street

To Garforth

Park West

Stone Brig Lane

Morrisons

Butcher Lane

A654 Carlton Lane

To Leeds City Centre

N

0   100m

A64(M)
A64
Leeds
A63
M1
Beeston
Rothwell Country Park
Rothwell
M1
Waterhaigh Woodland Park
Rothwell Pastures
M62
M62

Bladder campion

BEST SEASON TO VISIT

SEASONAL HIGHLIGHTS

⊞ SPRING
Common toad
Blackcap
Whitethroat
Willow warbler

◪ SUMMER
Bird's-foot trefoil
Bladder campion
Cinnabar

◪ AUTUMN
Hawthorn

⊞ WINTER
Yellowhammer

SALMON PASTURES

THE
wildlife
TRUSTS
Sheffield &
Rotherham

NEAREST POSTCODE
S4 7WT

NEAREST TOWN
Sheffield

GRID REFERENCE
SK 371 881

PUBLIC TRANSPORT
Frequent buses run from
Sheffield City Centre,
where the nearest train
station is located.

DIRECTIONS
From Sheffield City Centre
take Saville Street (A1609)
from the A61. Turn right
onto Attercliffe Road
(A6178) where there is
limited parking on the
road. Reached on foot
along the Five Weirs Walk.

**OTHER
INFORMATION**
Site designation: LNR
Size: 0.5 ha

TOP TIP Due to its easy
access for pushchairs, this is
a great nature reserve to visit
with the whole family and
introduce young children to the
wonders of wildlife.

Next to the River Don, nestled in the industrial Attercliffe area, this tiny but important wildlife haven is home to many birds and insects. Sit back and watch butterflies flit between the flowers and warm themselves in the sun.

This small nature reserve manages to pack in both woodland and river, as the Don meanders by. Home to the locally rare hoverfly, *Cheilosa mutablis,* this site attracts many insects. Dragonflies and butterflies are also notable, with gatekeeper and orange-tip among those seen here. Birds such as mistle thrush, bullfinch, goldfinch and long-tailed tit nest and feed in the woods, while kingfisher, little grebe, moorhen and mallard may be seen on the banks of the River Don.

Due to its closeness to Sheffield and its unique wild space, which provides a home to a range of birds and insects, this site play a vital role in the city's green corridor.

Orange-tip

Little grebe

Mistle thrush

Location

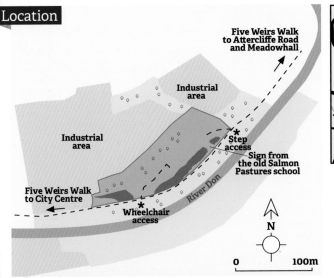

Five Weirs Walk to Attercliffe Road and Meadowhall

Industrial area

Industrial area

* Step access

Sign from the old Salmon Pastures school

Five Weirs Walk to City Centre

* Wheelchair access

River Don

N

0   100m

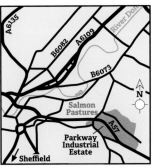

A6135
B6082
A6109
River Don
B6073
Salmon Pastures
N
Parkway Industrial Estate
A57
Sheffield

Goldfinch

BEST SEASON TO VISIT

SEASONAL HIGHLIGHTS

✿ SPRING
Orange-tip
Little grebe
Kingfisher
Mistle thrush

✿ SUMMER
Gatekeeper

✿ AUTUMN
Long-tailed tit

✿ WINTER
Bullfinch
Goldfinch

SALT LAKE QUARRY

NEAREST POSTCODE
LA6 3JF

NEAREST TOWN
Hawes

GRID REFERENCE
SD 774 784

PUBLIC TRANSPORT
Nearest train station is Ribblehead, from where it is a 1½ mile walk along the road to the nature reserve.

DIRECTIONS
Off the B6479, one mile south of the B6255 junction (Ribblehead).

OTHER INFORMATION
Site designation: SSSI
Size: 2 ha

TOP TIP This site is best visited in June and July to appreciate the flowering plants. Combine it with a trip to the nearby Ashes and Brae Pastures to make a day full of flora.

Despite its small size, Salt Lake Quarry Nature Reserve is a very diverse and complex site, with several fragile habitats. Comprising of limestone grassland, quarry cliff faces, pools, fen, flushes and willow scrub the nature reserve supports a rich flora with several nationally scarce plants.

This disused limestone quarry on the edge of the Settle to Carlisle railway is now managed for its botanical and invertebrate interest. It is a SSSI and home to several nationally rare or scarce plants such as rigid buckler fern on the cliff faces, bird's-eye primrose in the damp grassland and northern spike rush around the pools. The cliff faces support many ferns such as brittle bladder-fern, hart's-tongue fern, maidenhair spleenwort and moonwort. Flowering plants of interest include wood cranesbill, hare's-tail cottongrass and ox-eye daisy, along with several species of orchid including frog orchid and common twayblade. The damp scrub along the base of the cliff face also supports an impressive number of mosses and lichens.

The site has been undergrazed in the past and scrub and course grasses have encroached on the grassland. Since taking on the lease of the site in 1985 Yorkshire Wildlife Trust has worked to remove non-native species and manage the scrub encroachment. Salt Lake Quarry is now grazed by the Trust's Hebridean sheep in autumn, which are great at keeping on top of the coarse vegetation.

Salt Lake Quarry is a small and fragile site with difficult terrain, cliff faces and scree slopes. It is unsuitable for young children or dogs and we ask all visitors to remain on the single path and to take care on the uneven terrain and near to cliff faces.

Hart's-tongue fern

Elf cup lichen and moss

Location

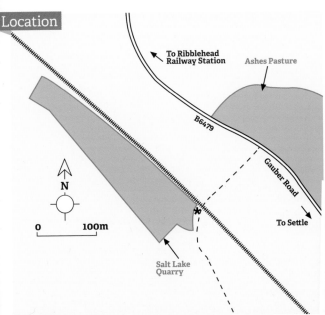

To Ribblehead Railway Station

Ashes Pasture

B6479

Gauber Road

To Settle

N

0   100m

Salt Lake Quarry

N

Ribblehead   Hawes
Ashes Pasture
Chapel le Dale   B6255   Salt Lake Quarry
B6479   Selside
Southerscales
Inglebrough Hill   South House Pavement   Brae Pasture
Ingleton   Horton in Ribblesdale
A65   Settle Carlisle Railway
Skipton   Clapham

Moonwort

BEST SEASON TO VISIT

SEASONAL HIGHLIGHTS

SPRING
Blue moor grass

SUMMER
Northern spike rush
Bird's-eye primrose
Frog orchid
Common twayblade
Moonwort

AUTUMN
Hart's-tongue fern

WINTER
Lichens

SALTMARSHE DELPH

NEAREST POSTCODE
DN14 7RP

NEAREST TOWN
Goole

GRID REFERENCE
SE 775 248

PUBLIC TRANSPORT
The nearest train station is at Saltmarshe, which is just over 2 miles from the nature reserve. A Trans-Pennine footpath passes the site.

DIRECTIONS
The nature reserve is 2½ miles south east of Howden. Turn off the A614 roundabout signed Kilpin and Laxton. Take the Skelton road and proceed through the village, then turn left away from the River Ouse before the railway swing bridge. The nature reserve is 400m along the road to Saltmarshe.

OTHER INFORMATION
Size: 5 ha

TOP TIP Visit in late spring for willow tits, marsh harriers and water rails. Or come late summer and be on the lookout for dragonflies.

Saltmarshe Delph is a small nature reserve with a diverse mix of wetland habitats. For a small site, some top quality wildlife can be discovered including marsh harriers and water rails.

Open water and reedbeds contain lesser reedmace and attract marsh harrier and water rail, whereas in the woodland fringe mature willow, oak and ash grow. Birds of prey often frequent the site so make sure you take the occasional look up during your visit.

The site is divided neatly into two compartments by the Hull to Doncaster railway, known as the Delph, which contains a large reed-fringed lake, and Willow Garth an area of wet woodland, scrub and ponds. In the north east corner is an area of wet willow carr, a habitat which is full of song in spring with sedge warbler, blackcap and chiffchaff. Reed warblers breed around the lake and a small number of willow tits have bred in recent years, some of which have used specially-designed nestboxes put up by volunteers. In high summer, dragonflies and damselflies make themselves at home, with 19 species recorded. Other insects, including the lesser stag beetle and ringed china-mark moth can also be found. This rich insect life attracts Daubenton's bats that skim low over the lake surface. Winter is a great time to see great crested grebes and several species of ducks on the main lake, including gadwall, teal and shoveler.

The Delph was excavated in 1864 to provide spoil for the approach to the railway bridge close by. The Willow Garth to the west of the railway was commercially worked until 1956, providing materials to make agricultural baskets. In 1972 the site become a nature reserve. Yorkshire Wildlife Trust works, with the help of volunteers, to keep the ponds and reedbeds in their present condition and to control willow encroachment.

Cuckoo

Ruddy darter

Location

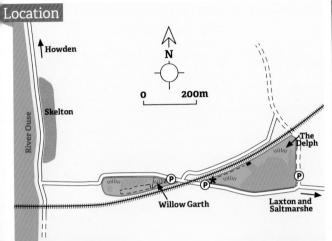

Howden

River Ouse

Skelton

N

0   200m

The Delph

Willow Garth

Laxton and Saltmarshe

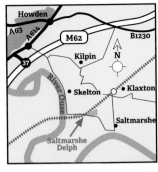

Howden

A63 A614 M62 B1230

Kilpin

N

37

Skelton Klaxton

Saltmarshe

Saltmarshe Delph

River Ouse

Water rail

BEST SEASON TO VISIT

SEASONAL HIGHLIGHTS

▣ SPRING
Mute swan
Marsh harrier
Cuckoo
Sand martin
Sedge warbler

▣ SUMMER
Emperor dragonfly
Small red-eyed damselfly
Broad-bodied chaser
Southern hawker
Hobby

▣ AUTUMN
Ruddy darter
Teal
Wigeon
Gadwall

▣ WINTER
Great crested grebe
Water rail
Willow tit

SEATA QUARRY

NEAREST POSTCODE
DL8 3AL

NEAREST TOWN
Hawes

GRID REFERENCE
SD 988 881

PUBLIC TRANSPORT
Buses from Leyburn and
Hawes.

DIRECTIONS

The quarry lies north of
the Aysgarth to Thornton
Rust road in Wensleydale.
A narrow green lane leaves
this road ½ mile from the
junction with the A684 in
Aysgarth, park at the start
of the lane and walk to
the nature reserve. After
two right-angled bends the
lane ends at the quarry
entrance. Footpaths also
link the quarry to the A684
and back to Aysgarth.

OTHER INFORMATION

Size: 41 ha

TOP TIP Although
an alien species amongst
wonderful natives, the fairy
foxgloves' ability to colonise the
narrowest of hairline cracks is
really impressive.

From May until late autumn there is an abundance
of wildflowers. In May, shelter from the west wind
encourages butterflies and allows the sweet scent
of cowslips to hang in the air.

Blue moor-grass is the most abundant grass and its metallic
blue flowers are impressive in April. Both meadow and hairy
oat-grasses are frequent along with quaking grass, but the
star of the grasses is the rare spiky fescue, a native of the Pyrenees.
Two other non-native Pyrenean plants occur: round-leaved St John's-
wort can be seen on a ledge and fairy foxglove is abundant on the
quarry walls. The thin soils have more typical calcareous grassland
species with abundant bird's-foot trefoil, purging flax, harebell and
especially small scabious. In a damp autumn the autumn gentians
can reach 20cms high. Where the soil is exceptionally thin field
madder, parsley piert and biting stonecrop join the fairy foxglove.
Four species of orchids also occur here. In mid-summer six-spot
burnet moth, common blue butterfly and ringlet enjoy the flower-
rich habitat. Curlew and grey partridge have nested here and
sometimes brown hares can be seen.

Sheep grazing within the nature reserve is limited to the winter
months to allow over 100 plant species to flower. In autumn the
deeper soils support a dense growth which is removed by strimming,
raking and burning. Seata Quarry is leased from Township of
Aysgarth and was once used to supply stone to the local area. Some
local properties retain the right to take stone, but practical difficulties
prevent uptake, which is fortunate for the wildlife here!

Harebell

Fragrant orchid

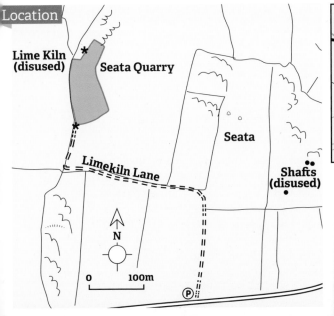

Location

Lime Kiln (disused)

Seata Quarry

Limekiln Lane

Seata

Shafts (disused)

N

0   100m

P

Carperby

Ballowfield

Seata Quarry

Aysgarth

N

Fairy foxglove

BEST SEASON TO VISIT

SEASONAL HIGHLIGHTS

⊞ SPRING
Blue moor-grass
Cowslip
Early purple orchid
Fairy foxglove

⊠ SUMMER
Spiky fescue
Round-leaved
St John's-wort
Small scabious
Fragrant orchid

⊡ AUTUMN
Autumn gentian

⊞ WINTER
Grey partridge

North Yorkshire Nature Reserves | 173

SEMER WATER

NEAREST POSTCODE
DL8 3DJ

NEAREST TOWN
Hawes

GRID REFERENCE
SD 988 881

PUBLIC TRANSPORT
Bus service to Bainbridge then walk up the River Bain footpath to the lake and on to the site.

DIRECTIONS
Take the A684 Leyburn-Hawes road and exit at Bainbridge. Follow signs for Semer Water. Park at Low Bean Farm for a small charge and take the footpath opposite the farm across the fields to the nature reserve. There is also limited free parking in Stalling Busk.

OTHER INFORMATION
Size: 37 ha

TOP TIP Visit when the ice breaks up: its music echoes around the dale.

From the air Semer Water resembles a pearl lying in the heart of Raydale. Ducks and wading birds wheel over the nature reserve with the calls of curlew, oystercatcher and snipe filling the air.

Semer Water is the largest of only three natural water bodies in Yorkshire; a glacial lake which was formed at the end of the last Ice Age when huge amounts of glacial till blocked the outflow. Crooks Beck takes the water from three feeder dales upstream through the nature reserve, which includes two wet meadows by the hamlet of Marsett. There is a full range of habitats from open water with swamp species like yellow water lily, through to fen, marsh, hay meadow and willow carr to developing ash woodland on the driest part. The sandy shore supports a fine growth of needle spike-rush and an abundance of sedge species dominate and it is here that the wading birds feed. The willow species are challenging with many hybrids but bay willow dominates.

Once the ground-nesting birds have fledged the site is grazed with cattle and sheep and excess rush is cut in late summer when possible.

Recently a belt of mixed ash woodland has been planted on the eastern boundary as part of a project to slow rainwater run-off into the lake. Much of the site is an old lake bed which still floods regularly and Yorkshire Wildlife Trust also control a wedge of the lake to a central buoy. The level of the lake was lowered by about one metre in 1937 and the old shore line is still visible.

Teal

Redshank

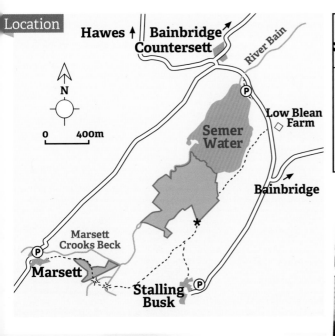

Hawes ↑ Bainbridge
Countersett

River Bain

N

0   400m

Low Blean
Farm

Semer
Water

Bainbridge

Marsett
Crooks Beck

Marsett

Stalling
Busk

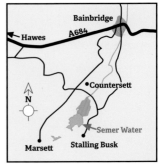

Bainbridge
Hawes → A684
Countersett
N
Marsett Stalling Busk
Semer Water

Mallard

BEST
SEASON
TO VISIT

SEASONAL
HIGHLIGHTS

❖ SPRING
Tufted duck
Great crested grebe
Lapwing
Curlew
Redshank

✿ SUMMER
Devil's-bit scabious
Sand martin
Willow warbler
Reed bunting

✿ AUTUMN
Roe deer

❖ WINTER
Wigeon
Teal
Mallard

SHERBURN WILLOWS

NEAREST POSTCODE
LS25 6AG

NEAREST TOWN
Sherburn in Elmet

GRID REFERENCE
SE 487 326

PUBLIC TRANSPORT
Sherburn in Elmet has a good bus service with a bus stop at the top of New Lane. The train station is 1½ miles away.

DIRECTIONS
Sherburn Willows is situated about two miles north-east of the A1-A63 junction and about one mile from the centre of Sherburn in Elmet. Half a mile from the traffic lights on Low Street in Sherburn travelling south towards South Milford turn right along New Lane. The nature reserve is at the end of the footpath that runs straight on from the end of this road. Park immediately beyond the end of the houses and continue on foot past the metal gate and straight along the farm track. When you reach the end of the track, turn left through the field gate and the nature reserve starts a little further on.

OTHER INFORMATION
Size: 3 ha

TOP TIP The grassland is a riot of colour from May through to August, with the best displays in June and July.

Enjoy colourful pasture where butterflies feed on the purple starbursts of greater knapweed flowers, birds sing from the scrub edge on the bank top and livestock regard you with curiosity as they graze.

This small nature reserve contains flower-filled magnesian limestone grassland which runs steeply down a slope to a wet area of fen and willow carr woodland. In spring and summer the grassland is a carpet of colour, changing with the months: cowslip, ox-eye daisy, hairy violet and common knapweed all bloom. A good show of common spotted orchid, bee orchid and common twayblade are not to be missed, bringing colour in mid-summer. Other species noted as rare locally include purple milk vetch, sainfoin and pale St John's-wort. The wildflowers attract many butterflies, moths and other insects. Reed warblers, chiffchaffs and reed buntings all breed on site along with whitethroats in the hedgerows. The grassland is being restored by removing scrub and grazing with the Trust's livestock. In the areas of wet woodland the Trust coppices the willow to keep it rich in wildlife.

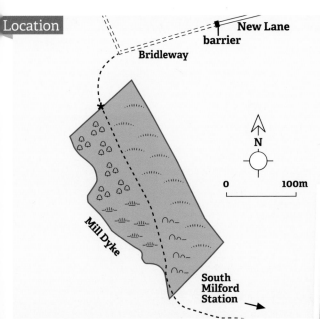

New Lane
barrier
Bridleway

Mill Dyke

N

0   100m

South
Milford
Station →

Church Fenton
Barkston
Sherburn in Elmet
Sherburn Willows
South Milford
Monk Fryston
A1   A63
Ledsham Bank

Sainfoin

BEST
SEASON
TO VISIT

SEASONAL
HIGHLIGHTS

SPRING
Ox-eye daisy
Cowslip
Chiffchaff

SUMMER
Sainfoin
Agrimony
Greater knapweed
Bee orchid
Whitethroat
Lesser whitethroat

AUTUMN
Redwing
Fieldfare

WINTER
Reed bunting

North Yorkshire Nature Reserves | 177

SKERNE WETLANDS

NEAREST POSTCODE
YO25 9HU (Cleaves Farm)

NEAREST TOWN
Driffield

GRID REFERENCE
TA 0638 5600 – Snakeholm
Pastures entrance at
Wansford Bridge; TA 0574
5428 – Skerne Wetlands
entrance

PUBLIC TRANSPORT
Closest train station in
Driffield. Bus to Wansford.

DIRECTIONS
Snakeholm Pastures lies
just south of Wansford
Bridge off the B1249
southeast of Driffield. A
small amount of roadside
parking exists. Skerne
Wetlands is accessed along
a farm track just east of
Skerne Village. Turn south
off the road, left at the
fork, right towards Cleaves
Farm and follow the track
past the farm to the end
where parking is available.

**OTHER
INFORMATION**
Site designation: SSSI
Size: 45 ha

A public footpath runs
along the West Beck at
Snakeholm Pastures.
Prior to visiting Skerne
Wetlands check our
website for opening
information as work is
currently underway.

TOP TIP Take time to
watch the chalk stream to
glimpse of a kingfisher or water
vole busy above the water, or
brown trout lazing below.

The jewel in the crown of this site is the nationally important, most northerly chalk river that is the River Hull headwater chalk streams. The West Beck with its crystal clear waters, lush bankside plants and stunning flowering beds of water crowfoot are not to be missed in the early summer.

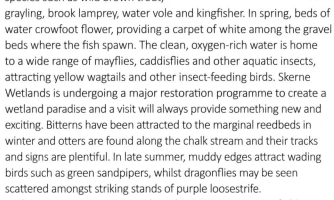

Caddisfly

This complex of sites lying along the crystal clear waters of the West Beck form a beautiful landscape in which to watch wildlife. The waters of this, the most northerly chalk stream in Britain, are a haven for charismatic species such as wild brown trout, grayling, brook lamprey, water vole and kingfisher. In spring, beds of water crowfoot flower, providing a carpet of white among the gravel beds where the fish spawn. The clean, oxygen-rich water is home to a wide range of mayflies, caddisflies and other aquatic insects, attracting yellow wagtails and other insect-feeding birds. Skerne Wetlands is undergoing a major restoration programme to create a wetland paradise and a visit will always provide something new and exciting. Bitterns have been attracted to the marginal reedbeds in winter and otters are found along the chalk stream and their tracks and signs are plentiful. In late summer, muddy edges attract wading birds such as green sandpipers, whilst dragonflies may be seen scattered amongst striking stands of purple loosestrife.

The nature reserve was purchased in 2008 as two grass fields – Snakeholm Pastures, adjacent to the Wansford Bridge, some four miles southeast of Driffield, in the heart of East Yorkshire. Then, in 2011 the Trust had the opportunity to acquire what at the time was a commercial fish farm covering 28 hectares along with around a mile of the West Beck chalk stream. This is now known as Skerne Wetlands and in 2014 the Trust completed the purchase of a further 12 hectares of land on the opposite side of the chalk stream to extend the nature reserve to over 40 hectares and 1½ mile of chalk stream. The site complex of over 80 former fish farm ponds is now being developed into a mosaic of wetland habitat to include wet grassland, wet woodland, reedbed and open water, alongside works being undertaken to restore degraded sections of the chalk stream.

(COPPER HALL & SNAKEHOLM PASTURES)

Location

Wansford Bridge

P

The Grange

Skerne Village

Snakeholm Pastures

Trout Farm

N

0   200m

Skerne Village

Copper Hall

Cleaves Farm

P

Balkend Field

Skerne Wetlands

Over Hills

A614   Nafferton

N

Driffield   B1249

Wansford

Skerne

Driffield Golf Course

A164

Snakeholm Patures, Copper Hall & Skerne Wetlands

Hutton

Brook lamprey

Brown trout

BEST SEASON TO VISIT

SEASONAL HIGHLIGHTS

SPRING
Orange-tip
Grass snake
Brook lamprey
Yellow wagtail

SUMMER
Emperor dragonfly
Brown trout
Water vole

AUTUMN
Common darter
Green sandpiper
Kingfisher

WINTER
Bittern
Barn owl
Fieldfare
Redwing
Otter
Roe deer

SOUTHERSCALES

Venture across the great expanse of limestone pavement at this impressive nature reserve, perched high on the side of Ingleborough. Off the pavement, the rare and delicate plants of limestone grassland and blanket bog should not be missed.

NEAREST POSTCODE
LA6 3AR

NEAREST TOWN
Settle

GRID REFERENCE
SD 742 769

PUBLIC TRANSPORT
A Sunday bus service runs between Darlington and Lancaster which stops at Chapel-le-Dale. The nearest train station is Ribbleshead.

DIRECTIONS
The nature reserve is off the B6255 Ingleton to Hawes road. Follow the path below the layby and small water company building on the B6255 through the gate. Follow the track towards Ingleborough for three fields to the nature reserve entrance. Parking is available by the Old Hill Inn, where you may also access the site walking south.

OTHER INFORMATION
Site designation: Part of the Ingleborough NNR
Size: 42 ha

TOP TIP Enjoy the nature reserve as part of a longer walk in the Yorkshire Dales soaking up the scenery and be sure to check out the grykes for interesting plants!

A landscape iconic of the Yorkshire Dales, Southerscales Nature Reserve boasts a large area of limestone pavement which is worthy of exploration. The fascinating pattern of blocks and tunnels, known as clints and grykes, which were formed as the glaciers retreated around 15,000 years ago, create the sort of conditions one might expect in a woodland with species like rigid buckler fern taking advantage of the sheltered spots within the deep, gaping grykes. In the shallower, grassy grykes, plants such as meadow rue, fragrant orchid and limestone bedstraw thrive. Whilst in the wetter spots stunning bird's-eye primrose grow.

Early purple orchids cover the neighbouring limestone grassland in their thousands come spring, followed later in the year by a succession of small scabious, harebell and eyebright – all easy to miss, but well worth the effort to find. The acid grassland on site provides habitat for yet more plants including the carnivorous round-leaved sundew, cross-leaved heath and bog asphodel – plants typical of these soils. Many interesting grasses and sedges can be found here. The wide variety of nectar sources provide rich pickings for a number of butterflies including dark green fritillary, common blue and small heath. In spring the UK's largest moth can also be found, the emperor moth.

Managed by Yorkshire Wildlife Trust since 1982, this site actually forms part of Ingleborough National Nature Reserve, and sits at an altitude of 335 metres. The Trust use cattle to graze the grassland in summer and sheep in the winter to keep a rich variety of plants and grasses on site using the traditional management method of conservation grazing. The pavement can be extremely slippery during wet weather and the limestone clints unstable so visitors are advised to walk across with caution. Nearby there are caves and potholes to explore for the more adventurous.

Wild thyme

180 | Discover Yorkshire's Wildlife

Location

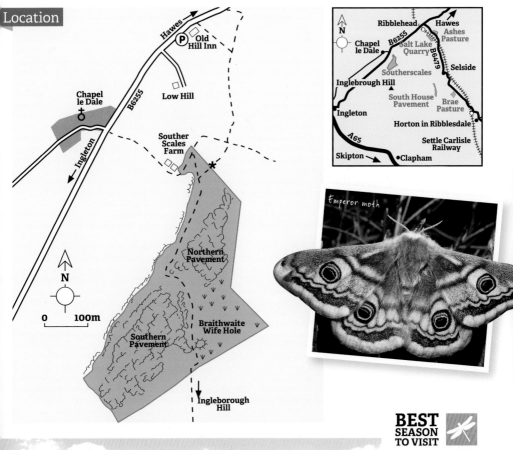

Hawes

(P) Old Hill Inn

Chapel le Dale

B6255

Low Hill

Souther Scales Farm

*

Ingleton

N

0   100m

Northern Pavement

Southern Pavement

Braithwaite Wife Hole

Ingleborough Hill

N

Ribblehead   Hawes
Ashes Pasture
Chapel le Dale   B6255   Salt Lake Quarry
Southerscales   Selside
Inglebrough Hill
South House Pavement   Brae Pasture
Ingleton
Horton in Ribblesdale
A65   Settle Carlisle Railway
Skipton →   •Clapham

Emperor moth

BEST SEASON TO VISIT

SEASONAL HIGHLIGHTS

⊞ SPRING
Early purple orchid
Primrose
Emperor moth
Wheatear

◪ SUMMER
Wild thyme
Fragrant orchid
Mouse-ear hawkweed
Dark green fritillary

◪ AUTUMN
Black darter
Painted lady

⊞ WINTER
Rigid buckler fern

SOUTH HOUSE PAVEMENT

NEAREST POSTCODE
BD24 0HU

NEAREST TOWN
Settle

GRID REFERENCE
SD 776 744

PUBLIC TRANSPORT
Train (Settle-Carlisle line) station and occasional buses at Horton-in-Ribblesdale 2½ miles away.

DIRECTIONS
Take the B6479 Horton to Selside Road and turn off for South House. The nature reserve lies beyond South House on the lower slopes of Simon Fell, east of Ingleborough Hill. There is limited roadside parking. Enter the nature reserve by a small gate in the wall.

OTHER INFORMATION
Size: 5 ha

TOP TIP The summer flowers in the meadow and around the limestone pavement areas are exceptional; visit in June to see them at their best.

Part of the spectacular Ingleborough National Nature Reserve, South House Pavement is a strip of fine limestone pavement, offering magnificent scenery and interesting plant life from ferns and grasses to rich mosses and lichens.

Surrounded by dry stone walls, typical in the Yorkshire Dales National Park, South House Pavement Nature Reserve is a fantastic example of a limestone pavement. A great site for the sure-footed, the mosaic of narrow clints (blocks) and grykes (fissures) does mean it can be rather difficult to venture across, particularly in wet weather when it is best avoided.

An excellent site for limestone grassland species you can find ferns including rigid buckler and hart's-tongue. Plants of interest include devil's-bit scabious, heath spotted and early purple orchids, whilst small trees and shrubs like rowan, bird cherry and hawthorn are scattered across the nature reserve. There are some patches with thicker soil where heather is found. Beautiful pink hairy stonecrop grows at the edge of pools that form in depressions on the clint surface when it rains or where the soil borders the bare rock.

South House Pavement was once grazed, the rocky areas cleared in previous centuries. However the grykes in the pavement make it a dangerous site for livestock and there is no water supply. Management is now focussed on maintaining the dry stone walls and occasionally removing sycamore seedlings and rosebay willowherb which would otherwise grow and shade out the rich ground flora. The land here is part of the Ingleborough National Nature Reserve.

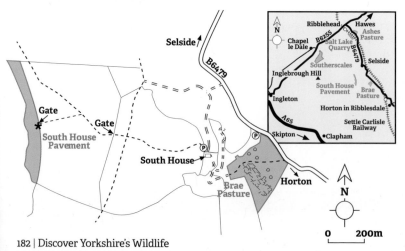

BEST SEASON TO VISIT

SEASONAL HIGHLIGHTS

SPRING
Blue moor-grass
Wheatear
Meadow pipit

SUMMER
Rigid buckler fern
Hairy stonecrop

AUTUMN
Rowan
Harebell

WINTER
Hart's-tongue

SPURN SAFARI

Visit the iconic Spurn National Nature Reserve on a unique wildlife safari, aboard our all-terrain vehicle. You will see and learn about Spurn's fantastic wildlife and rich history, and get the chance to explore the peninsula, including a trip to the Spurn Lighthouse. A must for all families!

Book today www.ywt.org.uk/whats-on

SPROTBROUGH FLASH

NEAREST POSTCODE
DN5 7NB

NEAREST TOWN
Doncaster

GRID REFERENCE
SE 536 013

PUBLIC TRANSPORT
Buses run to Sprotbrough village from Doncaster Interchange. The nearest train station is Conisbrough, approximately two miles west. The nature reserve is also located on the Trans-Peninne Trail, a long-distance walking and cycling route.

DIRECTIONS
Adjacent to the Boat Inn, half a mile south of Sprotbrough village. Public car parking is available next to the toll house on Nursery Lane, which is a two minute walk along the towpath from the nature reserve.

OTHER INFORMATION
Site designation: SSSI
Size: 28 ha

TOP TIP Stunning displays of wildflowers can be enjoyed in spring and summer, while interesting migrant birds may drop in during autumn and winter. Combine with a visit to nearby Denaby Ings Nature Reserve for a full day out. Denaby Ings is a three mile walk away.

Picturesque Sprotbrough Flash is one of the richest wildlife sites in South Yorkshire. A mosaic of open water, wetland, woodland and limestone grassland, the site offers a year-round treat for wildlife enthusiasts.

The impressive diversity of wildlife found at Sprotbrough Flash is due to the range of habitats that have established on the unusual magnesian limestone bedrock. The nature reserve is located in the Don Gorge, where the River Don cuts through the elevated limestone ridge to the west of Doncaster.

Magnesian limestone formed in a shallow tropical sea in the Permian period, some 280 million years ago. This rare rock type is found in a narrow band running approximately north-south from Durham to Nottinghamshire, upon which fantastic wildflower-rich meadows thrive. Due to the financial value of magnesian limestone as a building material large amounts have been quarried, which has shaped the site today.

Fragments of ancient woodland can be found on the slopes of the gorge, whilst wildflower grassland prospers on the plateau and in the restored quarry at the northern end of the site.

The limestone woodland is dominated by ash, wych elm and sycamore, with a varied shrub layer of hazel, spindle and guelder rose. There are some magnificent specimens of small-leaved lime and an avenue of mature yew trees, whilst the woodland immediately to the north-west supports a nationally notable array of invertebrates associated with ancient woodland. The wood is also home to good populations of breeding woodland birds – all three species of woodpecker have been recorded here.

The grasslands at the top of the wooded slopes support a variety of limestone wildflowers and insects. In recent years the area of this valuable habitat has significantly increased through scrub removal and the introduction of conservation grazing. Highlights include good displays of cowslip, common spotted and pyramidal orchids, with common twayblade, quaking grass and autumn gentian among many others. Brown hares and grass snakes are also a common sight. Bones found locally indicate that woolly mammoth and woolly rhinoceros lived in the area during the last Ice Age. When this period ended, approximately 12,000 years ago, water from the melting ice-sheets forced its way through a fault in the elevated limestone ridge, creating the Don Gorge which dominates the local landscape today. Coal mining also contributed to shaping the site.

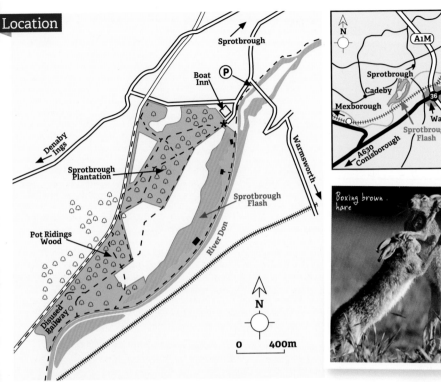

Sprotbrough

Boat Inn

P

Denaby Ings

Sprotbrough Plantation

Sprotbrough Flash

Pot Ridings Wood

River Don

Warmsworth

Disused Railway

N

0   400m

N

A1M

River Don

Sprotbrough

Cadeby

Mexborough

A630 Doncaster

36

Warmsworth

Sprotbrough Flash

A630 Conisborough

Boxing brown hare

SEASONAL HIGHLIGHTS

✖ SPRING
Early purple orchid
Sanicle
Greater stitchwort
Woodruff
Great crested grebe

✓ SUMMER
Common spotted orchid
Common twayblade
Ruddy darter
Comma

✓ AUTUMN
Small-leaved lime
Spindle
Bittern

✖ WINTER
Kingfisher
Brown hare

SPURN

NEAREST POSTCODE
HU12 0UB

NEAREST TOWN
Withernsea

GRID REFERENCE
TA 416 158

PUBLIC TRANSPORT
Buses from Hull stop in Easington. The nearest train station is in Hull.

DIRECTIONS
Spurn is located c.30 miles east of Hull. From Easington follow the B1445 to Kilnsea. From the village of Kilnsea, the nature reserve begins on the road past the Blue Bell. Toilets and a car park can be reached by driving down the side of the Blue Bell. From winter 2017 a new car park will be provided off Spurn road. Access to the point is on foot only, unless joining an organised trip. Great care must be taken when crossing the beach and this should never be attempted when water is washing across.

OTHER INFORMATION
Site designation: SPA, SAC, NNR, SSSI, RAMSAR
Size: 327 ha

No dogs are permitted on site.

TOP TIP **Visit in October** when northeasterly winds blow to witness the spectacle of bird migration, when flocks of thousands of redwings, fieldfares and blackbirds can be seen arriving from Scandinavia.

Spurn is an iconic National Nature Reserve, internationally renowned for bird migration, but also for a wide range of other important wildlife and cultural heritage.

A long, narrow, crooked finger of sand reaching out from the Holderness coast across the mouth of the mighty River Humber. This is Spurn, one of Yorkshire Wildlife Trust's most iconic nature reserves. It is a wildlife-rich mosaic of beach, mudflats, saltmarsh, dunes, grassland, open water, saline lagoons and native sea buckthorn scrub.

Spurn has formed from the sediment, sand and gravels washing down the Holderness coast and by the interaction between the North Sea and the River Humber. In the past, people have tried to fortify Spurn against these dynamic natural processes, but largely these have failed. The Trust now tries to work with nature, rather than against it. In December 2013, a huge tidal surge inundated large areas of the nature reserve and washed through the narrowest part of the peninsula, removing a long stretch of road preventing vehicle access.

Spurn is rich in wildlife but this may not be obvious at first glance. Plants are the first feature noticed, with the marram grass-topped dunes interspersed with stunted elder and orange-berried sea

buckthorn bushes. On the Humber side of Spurn, a strip of saltmarsh exists between the land and the mudflats, supporting colourful flowering plants including sea lavender, sea aster and sea rocket, along with common glasswort and eel grass. Curlew, grey plover and knot use the saltmarsh to roost at high tide. Look out for merlin and peregrine which cause panic among the flocks of roosting wading birds when they start to hunt. Shelduck and brent geese are conspicuous on the mudflats during the winter.

In spring and summer a range of wildflowers appear in the grassland areas which the Trust manages by grazing with sheep and cattle, and also by cutting. Magenta pyramidal orchids grow here and closer inspection of short grass may reveal the rare suffocated clover. Sea holly grows amongst the dunes. Roe deer are a regular sight in these grassy areas, particularly early in the morning, which is also a good time to see a fox. A look over the sea will not only reveal passing seabirds including locally breeding little tern in the summer but also a chance of a harbour porpoise or even a minke whale.

The Spurn lighthouse

SPURN

Red-veined darter

Spurn is famous for migration. Birds are the most visible migrants, but impressive movements of insects, including hoverflies, ladybirds, dragonflies and butterflies can occur. Due to its prominent position, huge numbers of birds pass through Spurn during the year. The numbers and types of birds varies from week to week and is influenced by the weather conditions. The adjacent Humber Estuary is of international importance for its vast numbers of wildfowl and wading birds, which can be seen on passage in spring and autumn and during the winter.

Evidence of Spurn's historical past still exists, including the remains of a railway track, built by the army in 1915 and maintained by them until the 1950s. Old gun emplacements can also be found on the point dating from the First World War. In 1819 lifeboat men came to live on the point with their families and did so until 2012. The station is still manned, however, with a full crew.

Ringed plover

The Spurn lighthouse underwent a programme of restoration in 2015 funded by the Heritage Lottery Fund and will enable visitors to enjoy the building and find out about Spurn's fascinating heritage.

Dogs are not permitted on site.

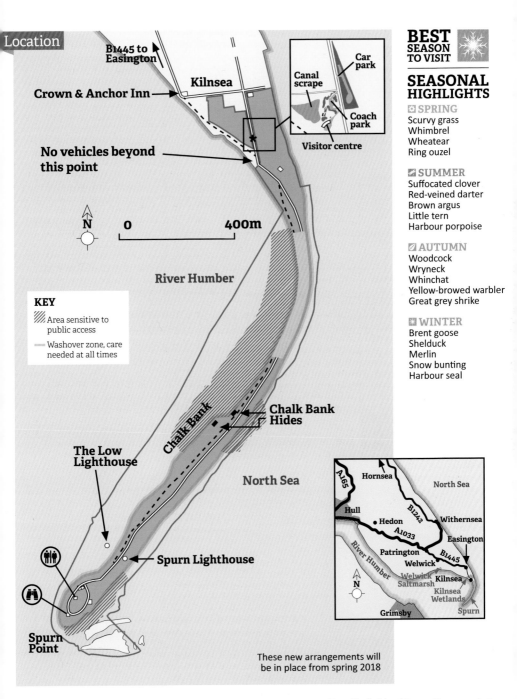

Location

B1445 to Easington

Crown & Anchor Inn

Kilnsea

Canal scrape

Car park

Coach park

Visitor centre

No vehicles beyond this point

N

0   400m

River Humber

KEY

Area sensitive to public access

Washover zone, care needed at all times

Chalk Bank

Chalk Bank Hides

The Low Lighthouse

North Sea

Spurn Lighthouse

Spurn Point

A165

Hornsea

North Sea

Hull

B1242

Hedon

A1033

Withernsea

Patrington

Welwick

Easington

B1445

River Humber

Welwick Saltmarsh

Kilnsea

N

Kilnsea Wetlands

Grimsby

Spurn

These new arrangements will be in place from spring 2018

BEST SEASON TO VISIT

SEASONAL HIGHLIGHTS

✤ SPRING
Scurvy grass
Whimbrel
Wheatear
Ring ouzel

☀ SUMMER
Suffocated clover
Red-veined darter
Brown argus
Little tern
Harbour porpoise

🍂 AUTUMN
Woodcock
Wryneck
Whinchat
Yellow-browed warbler
Great grey shrike

❄ WINTER
Brent goose
Shelduck
Merlin
Snow bunting
Harbour seal

STAVELEY NATURE RESERVE

NEAREST POSTCODE
HG5 9LQ

NEAREST TOWN
Harrogate

GRID REFERENCE
SE 369 630

PUBLIC TRANSPORT
Bus routes pass through
Staveley village.

DIRECTIONS
On the northern outskirts
of Staveley, 2½ miles south
west of Boroughbridge.
Car park just out of the
village on the Minskip
road and also disabled
access via radar key from
the track next to the
church on Main Street.
Public footpaths cross the
site from Staveley Main
Street next to the pub and
from the Minskip road.

**OTHER
INFORMATION**
Size: 79 ha

TOP TIP Look out
for tawny owls in the small
woodland near the East Lagoon
and also rare dune helleborines
that grow next to the path.

This superb wetland site lying close to the River Tutt holds year round interest for visitors with regular sightings of otters and several orchid species among the highlights.

Staveley Nature Reserve, part of a larger area known as Staveley Carrs, has been renowned for rare plants for centuries. Today, this large, accessible site has been sculpted through quarrying activities followed by decades of work by Yorkshire Wildlife Trust and dedicated volunteers.

The site is in two parts: the East Lagoon edged with vegetation that was allowed to develop naturally post quarrying, comprising fen, reed swamp, scrub and flower-rich grassland, and the West Lagoons, which was landscaped and returned to agricultural usage after quarrying, with arable and intensively grazed areas. This part of the site has seen much activity to create more interesting wildlife habitats, since the Trust's purchase of the land in 2010. An 11 hectare hay meadow has been created on a former arable field, islands, nesting platforms and a sand martin wall have been built around the lake, and ponds and scrapes put in to increase the area of wetland habitat. The nature reserve is bordered by the River Tutt on its northern boundary and there are footpaths and hides from which to observe the varied wildlife.

Small areas of fen are home to several relic species which were once widespread before the carrs were drained and transformed into farmland. Locally scarce species such as water violet, marsh helleborine and meadow rue can be found. Common breeding birds include summer visitors such as sand martin and several species of warbler, with common tern breeding on the rafts put out for them and barn owls in nest boxes. Wading birds such as little ringed plover and oystercatcher sometimes breed on the exposed bare ground and islands of West Lagoon. There have been 22 species of damselflies and dragonflies recorded in the main lagoons, small ponds and ditches. Red kites and buzzards are regular visitors.

Mammals are well represented with roe deer and fox amongst the larger species and water shrew and harvest mouse amongst the smaller species. Otters are seen regularly, quite often in the middle of the day on both lagoons. Management of the nature reserve is designed to maintain the site's diverse habitats with rotational reedbed management, scrub clearance and coppicing, cutting and raking of grassland, traditional haymaking and grazing with the Trust's Highland and white park cattle, and Hebridean sheep, amongst other activities.

Otter

Location

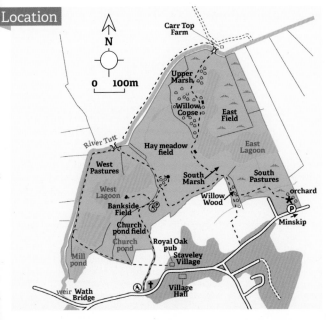

Meadow rue

BEST SEASON TO VISIT

SEASONAL HIGHLIGHTS

✣ SPRING
Large red damselfly
Orange-tip
Common tern
Sand martin
Otter

✣ SUMMER
Marsh helleborine
Common spotted orchid
Bee orchid
Peacock butterfly
Barn owl

✣ AUTUMN
Migrant hawker
Teal
Shoveler
Greenshank

✣ WINTER
Red kite
Tufted duck
Reed bunting
Tree sparrow

STIRLEY COMMUNITY FARM

NEAREST POSTCODE
HD4 6RP

NEAREST TOWN
Huddersfield

GRID REFERENCE
SE 145 137

PUBLIC TRANSPORT
Nearest train stations are Berry Brow and Honley. Buses from Huddersfield service Cold Hill Lane and the junction of Hall Bower Lane and Ladyhouse Lane.

DIRECTIONS
From the M1 take junction 38 to Huddersfield. Take the second exit at the roundabout onto the A637. Cross two roundabouts then at the third take first exit onto the A642. Turn right onto Station Road, then right onto the A629. Turn left onto Fenay Lane and continue to Ashes Lane. Turn right onto High Lane down a steep hill. Take the first left onto Hall Bower Lane. Follow the road until it drops down, turn left on the sharp bend past the houses onto a tarmac drive. Follow the track until the crossroads and drive straight across to car park.

OTHER INFORMATION
Contact information:
01484 663185
Size: 94 ha

TOP TIP Visit in summer when the beef shorthorn herd are grazing the fields with calves at foot, swallows sweep through the air and wildflower borders around the farm buildings are in full bloom.

Stirley Community Farm is an inspirational place in West Yorkshire, which is bringing back wildlife to farming, and working with local people to achieve healthy living and a healthy environment in this corner of Huddersfield.

Abandoned around the start of the 21st Century after being intensively farmed, Yorkshire Wildlife Trust took on the land and farm buildings, which had fallen into disrepair in 2011. Seeing an opportunity to transform the farm into a showcase for wildlife-friendly farming and somewhere that could inspire thousands of people, young and old, the Trust has been improving both the landscape and buildings ever since.

Progress has been steady, with an old barn now transformed into an excellent education facility known as the Cre8 Barn. Thriving food training gardens are abundant with healthy vegetables and salad. An orchard, pond, bee hives and beef shorthorn cattle herd have all

been established on site, whilst a visitor information point, cattle barn and volunteer hub are near completion.

For much of the year, the beef shorthorn herd can be seen grazing the fields at a low density, and with little chemical input it is hoped in time the extensive grasslands of the farm will return to a wildlife-rich habitat. These cows also help out at nearby nature reserves Stocksmoor Common and Broadhead Clough when in need of grazing. A Beef Box scheme, available to local people through the farm, helps towards making this farm sustainable: a step towards the aim of making it a showcase for workable wildlife-friendly farming methods.

The local community is key to the success of the farm, with training opportunities offered to young adults and a growing team of volunteers assisting in all sorts of tasks, from herd checking to harvesting vegetables to carrying out butterfly **surveys.**

Swallow

Cre8 Barn

STIRLEY COMMUNITY FARM

A busy family events and education programme engages huge numbers of people, teaching everything from healthy eating and where food comes from, to the wildlife found here, and how farming methods can complement, rather than destroy wildlife and its habitats.

Public footpaths wind their way through the fields at Stirley Community Farm, with fantastic views afforded from the main farm buildings across the valley and up to local landmark, Castle Hill, which looms above the farm. Look out for returning wildlife including swallows swooping through the air and butterflies feeding on the nectar provided by clever planting in the vegetable beds and the surrounding hedgerows.

Family events held at the farm

Location

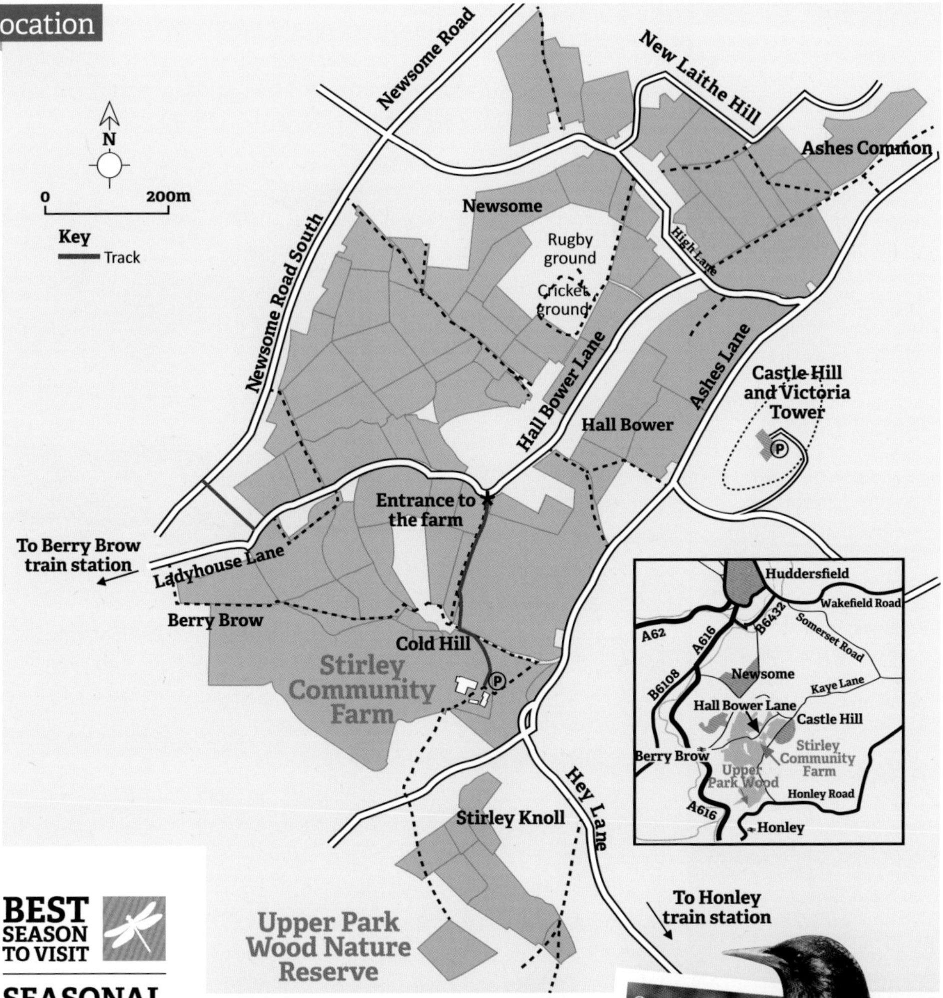
Newsome Road
New Laithe Hill
N
0
200m
Key
Track
Ashes Common
Newsome
Rugby ground
Cricket ground
High Lane
Newsome Road South
Ashes Lane
Castle Hill and Victoria Tower
Hall Bower Lane
Hall Bower
Entrance to the farm
To Berry Brow train station
Ladyhouse Lane
Berry Brow
Cold Hill
Stirley Community Farm
Hey Lane
Stirley Knoll
To Honley train station
Upper Park Wood Nature Reserve
Huddersfield
Wakefield Road
A62
A616
B6432
Somerset Road
B6108
Newsome
Kaye Lane
Hall Bower Lane
Castle Hill
Berry Brow
Stirley Community Farm
Upper Park Wood
Honley Road
A616
Honley

BEST SEASON TO VISIT

SEASONAL HIGHLIGHTS

SPRING
Brimstone
Little owl

SUMMER
Meadow brown
Swallow
Pied wagtail

AUTUMN
Starling

WINTER
Lapwing

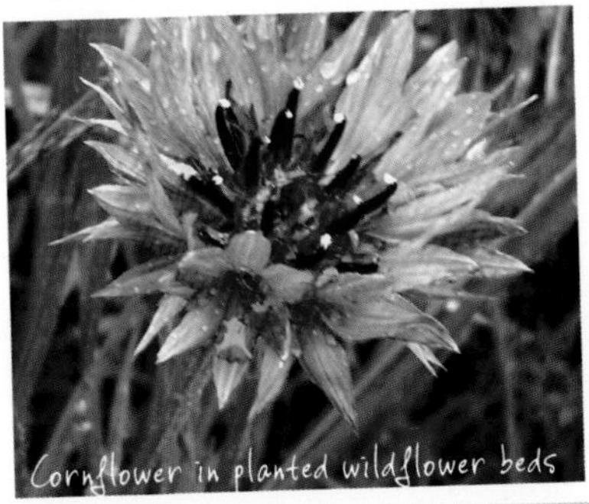
Cornflower in planted wildflower beds

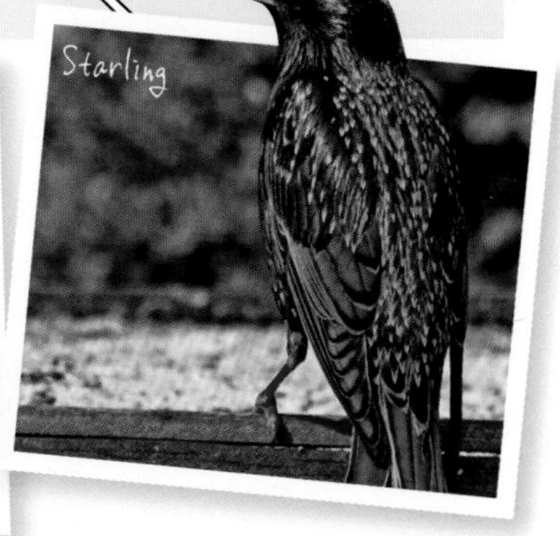
Starling

STOCKSMOOR COMMON

NEAREST POSTCODE
WF4 4JF

NEAREST TOWN
Wakefield

GRID REFERENCE
SE 275 150

PUBLIC TRANSPORT
Buses run to Midgley
from Wakefield, which is
five miles south-west.
The nearest train station
with bus connections is
at Wakefield.

DIRECTIONS
Leave the M1 at junction
38 and take the A637
towards the Yorkshire
Sculpture Park. Carry
on past the park into
Midgley and take a right
after the Black Bull onto
Stocksmoor Road/B6117.
Park on the roadside
either along the B6117 or
on South Lane, which is on
the right.

**OTHER
INFORMATION**
Size: 12 ha

TOP TIP A stone's throw
away from Stoneycliffe Wood,
make a day of it and combine
a visit to the two during early
summer, when the flowers will
be at their best!

Tree pipits and linnets sing from the trees in the young woodland at Stocksmoor Common, whilst wavy hair-grass sways in the breeze in the acid grassland: a snapshot of a once widespread habitat created by rough grazing, which is all but lost in today's intensively used landscape.

Wood mouse

B roadly split into two parts the nature reserve is home to rough acid grassland, which covers approximately half of the area. Moist for most of the year, marshy patches nestle in among the grassland. Elsewhere woodland has encroached onto the site, where historical grazing ceased.

Mat grass, wavy hair-grass and tufted hair-grass dominate the damper grassland, a mix of grasses that demonstrate a halfway house between the extensively sheep-grazed uplands of the Pennines and the drier lowland grassland and heaths of the Vale of York. In the drier areas adder's-tongue fern, common spotted orchid and common fleabane can be found.

In the woodland, pioneering species including birch have established, which today are strewn with bracket fungi that can grow as big as dinner plates! Oak, willow, gorse and hawthorn have taken root and their leaf litter dispersed amongst the tufted-hair grass make for important micro-habitats for all sorts of beetles, flies and other types of insect. A pond, which was dug in 1997, provides another key habitat for insects on site and important populations of toads and newts. Birds including tree pipit, linnet, yellowhammer, willow tit and long-tailed tit all feed on this bounty. Small mammals such as bank voles and wood mice also thrive, food themselves for foxes and tawny owls which use the site.

Leased since April 1965 from Messrs Job Earnshaw and Bros. Limited, the Trust manage the site through conservation grazing, using cattle from the Trust's Stirley Community Farm to keep coarse vegetation and invading scrub plants in check. Bracken is also removed to let more delicate wildflowers to flourish.

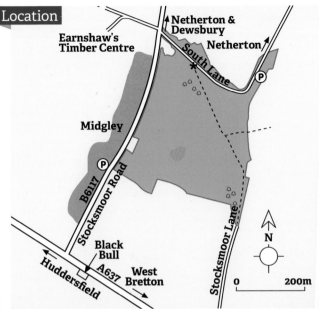

Earnshaw's Timber Centre

Netherton & Dewsbury

Netherton

South Lane

P

Midgley

Stocksmoor Road

B6117

P

Black Bull

Huddersfield

A637

West Bretton

Stocksmoor Lane

N

0   200m

B6117

Dewsbury

Stocksmoor Common

A642

Huddersfield

Netherton

39

Midgley

A637

A636

M1

N

Denby Dale

Barnsley

38

Common fleabane

BEST SEASON TO VISIT

SEASONAL HIGHLIGHTS

✣ SPRING
Tree pipit
Willow tit

☀ SUMMER
Common spotted orchid
Common fleabane
Yellowhammer

🍂 AUTUMN
Fungi

❄ WINTER
Long-tailed tit

STONEYCLIFFE WOOD

NEAREST POSTCODE
WF4 4NF

NEAREST TOWN
Wakefield

GRID REFERENCE
SE 274 161

PUBLIC TRANSPORT
Wakefield to Huddersfield buses call at Netherton. Exit on Upper Lane (Coxley View).

DIRECTIONS
Travelling south on the M1, leave at Junction 39 and take the B6117 to Netherton. The site is on the western edge of the village. A footpath enters the site south of the Star Inn. Another entrance is alongside Netherton Cemetery, whilst a third enters from the signposted entrance road to Earnshaw's Timber Centre near Midgley.

OTHER INFORMATION
Size: 40 ha

TOP TIP A visit in spring is a must as the carpet of bluebells provide a picturesque backdrop to the meandering beck, birds are singing and the scent of wild garlic fills the air.

A stunning woodland with a meandering beck trickling through, this semi-natural ancient woodland is a joy to behold come spring when bluebells and wild garlic abound, or summer when breeding birds are busy raising their broods.

Oak and birch are plentiful in Stoneycliffe Wood Nature Reserve, whilst holly, hazel and, in one spot, heather grow below the canopy. Historically managed for timber production, some areas have since become dominated by sweet chestnut. Benefitting from adjoining woodland to the north and south, this collection of woodlands form a significant part of a tree-covered belt in the wider landscape.

Come spring there are magnificent displays of bluebells and wild garlic, also known as ramsons, with yellow archangel in summer, all of which are considered as ancient woodland indicator species. Streamside plants include wood club-rush, hemlock water dropwort and Sprengel's bramble.

Birds fill the woodland with their songs in the spring and summer, with a variety of summer migrants including chiffchaff, garden warbler and lesser whitethroat breeding on site. All three species of woodpecker frequent the woodland, feeding on the plethora of insects in the dead wood, which provides an important habitat for them. Several rare spiders have been recorded here, and mammals are regularly recorded including bank and field voles, wood mice, stoats and foxes. In recent years the Trust has been improving footpaths on site to provide good access for visitors. Practical conservation work has included thinning the woodland to increase structural and age diversity and to create more deadwood for insects. Bracken and Himalayan balsam are also controlled annually to prevent them from swamping the woodland flowers.

Wild garlic

Field vole

Location

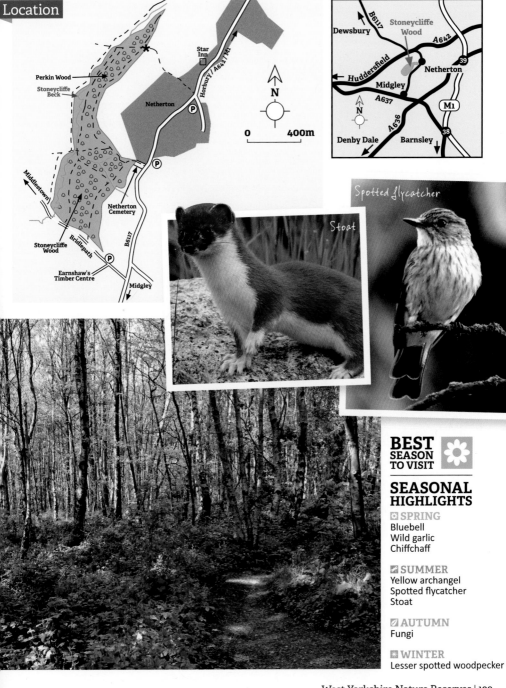

Perkin Wood
Stoneycliffe Beck
Netherton
Star Inn
Horbury / A642 / M1
N
0 — 400m
Middlestown
Netherton Cemetery
Stoneycliffe Wood
Bridlepath
B6117
Earnshaw's Timber Centre
Midgley

Dewsbury
Stoneycliffe Wood
B6117
A642
Huddersfield
Netherton
39
Midgley
A637
N
A636
M1
Denby Dale
Barnsley
38

Stoat

Spotted flycatcher

BEST SEASON TO VISIT

SEASONAL HIGHLIGHTS

SPRING
Bluebell
Wild garlic
Chiffchaff

SUMMER
Yellow archangel
Spotted flycatcher
Stoat

AUTUMN
Fungi

WINTER
Lesser spotted woodpecker

STRENSALL COMMON

NEAREST POSTCODE
YO60 7QY

NEAREST TOWN
York

GRID REFERENCE
SE 674 615

PUBLIC TRANSPORT
A regular bus service from
York runs to Strensall.

DIRECTIONS
Follow the A1237 from
York into Strensall village,
follow the signs for Flaxton.
After a mile you cross a
cattle grid onto Strensall
Common. The nature
reserve is to the left.
There are various parking
areas within the common –
a central parking point
is by the Common Road
level crossing.

**OTHER
INFORMATION**
Site designation: SSSI, SAC
Size: 42 ha

TOP TIP Visit on a warm
August afternoon to enjoy the
purple heather which carpets
the common at this time of
year and look for black darter
dragonflies around the pools.

Strensall Common is a fabulous large heathland close to York where the pink heads and grey green leaves of cross-leaved heath intermingle with the purple spikes and green foliage of ling heather. Common lizards and black darter dragonflies bask on the stumps of silver birch.

Strensall Common forms part of a larger tract of internationally important lowland heath that lies within the Vale of York. Close to the City of York, the nature reserve supports a mosaic of wet heath, dry heath, mire, open water, woodland and acid grassland. Over 150 plant species grow here including marsh cinquefoil, the beautiful blue marsh gentian and carnivorous round-leaved sundew. Ling heather and cross-leaved heath turn the heathland purple in August. Less showy, but just as pretty are the flowers found within some of the drier grassland: pinky-red sheep's sorrel and the tiny white crosses of heath bedstraw can be seen if you look closely.

The Common is home to a host of insects including a nationally important population of dark-bordered beauty moth. Green and purple hairstreak butterflies occur here and bog bush-cricket live in the rushy grassland.

Birds using the site include woodlark, green woodpecker, stonechat, coal and willow tits. Cuckoo and long-eared owl have bred and hobby sightings are increasing.

Conservation management here aims to maintain the open areas of heath. Grazing using Hebridean sheep has helped control birch seedlings. Bracken is controlled along with invasive coniferous species that are not native to heaths in this part of the UK. Ponds are cleared out from time to time, which maintains patches of open water.

Oyster fungus

Dark-bordered beauty

Location

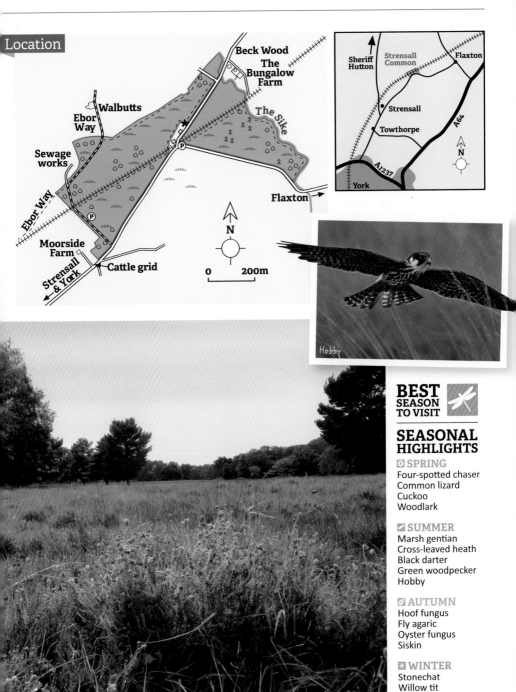

Beck Wood
The Bungalow Farm
Walbutts
Ebor Way
The Sike
Sewage works
Ebor Way
Flaxton
Moorside Farm
Cattle grid
Strensall & York

N

0   200m

Sheriff Hutton
Strensall Common
Flaxton
A64
Strensall
Towthorpe
A1237
York
N

Hobby

BEST SEASON TO VISIT

SEASONAL HIGHLIGHTS

✤ SPRING
Four-spotted chaser
Common lizard
Cuckoo
Woodlark

✿ SUMMER
Marsh gentian
Cross-leaved heath
Black darter
Green woodpecker
Hobby

❃ AUTUMN
Hoof fungus
Fly agaric
Oyster fungus
Siskin

❄ WINTER
Stonechat
Willow tit
Brown hare

SUNNYBANK

NEAREST POSTCODE
S10 2DF

NEAREST TOWN
Sheffield

GRID REFERENCE
SK 346 864

PUBLIC TRANSPORT
From Sheffield City Centre take a bus towards Bakewell, Castleton or Matlock and alight on Eccleshall Road.

DIRECTIONS
From Sheffield City Centre turn off the A61 onto Eccleshall Road (A625) and follow it round, so you head back to the A61, but turn left into William Street. Turn right onto Exeter Drive, where metered parking is available.

OTHER INFORMATION
Site designation: LNR
Size: 0.8 ha

The Wildlife Trusts — Sheffield & Rotherham

Despite its small size and location behind a petrol station at the end of Eccleshall Road, Sunnybank is Sheffield and Rotherham Wildlife Trust's most visited nature reserve. It is a hugely valuable greenspace where people can find trees and tranquillity away from the noise of the ring road.

The pool at Sunnybank is surrounded by wetland plants and is home to several types of dragonfly, pond skaters and common frogs.

The scrubby woodland and hedgerows provide plenty of food and shelter for the many birds that feed and nest here, while butterflies abound on the hay meadow in summer. Species found here include small skipper, green-veined white, red admiral and common blue, while six-spot burnet and cinnabar moths have also been seen. Mammals seen here include foxes, hedgehogs and common pipistrelle bats.

Green-veined white

TOP TIP Due to its closeness to the city centre this is a fantastic, tranquil place to spend a lunch hour.

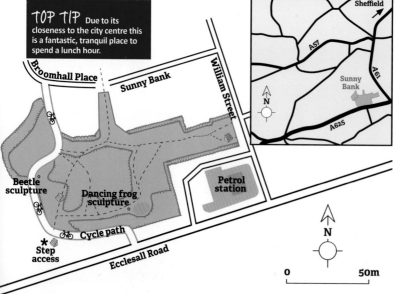

BEST SEASON TO VISIT

SEASONAL HIGHLIGHTS

SPRING
Common frog
Flag iris

SUMMER
Common pipistrelle
Six-spot burnet
Green-veined white

AUTUMN
Hedgehog

WINTER
Fox

THE LINES WAY

A superb corridor for people and wildlife, this route abounds with wildlife moving between one of several nature reserves in the nearby area.

The Leeds, Castleford and Pontefract Junction Railway was opened in 1878 and the Bowers Junction to Garforth section closed in 1969 – it is this that now forms the Lines Way. Happily, today it still provide a valuable route, albeit for walkers, cyclists and horse riders travelling under their own steam! The Lines Way has been developed into a recreational corridor, running between the settlements of Garforth and Allerton Bywater. It also provides a vital link between wildlife habitats which so often become isolated by suburban development. With a range of habitats that include sunny glades, mature trees and ponds there are plenty of wildlife watching opportunities, as well as interesting views out over the landscape. Along the route there is the opportunity to visit other nature reserves in the area. Townclose Hills is adjacent to the Lines Way, while Letchmire Pastures, Hollinhurst Wood, Owl Wood and Pit Plantation are only a short detour away. The Lines Way is owned by Leeds City Council and managed in partnership with Yorkshire Wildlife Trust.

NEAREST POSTCODE
WF10 2DJ

NEAREST TOWN
Castleford

GRID REFERENCE
SE 406 294

PUBLIC TRANSPORT
Regular buses run between Castleford and Allerton Bywater.

DIRECTIONS
On the M1 south take Junction 47 onto the A656 and follow this down to Allerton Bywater. On approach take a right turn onto Park Lane and the entrance is on your right as you travel along the lane. Parking is on the roadside.

OTHER INFORMATION
Size: 4 miles long

TOP TIP Listen out for the unmistakeable call of a cuckoo in spring.

BEST SEASON TO VISIT

SEASONAL HIGHLIGHTS

SPRING
Common frog
Cuckoo

SUMMER
Ringlet
Whitethroat

AUTUMN
Long-tailed tit
Bullfinch

WINTER
Linnet

The Lines Way

Kippax

Townclose Hills

A63

A656

Kippax Meadows

Great Preston

Owl Wood & Pit Plantation

Hollinhurst Wood

Park Lane

Allerton Bywater

N

0   100m

THORPE MARSH

NEAREST POSTCODE
DN3 1ET

NEAREST TOWN
Doncaster

GRID REFERENCE
SE 603 090

PUBLIC TRANSPORT
Catch the Doncaster
to Askern service via
Almholme from
Fordstead Lane.

DIRECTIONS
Park on Marsh Lane, near
the electricity sub station
and follow the bridleway to
Thorpe Marsh drain. Turn
left and follow down to a
bridge. Cross the bridge
and turn left again following
the bank along to where
it turns right over a small
drain and go left into a
field. Paths lead you around
the site.

**OTHER
INFORMATION**
Size: 77 ha

TOP TIP Make sure you
make a trip during summer
to see around 20 species of
butterfly and 15 species of
damsel and dragonflies.

Enjoy a peaceful walk around Thorpe Marsh Nature
Reserve with pastures lined with hedgerows, ponds,
lakes and small woodlands.

With such varied habitats supporting a wide range of
plants and animals you are guaranteed to see or hear
something of interest.

On the east bank of the River Don floodplain, Thorpe Marsh
Nature Reserve is a mixture of semi-improved and unimproved
grassland, small patches of woodland and open water. It was never
intensively farmed due to the surrounding railway lines and Ea Beck,
as well as being purchased by the Central Electricity Generating
Board in the 1960s for tipping fly ash. This has meant that a great
mix of plant species have flourished. Reedholme and Cockshaw
Fields have centuries-old ridge-and-furrow corrugations with plants
not now commonly seen in pastures, such as adder's-tongue fern,
pepper saxifrage, devil's-bit scabious, great burnet and common
figwort. Voles, mice and shrews thrive here and so do the owls that
feed on them, including long-eared owls in winter.

The disused railway embankments, open in parts and wooded
in others, give excellent views over the site and support many
plants such as red and white campions, lady's bedstraw and
broad-leaved helleborine, as well as plentiful insects and breeding
birds. Hedgerows of varying age provide food, cover and highways
for insects, birds, mammals and grass snakes. Small patches of
woodland and scrub with oak, ash, hawthorn, blackthorn, willow,
birch, and, in the wetter areas, alder, give many feeding and nesting
opportunities for great spotted woodpeckers, long-
tailed and willow tits, treecreepers and tawny owls.

Thorpe Mere is the largest of the water bodies.
Grey heron, geese and ducks are regulars but
wading birds like oystercatcher, green sandpiper and
redshank are often seen here. In winter wigeon and
goosander are frequently seen. At the Mere Scrape
little grebe, moorhen, coot and mallard usually
breed and water rail are shy visitors too. Applehurst
Pond is also worth watching for water birds.

Recently, land by the substation has come
under management by the Trust in partnership
with National Grid, with plans to open it up to the
public in the future.

Long-eared owl

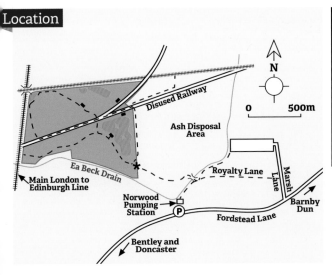

Disused Railway

Ash Disposal Area

0   500m

N

Ea Beck Drain

Main London to Edinburgh Line

Royalty Lane

Marsh Lane

Norwood Pumping Station

P

Fordstead Lane

Barnby Dun

Bentley and Doncaster

Selby
Barnby Dun
A19
A18
Thorpe Marsh
Almholme
Bentley
A630
A630
Doncaster
4
M18
N

Comma

BEST SEASON TO VISIT

SEASONAL HIGHLIGHTS

❂ SPRING
Cuckooflower
Common spotted orchid
Orange-tip
Cuckoo
Blackcap

SUMMER
Cinnabar moth
Kingfisher

AUTUMN
Comma
Migrant hawker
Common darter
Teal

WINTER
Wigeon
Long-eared owl
Fieldfare
Lesser redpoll
Bullfinch

TOWNCLOSE HILLS

NEAREST POSTCODE	LS25 7LJ

NEAREST TOWN
Garforth

GRID REFERENCE
SE 406 303

PUBLIC TRANSPORT
A regular bus runs between Castleford, Kippax and Leeds.

DIRECTIONS
From Castleford take the A656 north, then turn left onto the B6137 into Kippax. Head through the centre of Kippax and take the first exit off the roundabout onto Cross Hills, followed by a slight right onto Station Road. Park at Kippax Leisure Centre on the right.

OTHER INFORMATION
Site designation: SSSI, Local Nature Reserve
Size: 20 ha

TOP TIP Visit in June when the wildflowers will be at the height of their season, adorning the grassland plateau.

Townclose Hills, or Billy Wood as it is commonly known, is a prominent knoll of magnesian limestone which gives a stunning show of wildflowers, surrounded by low-lying arable land in the surrounding Kippax area.

This nature reserve comprises a steep-sided grassland plateau with woodland, wildflower meadows, extensive scrub and a disused railway cutting with exposed limestone and shallow, spring-fed pools. The grassland plateau received Site of Special Scientific Interest (SSSI) designation in 1984 due to it being the largest example of magnesian limestone grassland over one hectare recorded in the county. The grassland is important for its diverse assemblage of wildflowers and plants. During the summer the nature reserve comes alive with an array of orchids followed by clustered bellflower, field scabious and others.

The woodland at Townclose Hills is also strongly influenced by the underlying magnesian limestone. The steep undulating ground is a remnant of past quarrying and the woodland has colonised this previously disturbed site with species such as ash, wych elm and hazel. Common woodland birds can be found and lesser spotted woodpeckers are occasionally seen – early spring is usually best, when their high-pitched repetitive call can sometimes be heard.

The area of the SSSI and the two adjoining hay meadows nearest to Kippax Leisure Centre were designated as a Local Nature Reserve in 1994 and are well worth a visit, especially in the summer months. As you walk through the nature reserve, keep your eyes open for butterflies such as gatekeeper, speckled wood and comma, as well as birds such as yellowhammer and whitethroat.

On a clear day the views from the grassland plateau are well worth the short but sometimes steep walk to the top. If you fancy a late night stroll, Townclose Hills is home to a small glow worm population and during the summer months the females can be spotted amongst the grass, shining to attract a mate.

Townclose Hills is owned by Leeds City Council and managed in partnership with the Trust. Management on site includes traditional coppicing and scrub control, which adds to the site's appeal for nesting birds. A volunteer group in the Lower Aire Valley help out with much of this work, as well as on other local nature reserves.

Gatekeeper

Location

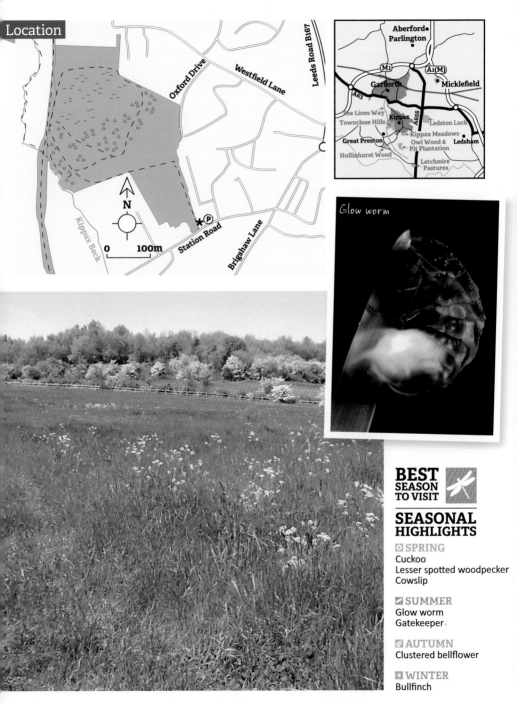

Glow worm

BEST SEASON TO VISIT

SEASONAL HIGHLIGHTS

✚ SPRING
Cuckoo
Lesser spotted woodpecker
Cowslip

☀ SUMMER
Glow worm
Gatekeeper

☂ AUTUMN
Clustered bellflower

❄ WINTER
Bullfinch

UPPER DUNSFORTH CARRS

NEAREST POSTCODE
YO26 9RU

....

NEAREST TOWN
York

....

GRID REFERENCE
SE 440 631

....

PUBLIC TRANSPORT
Buses run to nearby
village Great Ouseburn
from Boroughbridge, York
and Ripon.

....

DIRECTIONS
Head south on the B6265
from Boroughbridge.
After three miles turn left
following signs for Upper
Dunsforth. Turn left again
and park on the left after
about half a mile and just
before a T-junction.

....

**OTHER
INFORMATION**
Site designation: SSSI
Size: 10 ha

Can get very boggy and wet.

TOP TIP Look for flocks of
lesser redpoll and siskin feeding
on alder seeds during the
winter months.

A host of wetland plants and insects thrive in the wet
meadows and woodland of Upper Dunsforth Carrs.
The scene is stunning come summer, with orchids,
ragged robin and flag iris delighting the eye.

Upper Dunsforth Carrs is home to a number of habitats that are increasingly rare in lowland Yorkshire, as a result of the intensification of agriculture, which has seen land drained and soil nutrients enhanced. The permanently waterlogged soils over much of the site has produced a variety of wetland communities that represent different stages of ecological succession (where a series of species colonise a patch of land, which changes over time as the physical and chemical environment changes).

Come summer, cattle graze part of the site and this has encouraged diverse rush-pasture, fen meadow and swamp habitats to develop. In the ungrazed areas willow and alder have grown up, creating a wet woodland – an important habitat for many insects. In contrast the lighter and sandier soil at the south end of the nature reserve has meant a drier grassland habitat has endured, reminiscent of the hay meadows that would once have covered much of the Vale of York.

Birds, characteristic of the farmed landscape surrounding the nature reserve, can be enjoyed here, including chaffinch, greenfinch and yellowhammer. Listen out for the latter's distinctive 'little bit of bread and no cheese' song. Snipe may also be found in the winter, along with mixed flocks of lesser redpoll and siskin, whilst reed bunting may be seen all year round. Green woodpecker is another noisy resident of the nature reserve.

Lesser redpoll

The site is special for insects with an impressive 120 species of beetle recorded on site, including the nationally scarce diving beetle *Agabus uliginosus* and the large click beetle *Ctenicera pectinicornis* – an important indicator of damp grassland.

Much of the habitat work here has been to control the spread of invasive non-native plant species like Himalayan balsam, which could outcompete the more delicate flowering plants that make the site special. In recent years a boardwalk has also been built to improve visitor access to this attractive spot.

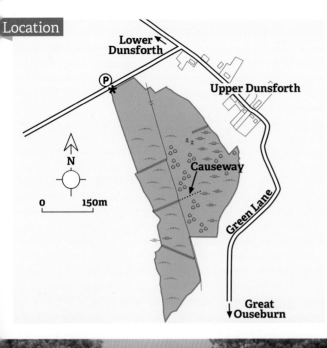

Lower Dunsforth

Upper Dunsforth

P

Causeway

Green Lane

N

0   150m

Great Ouseburn

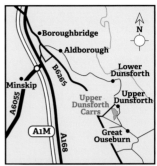

Boroughbridge

Aldborough

Lower Dunsforth

B6265

Minskip

Upper Dunsforth Carrs

Upper Dunsforth

A6055

A1M

A168

Great Ouseburn

N

Willow catkins

 BEST SEASON TO VISIT

SEASONAL HIGHLIGHTS

✦ SPRING
Great spotted woodpecker
Willow warbler
Willow tit

✦ SUMMER
Ragged robin
Flag iris
Marsh orchid
Sedge warbler

✦ AUTUMN
Migrant hawker
Common darter

✦ WINTER
Snipe
Reed bunting
Lesser redpoll

UPPER PARK WOOD

NEAREST POSTCODE
HD9 6QN

NEAREST TOWN
Holmfirth

GRID REFERENCE
SE 145 130

PUBLIC TRANSPORT
Nearest train station is
Honley, which is connected
by a Huddersfield to
Sheffield train.

DIRECTIONS
Approach via Northgate
– take a left turn off the
A616 from Huddersfield,
immediately after the
A6024 turn-off towards
Holmfirth. After a steep
climb of approximately
¾ miles reach a high
wall that can be parked
against. A footpath
also leads from Stirley
Community Farm.

**OTHER
INFORMATION**
Site designation: LNR
Size: 40 ha

TOP TIP An excellent
network of paths offer
opportunities to explore the
wider landscape, with a geology
trail that starts at Castle Hill
passing through the site.

Visit Upper Park Wood for fantastic panoramic views of the 'Last of the Summer Wine' countryside of the Holme Valley – a colourful mosaic of meadow, woodland and moorland.

Thought once to be part of a game park in the Manor of Almondbury, today Upper Park Wood is primarily an oak woodland with an understorey of holly. Come spring the ground is carpeted with bluebells, whilst summer brings the blooms of foxglove, heath bedstraw and sheep's sorrel, which thrive in the acid grassland.

Bilberry and heather also do well in the acid soils, and many typical woodland birds breed among the trees, particularly favouring a new patch planted just over a decade ago.

A good network of paths provides visitor access, with excellent views from the nature reserve of the surrounding area. They also lead through a number of habitats, from woodland edge to field margins, wet areas and hedgerows. A small pond, which was created by the damming of a stream, provides breeding habitat for common frogs.

The south facing hillside lies on the lower coal measures, made up of layers of shale and sandstone, with coal seams above some of the sandstone beds. Until the 1900s the richer seams were worked along the valley and evidence of two coal pits can be seen adjacent to the steps up the side of the wood, where gorse now flourishes.

Designated as a Local Nature Reserve in 1987, the site took its name from a tiny remnant of ancient deciduous woodland. Owned by Kirklees Metropolitan Council and managed jointly with Yorkshire Wildlife Trust, the site has grown with acquisition of adjacent fields which have since been planted with mix of native trees and shrubs. Much of the woodland work is undertaken by a group of enthusiastic volunteers, who aim to increase the diversity of life there as much as possible.

Bilberry

Gorse

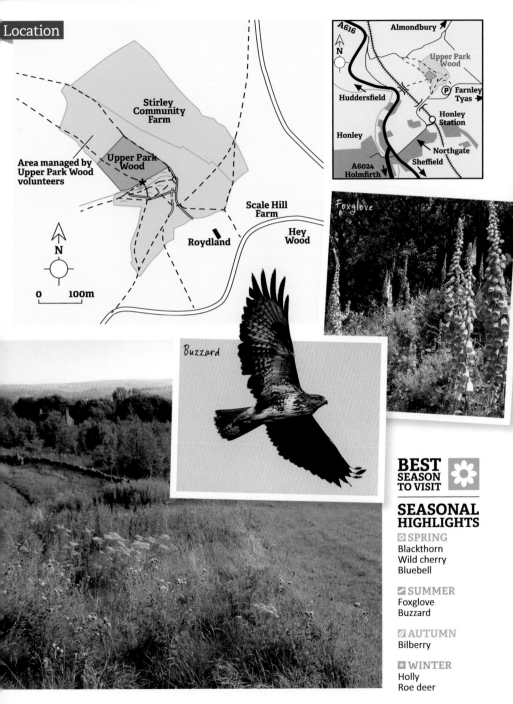

Stirley Community Farm

Upper Park Wood

Area managed by Upper Park Wood volunteers

N

0   100m

Scale Hill Farm

Roydland

Hey Wood

A616

Almondbury

N

Upper Park Wood

Huddersfield

P Farnley Tyas

Honley Station

Honley

Northgate

Sheffield

A6024 Holmfirth

Foxglove

Buzzard

BEST SEASON TO VISIT

SEASONAL HIGHLIGHTS

✜ SPRING
Blackthorn
Wild cherry
Bluebell

✎ SUMMER
Foxglove
Buzzard

✐ AUTUMN
Bilberry

✖ WINTER
Holly
Roe deer

WATER HAIGH WOODLAND PARK

NEAREST POSTCODE
LS26 8WW

NEAREST TOWN
Rothwell

GRID REFERENCE
SE 376 287

PUBLIC TRANSPORT
A train service runs
between Leeds and
Woodlesford, a short walk
away from the site.

DIRECTIONS
Take Junction 44 off the M1
onto the A639/Leeds Road
south. Follow the A639
past the petrol station and
onto the roundabout. Take
the first exit onto A642/
Calverley Road, then a right
turn onto Fleet Lane. Park
at the end of the road or on
Eshald Lane.

**OTHER
INFORMATION**
Size: 97 ha

TOP TIP **A walk along the
canal tow path may provide a
chance sighting of an otter.**

Water Haigh Woodland Park is an attractive site with
leafy areas of woodland and a pleasant walkway along
the canal tow path.

This nature reserve is located on the footprint of the former
Water Haigh colliery, which has now been transformed from a
spoil heap to a green oasis.

Split in half by the railway lane with the Aire and Calder Navigation
also passing through, this site is a patchwork containing broadleaved
woodland, hedgerow and pasture, along with many surfaced paths
throughout, which include part of the TransPennine Trail and the Leeds
Country Way.

Additional woodland compartments have been planted in recent
years and a large flood alleviation scheme near Swillington Bridge
is nearing completion. Habitat creation on this heavily engineered
part of the site will take the form of reedbed and wet woodland with
wildflower meadow and drier woodland on higher ground.

Part of the important green corridor that is the Lower Aire Valley
this site is also a valuable recreational space. Sensitive management is
needed on this site to ensure benefit for both people and wildlife for
years to come.

Water Haigh Woodland Park is owned by Leeds City Council and
managed in partnership with Yorkshire Wildlife Trust.

Roe deer

Tawny owl

A642
Cockpit Round
St Aidan's
Woodlesford Station
River Aire
Aire & Calder Navigation
Eshald Lane
Fleet Lane

A64(M)
Leeds
A64
A63
M1
Beeston
Rothwell Country Park
Rothwell
Water Haigh Woodland Park
M1
Rothwell Pastures
M62
M62

Coot

BEST SEASON TO VISIT

SEASONAL HIGHLIGHTS

✤ SPRING
Skylark
Song thrush

✐ SUMMER
Otter

✐ AUTUMN
Marsh harrier
Roe deer

✤ WINTER
Buzzard
Tawny owl

WELWICK SALTMARSH

NEAREST POSTCODE
HU12 0SG

NEAREST TOWN
Withernsea

GRID REFERENCE
TA 338 191

PUBLIC TRANSPORT
Nearest bus stop in
Welwick village around
two miles away.

DIRECTIONS
From Welwick village
head south down Humber
Lane which becomes Row
Lane. At the end take
a sharp right and park
considerately along
Sheep Trod Lane. Walk
south down a dust track
to the site.

**OTHER
INFORMATION**
Site designation: SSSI
Size: 44 ha

TOP TIP Enjoy a winter's
afternoon walk to experience
the best views of raptors as they
hunt along the Humber. Take in
the big horizons from Spurn to
the Humber Bridge as the sun
goes down.

For a windswept Humber Estuary experience, Welwick Saltmarsh is a great place. Big skies with wheeling flocks of wading birds and a great chance of a bird of prey or two enliven a winter's day.

Welwick Saltmarsh is the most extensive area of saltmarsh on the north bank of the River Humber. It is advisable to view this nature reserve from the riverbank as accessing the saltmarsh itself can be dangerous and would cause disturbance to wildlife. From the floodbank you can enjoy spectacular views across the mouth of the Humber. Thousands of birds use the Humber estuary including large flocks of golden plover, which appear bronze against the mudflats in the evening sun. Hundreds of large, curve-billed curlew feed on the edge of the saltmarsh whilst grey plover, bar-tailed godwit, knot and dunlin whir past and drop down to feed on the mudflats. Many of these flocks pass right overhead as they transfer to their inland roosting sites as the incoming tide pushes them from the river edge.

Welwick Saltmarsh is also a fantastic location to view hunting raptors and owls. Short-eared owl, merlin, peregrine, marsh harrier, hen harrier and kestrel are all regularly seen, particularly during the winter months.

In spring, scurvy grass creates hundreds of white tussocks across the marsh and mid-summer sees a real show of purple flowers from sea lavender and sea aster. The saltmarsh also supports sea purslane, sea arrowgrass and cord grass. On the land side of the saltmarsh a small area of relic dune containing two ponds supports common reed, bird's-foot trefoil, spiny restharrow and the curious non-native spring beauty.

Management of the saltmarsh has previously involved cutting but the Trust has been working with local farmers to reintroduce grazing in recent years as part of a project to improve the conservation management of the Outer Humber.

Peregrine

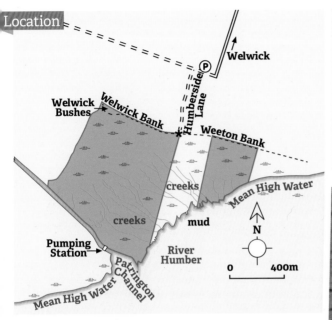

Welwick

P

Humberside Lane

Welwick Bushes

Welwick Bank

Weeton Bank

creeks

mud

Mean High Water

creeks

creeks

N

Pumping Station

River Humber

Patrington Channel

Mean High Water

0   400m

A165
Hornsea
North Sea
Hull
B1242
Hedon
A1033
Withernsea
Patrington
Easington
B1445
Welwick
Kilnsea
River Humber
Welwick Saltmarsh
Kilnsea Wetlands
Grimsby
Spurn
N

Grey plover

BEST SEASON TO VISIT

SEASONAL HIGHLIGHTS

✿ SPRING
Marsh harrier
Skylark
Linnet

☀ SUMMER
Scurvy grass
Sea lavender
Sea purslane
Spiny restharrow

🍂 AUTUMN
Short-eared owl
Hen harrier
Merlin
Curlew
Dunlin

❄ WINTER
Barn owl
Peregrine
Golden plover
Knot
Curlew

WHARRAM QUARRY

A species rich chalk grassland, Wharram Quarry is home to many of the characteristic flowering plants that once thrived on the thin, chalky Wolds soil. Butterflies flit among the wide variety of wildflowers on the quarry floor.

NEAREST POSTCODE
YO17 9TW

NEAREST TOWN
Malton

GRID REFERENCE
SE 858 653

PUBLIC TRANSPORT
Nearest train station is in Malton.

DIRECTIONS
At the crossroads on the B1248 in Wharram-le-Street, head west towards Birdsall and the nature reserve is about half a mile on the left as the road descends. Parking is limited in the gateway, or continue further down the hill to park by the side of the road and walk back to the site.

OTHER INFORMATION
Site designation: SSSI
Size: 7 ha

TOP TIP June to August are the best months to visit. Try to pick a warm and sunny day to see specialist butterflies like dingy skippers and the best orchid displays.

The nature reserve was actively quarried for chalk between 1919 and the 1940s and was offered to Yorkshire Wildlife Trust in the 1960s by owner Lord Middleton after he noticed bee orchids growing on the quarry floor. The quarry floor has variable depths of soil and consequently different plant communities. The west end, where the spoil was deposited, is now dominated by coarse grasses and hawthorn scrub. Several species of grasses can be found including cock's-foot, meadow and false oat-grasses, red and sheep's fescues, and quaking grass. Glaucous sedge is widely distributed.

The wildflowers present a beautiful scene; they include the yellow flowers of cowslip, rough hawkbit, mouse-ear hawkweed and bird's-foot trefoil, purple wild thyme and clustered bellflower, pink restharrow and blue common milkwort. Common spotted, twayblade, pyramidal and bee orchids can all be found in June and July, followed by autumn gentian in late summer.

The quarry is one of the few Wolds sites for thistle broomrape which parasitizes woolly thistle. Its large creamy spikes can be seen growing from the base of thistles in June. The endangered red hemp-nettle has been introduced from nearby populations along with small-flowered buttercup on the quarry face.

Butterflies abound on sunny days, including plentiful marbled white, small heath, meadow brown, ringlet and common blue. Dingy skippers can be seen, particularly in the north east corner along with large hills made by yellow meadow ants.

In order to maintain the succession of plants areas of the floor have been periodically scraped back to the chalk. Grazing using the Trust's Hebridean sheep in winter prevents the open flower-rich sward from swamped by dense coarse grasses and hawthorn. The floor is also mown in late summer, once the flowers have set seed.

Common milkwort

Location

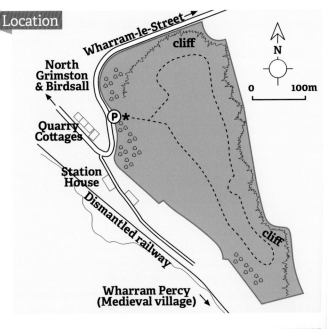

Wharram-le-Street →

cliff

North
Grimston
& Birdsall

P *

Quarry
Cottages

Station
House

Dismantled railway

cliff

Wharram Percy
(Medieval village) ↘

N

0   100m

N

Malton

Dismantled railway

B1248

Duggleby

Wharram-
le-Street

Wharram
Quarry

B1248

Birdsall

Wetwang

Colt's-foot

**BEST
SEASON
TO VISIT**

SEASONAL HIGHLIGHTS

✤ SPRING
Dingy skipper
Colt's foot
Cowslip

✤ SUMMER
Marbled white
Small heath
Thistle broomrape
Woolly thistle
Pyramidal orchid

✤ AUTUMN
Autumn gentian
Carline thistle

✤ WINTER
Stoat
Fieldfare
Redwing

WHELDRAKE INGS

NEAREST POSTCODE
YO19 6AS

NEAREST TOWN
York

GRID REFERENCE
SE 694 444

PUBLIC TRANSPORT
There is a regularly service between Wheldrake village and York Merchantgate (bus 36 to Sutton on Derwent and 18 to Holme Upon Spalding Moor). This service also passes through Skipwith, North Duffield and Bubwith.

DIRECTIONS
Eight miles south east of York, four miles east of the A19. From Wheldrake follow the road (Carr Lane) towards Thorganby and out of the village where the road takes a sharp right turn. Half a mile further on a narrow road to your left (after the Yorkshire Water compound) takes you down to the nature reserve. Park on the stony area before the bridge over the River Derwent and follow the footpath along the river to the viewing hides. Please do not enter the meadows.

OTHER INFORMATION
Site designation: SPA, SAC, RAMSAR, SSSI, NNR
Size: 157 ha

TOP TIP Visit on a spring evening at the end of April for a chance of seeing whimbrel, a spectacular migrant wading bird that pauses here on its way north to Iceland to breed.

A spectacular, flower-filled meadow filled with the bubbling cries of curlew in summer, gives way to vast floodlands, home to thousands of wintering wildfowl come winter.

For several centuries Wheldrake Ings, at the heart of the Lower Derwent Valley, has been managed consistently, which has maintained the superb floodplain meadows. As winter floodwaters recede the rich meadows begin to grow, with marsh marigold and cuckooflower the first to add splashes of colour.

Tucked within the growing grassland, lapwings, redshank, snipe and curlew raise their young and flotillas of mallard and gadwall ducklings scoot into the overhanging willows around the pool edges. Late June sees the meadows at their best with the best areas supporting up to 35 plant species per square metre. Look for crimson raspberry-like heads of great burnet, plus rarities like fine-leaved water dropwort and grasses such as meadow foxtail and sweet vernal grass. This type of meadow community is very rare in the UK and the area at Wheldrake Ings is of international importance. In early July the land is dry, chicks have fledged and the meadows are cut for hay by local farmers.

By August sheep and cattle are turned out to graze the re-growth of grass or 'fog' as it is known. In autumn, water from the River Derwent starts to flood the meadows and impressive expanses of open water attract a spectacle of thousands of ducks, geese and wading birds. 40,000 birds use the Lower Derwent Valley each winter, with a significant proportion of these at Wheldrake Ings.

Spring and autumn can be exciting on the wetlands as migrant wading birds, terns and raptors pass through. Spotted crake, water rail and willow tit all breed along with many wading birds and ducks. Marsh harrier, red kite, hobby and peregrine are all seen regularly. The Lower Derwent Valley supports one of the densest populations of barn owls in Europe and a visit early or late in the day almost guarantees a sighting.

The site also supports a host of grassland and wetland insects including some very rare beetles. Otters have bred on several occasions in the past few years and roe deer and brown hare are seen regularly in the meadows, especially during the winter and spring.

Management here is a fine balance of controlling water levels to support the wintering, passage and breeding birds, whilst also creating the right conditions for the rare floodplain grassland to thrive. On top of this regular maintenance and cleaning of the ditches is required, which each winter receive silty deposits from the floodwater.

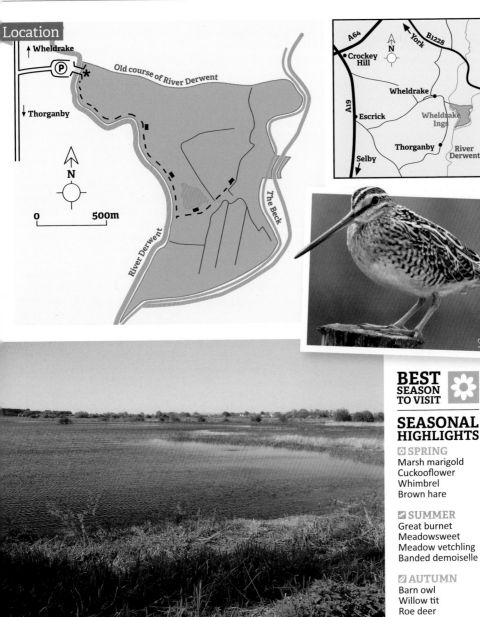

Location

Wheldrake

Old course of River Derwent

Thorganby

N

0   500m

River Derwent

The Beck

A64
York
B1228
Crockey Hill
N
Wheldrake
A19
Escrick
Wheldrake Ings
Thorganby
Selby
River Derwent

Snipe

BEST SEASON TO VISIT

SEASONAL HIGHLIGHTS

✦ SPRING
Marsh marigold
Cuckooflower
Whimbrel
Brown hare

✦ SUMMER
Great burnet
Meadowsweet
Meadow vetchling
Banded demoiselle

✦ AUTUMN
Barn owl
Willow tit
Roe deer

✦ WINTER
Whooper swan
Wigeon
Teal
Pintail
Peregrine

WILLOW GARTH

NEAREST POSTCODE
WF11 8TH

NEAREST TOWN
Knottingley

GRID REFERENCE
SE 516 241

PUBLIC TRANSPORT
Buses and trains run to
Knottingley from Leeds,
Castleford and Pontefract
Monkhill.

DIRECTIONS
From Knottingley head
east along the A645
crossing the Leeds to
Goole Canal (near the
former works of Croda).
Turn left into Trundles
Lane just before the
bridge. After 200m, where
a narrow footbridge
crosses the canal ahead,
turn a sharp right – the
unfenced canal should be
on your left and disused
Croda works on your right.
Continue three quarters
of a mile until the track
leaves the fence and park
on the roadside. The
entrance is 200m ahead
on the right.

**OTHER
INFORMATION**
Size: 5 ha

TOP TIP A trip in
early spring will provide the
ideal conditions to see both
emerging and returning wildlife
before the vegetation grows up
and restricts some views!

A window to the past, Willow Garth is resonant of a
countryside once filled with a mosaic of different
habitats, each one varied and special in its own right.
Primarily reedbed and wet woodland, this spot is ideal
for summer warblers.

A multitude of wetland habitats fills the generally flat and
low-lying land found on the nature reserve, with some open
water, marsh, willow carr and reedbed being dominant. As
its name suggests, this site, which is excellent for willow, was once a
commercial osier bed, where the whips were grown to be made into
baskets and furniture.

Marshland species can be found in the central area of the site,
whereas woodland and scrub plants grow in the north and east. Close
to 140 species of birds have been recorded at Willow Garth. Reed and
sedge warblers, long-tailed tit and chiffchaff are just a few of those
that breed on site. The variety of habitats also supports a diverse
mix of plants including water chickweed, common meadow-rue and
alder buckthorn. Crack and grey willow make up the majority of the
woodland on the nature reserve with some silver birch and hawthorn.
Mammals recorded on site include harvest mice, bank vole, common
and pygmy shrew, roe deer and fox.

Owned by Croda and managed by Yorkshire Wildlife Trust, the main
aim of the work here is to maintain a traditional willow coppice, with
woodland coupes cut on a rotational basis. Himalayan balsam and
giant hogweed are invasive non-native species and are controlled and
the reedbed is cut on rotation each winter to promote vigorous new
growth. Ditch maintenance is also carried out to ensure the flow of
water around the site.

Pygmy shrew

Reed warbler

Location

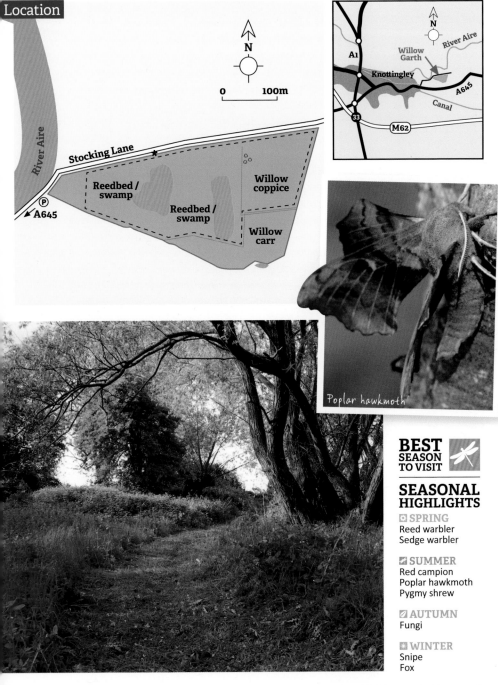

Willow Garth

River Aire

A1

Willow Garth

Knottingley

A645

Canal

M62

33

Stocking Lane

Reedbed / swamp

Reedbed / swamp

Willow coppice

Willow carr

River Aire

P

A645

0   100m

Poplar hawkmoth

BEST SEASON TO VISIT

SEASONAL HIGHLIGHTS

SPRING
Reed warbler
Sedge warbler

SUMMER
Red campion
Poplar hawkmoth
Pygmy shrew

AUTUMN
Fungi

WINTER
Snipe
Fox

WOODHOUSE WASHLANDS

NEAREST POSTCODE
S13 9WG

NEAREST TOWN
Sheffield

GRID REFERENCE
SK 438 852

PUBLIC TRANSPORT
Buses stop at nearby Furnace Lane. The nearest train station is at Woodhouse Station, half a mile from the entrance.

DIRECTIONS
Take junction 31 off the M1 and join the A57 towards Sheffield. At the second roundabout take the second exit onto the B6200 and follow it round to the Princess Royal pub. Parking is available here. There is also an entrance to a small section of the nature reserve from Furnace Lane by walking along a tree-lined path and from Rotherham Road, which is accessible from Beighton and Swallownest.

OTHER INFORMATION
Site designation: LNR
Size: 73 ha

Sheffield & Rotherham

Woodhouse Washlands are an ever changing tapestry of colours and textures throughout the seasons. The winter wetlands attracts great flocks of lapwing, which come spring give way to a buttercup-filled meadow.

Lying in the floodplain of the River Rother, the nature reserve straddles the boundary between Sheffield and Rotherham. This suburban site, whilst surrounded by roads, housing and industry, has a rich and varied history. The river meandered through extensive marshland right up until the 1950s, and flooded so regularly that a rowing boat was kept at the nearby Methodist Chapel to transport people between housing and factories. The disruption this caused to working life resulted in a flood alleviation scheme being put into operation and by 1960 the river channel had been straightened, flood banks built and ditches dug to control the water. Since then the river has only flooded the washlands three times; latterly during the major floods in June 2007.

The scheme transformed the widespread marshland into a mosaic of grassland, marsh, ponds, ditches and temporary pools with willows and remnant hawthorn hedges dotted across the site creating additional habitat. Divided by the River Rother and a railway viaduct, the site is split into compartments, each with their own distinct characteristics. The river was once the most polluted in Europe, a legacy of its industrial past, however today it happily supports a good fish population as well as a range of insects and plants.

When enjoying the site, watch out for the occasional flash of turquoise as a kingfisher darts by, or in winter see goosander and gulls bobbing about on the water. Dragonflies and damselflies are also plentiful on sunny days during the summer and early autumn.

Management on the nature reserve has consisted of cattle grazing to keep competitive plant species in check and allow for a greater diversity, and periodic management of the ditches, ponds and hedges.

Look out for metal sculptures which help to describe the site's industrial past, as well as explain more about the plants and animals that can be seen here.

Whilst currently managed by Yorkshire Wildlife Trust, this site is in the process of being transferred to Sheffield and Rotherham Wildlife Trust due to its proximity to the city.

TOP TIP Enjoy skylarks singing and meadows filled with wildflowers come early summer. The jewel-like banded demoiselle can be seen holding territory over the river, whilst emperor dragonflies patrol the ponds.

Location

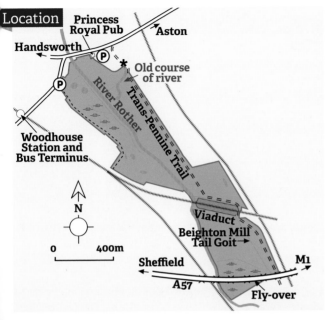

Princess Royal Pub
Aston
Handsworth
Old course of river
River Rother
Trans-Pennine Trail
Woodhouse Station and Bus Terminus
Viaduct
Beighton Mill Tail Goit →
Sheffield ← A57 M1
Fly-over

0 — 400m

N

Treeton
A618
Ulley
B6067
Woodhouse Washlands
Fence
Aston
A57
31
M1
A57
A618
Sheffield
N

Rosehip

BEST SEASON TO VISIT

SEASONAL HIGHLIGHTS

✿ SPRING
Pignut
Cuckooflower
Marsh marigold
Skylark

✿ SUMMER
Great burnet
Banded demoiselle
Green woodpecker

✿ AUTUMN
Rosehips
Goldfinch

✿ WINTER
Hawthorn berries
Alder
Goosander
Lapwing

WYMING BROOK

Sheffield & Rotherham

A little bit of wilderness on the edge of Sheffield, this site is enjoyable for both its landscape and rich wildlife.

NEAREST POSTCODE
S10 4LJ

NEAREST TOWN
Sheffield

GRID REFERENCE
SK 269 858

PUBLIC TRANSPORT
Buses from Sheffield City Road/Stafford Road and from Eyre Street, along Redmires Road.

DIRECTIONS
From Sheffield take Manchester Road (A57) towards Rivelin Dams. Just past the dam turn left onto Wyming Brook Drive. Follow this to the end.

OTHER INFORMATION
Site designation: LNR/SSSI
Size: 70 ha

TOP TIP Keep one eye on the sky, particularly in spring, when ospreys linger over the nearby reservoir and sometimes pass over the nature reserve.

Once set aside for the exclusive use of the nobility as part of the hunting and hawking grounds of the Rivelin Chase, Wyming Brook's babbling stream, mossy crags and sweet smelling pines are still protected today as a valuable home for wildlife.

Today, all visitors can enjoy this little bit of wild on the western edge of Sheffield, with easy strolls by the streams or higher, rockier routes with dramatic views of the Rivelin Reservoirs, the source of the brook and the city beyond. Part of the Eastern Moors SSSI, there is an abundance of wildlife at this nature reserve including bizarrely named moths: the common lutestring and northern spinach.

The nature reserve is also home to many kinds of birds including pine seed-eating crossbills, which breed in late winter and can be seen in noisy family parties among the pines. Listen out for their sharp 'chip' calls as they fly overhead. Nearby, resident dippers sporting smart white breasts forage for aquatic insects including caddisfly larvae along the fast flowing stream. In autumn the mossy banks, deadwood and boulders become coloured by the fruiting bodies of many fungi, including the wonderfully named plums and custard, and amethyst deceiver.

Dipper

Amethyst deceiver

Location

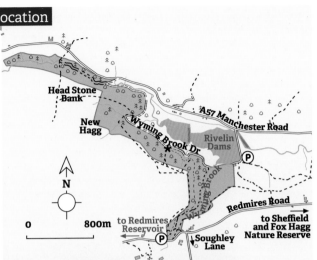

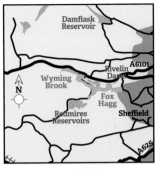

Crossbill

BEST SEASON TO VISIT

SEASONAL HIGHLIGHTS

✿ SPRING
Dipper
Nuthatch
Treecreeper
Great spotted woodpecker

✿ SUMMER
Speckled wood
Blackcap
Chiffchaff

✿ AUTUMN
Amethyst deceiver

✿ WINTER
Crossbill

YELLANDS MEADOW

NEAREST POSTCODE
DL11 6QJ

NEAREST TOWN
Hawes

GRID REFERENCE
SD 918 977

PUBLIC TRANSPORT
A very limited bus service
runs along Swaledale.

DIRECTIONS
Situated between the River
Swale and the B6270, about
one mile east of Muker. A
small parking area exists in
an informal lay by near the
field gate on the B6270.

OTHER INFORMATION
Site designation: SSSI
Size: 1 ha

TOP TIP To see the meadow at its colourful best visit in June and July. With the flowers in bloom, the meadow is alive with the sight and sound of bees, grasshoppers and butterflies.

A traditionally managed hay meadow set amid steep hills in the beautiful limestone landscape of Swaledale in the Yorkshire Dales National Park.

Yellands Meadow is a tiny meadow lying next to the River Swale and is one of twelve included in the 'The Muker Meadows' SSSI. A stream, lined with alders, runs diagonally across the meadow. There is a small stone barn on the western boundary containing the original stone cow stalls.

The meadow has resulted from traditional management in the harsh climate of the hills. It is of a type that is now almost entirely restricted to a few valley heads in the North of England. The flowering plants in the meadow include an abundance of pignut, lady's mantle, meadow buttercup, wood cranesbill, clovers and hawkbits. Other flowers include yellow rattle, cuckooflower, meadow vetchling, bugle, eyebright, bird's-foot trefoil and common spotted orchid.

Along the moist banks of the steam are meadowsweet, melancholy thistle and marsh marigold. There is a range of grasses in the sward with sweet vernal grass, the grass that gives cut hay its characteristic and evocative smell, predominant.

There are no clearly defined footpaths on site. To enjoy the meadow it is suggested that visitors cross the bridge over the steam to the right of the entrance gate and, keeping close to the boundary wall and river fence, go clockwise round the meadow, return across the footbridge at the eastern end and then walk back along the stream. Look out for sand martins and grey wagtails along the River Swale on the northern boundary. The meadow has been managed in a traditional way by the same tenant family for a number of generations and is grazed in the autumn and early spring and a hay cut is taken in July.

Meadow buttercup

Meadowsweet

N

0   400m

River Swale

barn

P
★
Muker

B6270

Gunnerside

Keld
River Swale
Angram
Thwaite   Muker
Yellands
Meadow
Buttertubs
Pass
B6270
S w a l e d a l e

Yellow rattle

Bugle

BEST
SEASON
TO VISIT

SEASONAL
HIGHLIGHTS

✤ SPRING
Marsh marigold
Cuckooflower
Sand martin

☀ SUMMER
Eyebright
Yellow rattle
Meadow vetchling
Lady's mantle
Redstart

🍂 AUTUMN
Autumn hawkbit

❄ WINTER
Grey wagtail

Glossary

Agricultural improvement
This refers to land that has had additional inputs such as fertilisers and pesticides applied to increase its productivity for growing crops or rearing livestock. Often land that has undergone this treatment has seen a corresponding decline in wildlife as the inputs are usually designed to be effective for a narrow range of crops.

Calcareous grassland
Grassland found over limestone and chalk rock. These soils are often shallow and are typically low in nutrients, well-drained and support a rich diversity of flowering plants.

Conservation grazing
The use of traditional and rare breed cattle and sheep can help maintain or improve the range of different plants growing in an area. They prevent bushes, trees or species with vigorous growth from dominating existing habitat e.g. flower-rich grassland.

Diversity/ Biodiversity
These two words are often used interchangeably, but in the case of this book essentially mean wildlife richness or number of species on a nature reserve. More generally it is a measure of variety, which could be at genetic or species level within an area.

Ings
Of Norse origin, this word is commonly used in Yorkshire to refer to seasonally-flooded land alongside rivers. Another common term used in other regions is 'washes'.

Local Nature Reserve (LNR)
Contain wildlife or geological features deemed of interest locally. Designated by local authorities, who either own or lease them, they are places for people to learn and enjoy wildlife close to where they live.

Local Wildlife Site (LWS)
An area recognised for having high wildlife value and containing rare or threatened habitats and species. No legal protection exists and they are often in private ownership, so survival depends on landowners' goodwill.

Magnesian limestone grassland
A type of calcareous grassland that occurs on an outcrop of magnesian limestone that stretches from Nottingham, through Yorkshire and into County Durham. Important habitat for plants and insects, although much of it has declined through the intensification of agriculture.

National Nature Reserve (NNR)
Designated by the Government to protect some of the UK's best wildlife sites. Most contain habitats or species that are nationally or internationally important. Managed to retain the wildlife, but also so that people can enjoy the site without damaging it.

Saltmarsh
Important habitat providing food for breeding and wintering wading birds and wildfowl. Can also act as a natural flood defence. Often forms a transitional zone between the sea and land.

Site of Ecological or Geological Importance (SEGI)

Area identified as being of county importance for its wildlife or geological features by a local authority.

Site of Special Scientific Interest (SSSI)

An area of land protected by law to conserve either its wildlife or geology, one or the other being considered special or rare. These designated sites have some restrictions in place, which are regulated by Natural England (non-departmental public body of the UK Government to protect and improve England's natural environment).

Special Area of Conservation (SAC)

These are areas that are designated under the EU Habitats Directive to conserve a network of sites that are internationally important for threatened habitats and species. They are also known as Natura sites.

Special Protection Area (SPA)

Areas designated under the EU Birds Directive to conserve rare, threatened or vulnerable birds, or regular migratory bird species. Together with SACs, they can be referred to as Natura sites.

Grasshopper warbler

Photograph Credits

Acknowledgements

This revised second edition of *Discover Yorkshire's Wildlife* is a fully refreshed version of the book that was published in 2012. It includes updated information about both Sheffield and Rotherham Wildlife Trust and Yorkshire Wildlife Trust nature reserves included in the previous versions and also a handful of new sites that Yorkshire Wildlife Trust has acquired.

Yorkshire Wildlife Trust's editorial and design team would like to thank the many volunteers who provided the original copy for inclusion in this book and updated information to bring this new edition up to date.

All photographs have been provided free of charge by members of the public, and staff and volunteers of the Trust. We would like to extend our thanks to them for allowing use of these fantastic images.

The range of nature reserves looked after for wildlife across Yorkshire is simply tremendous and we hope you will enjoy reading about them in these pages. If you are able, we hope the words and images inspire you to go and look for yourselves.

Researched, written and edited by
Jonathan Leadley and Joanna Richards
Yorkshire Wildlife Trust, May 2017

Designed by
Sally Henderson
Yorkshire Wildlife Trust, May 2017

Many thanks to the following for their support and assistance:
Dame Judi Dench, Andy Gibson, Jenny Hayward
Anna Honing, Jim Horsfall, Kara Jackson,
Ben Keywood, Brian Lavelle, Andy Mason,
Karen McDiarmid and Phillip Whelpdale.

Sheffield Wildlife Trust
37 Stafford Road, Sheffield, S2 2SF
T: 0114 263 4335
E: mail@wildsheffield.com
www.wildsheffield.com

Contributors

Nabil Abbas – Sprotbrough Flash
Chris Alder – Globeflower Wood, Grass Wood
Judith Allinson – Brae Pasture, Salt Lake Quarry, South House Pavement
Derrick Bateman – North Cliffe Wood
Roger Bird – Potteric Carr
Michael Brook – Upper Park Wood
David Burtell – Agden Bog
Charles Clarkson – Jeffry Bog, Kirkham Wood
Alastair Fitter – Askham Bog
Andrew Gibson – Kilnsea Wetlands, Spurn, Welwick Saltmarsh
Keith Gittens – Garbutt Wood
Julie Gough – Sheffield Wildlife Trust nature reserves
Barry Greenacre – Saltmarshe Delph
Christine Handley – Woodhouse Washlands
John Lawton – Foreword
John MacArthur – Adel Dam
Stephen Martin – North Cave Wetlands
Tony Martin – Paull Holme Strays
Jo Milborrow – Ashes Pasture, Salt Lake Quarry
Deborah Millward – Seata Quarry
Peter Nash – Denaby Ings
Roger Neale – Southerscales
Helen Pedley – Broadhead Clough
Kate Phillips – Sites managed in partnership with Leeds City Council
Martin Phillips – Wharram Quarry
Jonathan Proud – Allerthorpe Common
Elizabeth Round – Birch Wood, Burton Riggs, Chafer Wood, Ellerburn Bank, Fen Bog, Garbutt Wood, Harland Mount
Gordon Scaife – Rifle Butts Quarry
Dale Scott – Low Wood
Joyce Simmons – Brockadale
John Smith – Yellands Meadow
Jim Staveley – Maltby Low Common
Rob Stoneman – Foreword
Mary Sykes – Moorlands
Mick Townsend – Thorpe Marsh
Jon Traill – Snakeholm Pastures, Skerne Wetlands
Peter Treloar – Staveley Nature Reserve
Don Vine – Kirkstall Valley
Pete Wall – Sites managed in partnership with Barnsley Council
Jonathan Watkins – Leyburn Old Glebe
Jack Whitehead – Filey Dams
David Woodmansey – Flamborough Cliffs